Malawi's Lost Years (1964-1994): and Her Forsaken Heroes

by

Kapote Mwakasungura

and

Douglas Miller

All rights reserved. No part of this publication may be reproduced, stored in a retrieval system, or transmitted in any form or by any means, electronic, mechanical, photocopying, recording or otherwise, without prior permission from the publishers.

Published by

Mzuni Press
P/Bag 201
Luwinga, Mzuzu 2
Malawi
ISBN   978-99960-45-19-6

2016

Mzuni Press is represented outside Africa by:
African Books Collective Oxford (also for e-books)
(orders@africanbookscollective.com)
www.africanbookscollective.com
www.mzunipress.blogspot.com

Printed in Malawi by Baptist Publications, POB 444, Lilongwe

Cover design by Benoit Bessette

Table of Contents

Preface III

Acknowledgement V

List of Acronyms and Vernacular Terms VI

Foreword VIII

Chapter One   Introduction 9

Chapter Two   The Gathering Storm 28

Chapter Three   State Terrorism - Detention and Complicity 62

Chapter Four   Exile - The First Generation 100

Chapter Five   Exile – Second and Third Generation 135

Chapter Six   State of Terror - Suffering in Bitter Silence 156

Chapter Seven Organised Opposition 176

Chapter Eight   Living With the Pain 208

Chapter Nine   The Promised Land and the Democracy Bubble 227

Chapter Ten   Conclusion 240

Appendix 248

List of references 257

Preface

Good friends we have had,
Oh good friends we've lost along the way
No woman, No cry
Bob Marley

For befriending the dictator
we lost many patriotic friends,
defenders of democracy
and condemned the Malawi people to a state of terror.
For befriending Taiwan
we lost the friendship of the Peoples Republic of China
and all the benefit we could have derived
from aligning ourselves with the most populous nation in the world.
For befriending Jorge Jardim, Ian Smith and Johannes Vorster
we lost the friendship of
our friends in Africa and further afield
KM & DM

This is a modest attempt by two people who have been greatly touched, one by virtue of origin and birth, the other by marriage and compassion, to try and rehabilitate the lives of a number of Malawians who suffered the indignity of exile on the one hand, and detention on the other during the 30 year misrule under Dr Hastings Kamuzu Banda. They serve as representatives for many others who suffered the same fate, many of whom did not survive to tell their stories.

On the surface of it, the casual reader of this book may find it presumptuous of the authors, because after all it will be argued, Malawi today and specifically in the thirty years of the Kamuzu era made great strides vis à vis the University of Malawi, the Lakeshore Road, the new capital city of Lilongwe, and much else. Malawi also established diplomatic relations with many friendly countries in Africa and the world at large. It will also be argued that Malawi under Kamuzu was able to feed its population and with food to spare which the country was able to export. We do not deny that much was accomplished.

The argument about "Malawi's Lost Years" is not that Malawi in the 30 years stood still. No country ever stays still under nature's dialectic. Nations, like all living organisms, forever evolve. People lived their lives and infrastructure projects brought an element of development for some of the population. However, much was lost through the excesses of the misrule and the culture of predation that was implanted during that period and that persists today. Kamuzu Banda established the practice that has become the rule - taking over the reins of government entitles the rulers to exploit the country and its people for personal gain.

Indeed the period of history covered by the Lost Years was a tumultuous one for the world as well as Malawi. Internationally, the Cold War was at its worst point and manifest itself through wars and repression from Vietnam to the dictatorships imposed throughout Latin America, Asia and Africa. At the same time the winds of change that swept Africa had not yet accomplished their final goal and culminated with the popular, national struggles leading to the independence of Portugal's African colonies, Zimbabwe, Namibia and finally South Africa. These countries worked their way through the familiar cycle of early hope and expectation to be eventually disappointed as conditions worsened rather than improved under their new independence rulers. Malawi, like the rest of Africa, lived the tragedy of Structural Adjustment Programmes through the 1980s and 90s. The macro scheme certainly set the scene for the micro reality of Malawi.

Our own life stories were very directly tied to the vagaries of world events and personal circumstance. However, they were also shaped by our respective commitments to social justice, democracy and equality. They were also strongly influenced by the many men and women of great integrity and fortitude who guided, wrote about, participated in and sacrificed in their effort and by their shared commitment.

Trying to produce the unwritten story of the Kamuzu Banda regime has been a long process. We were limited by the very small personal resources we could draw on as two retirees with fixed and very modest incomes. We are two amateur historians with a commitment to setting the record straight. This book is not what we had originally set out to do. We thought we would write about our own personal reminiscences and perhaps something of a polemic. Nonetheless we are extremely pleased with the way it has turned out as a collaborative effort. It stands as an eloquent testimony to the many lives buffeted by the powerful currents and counter-currents that dragged people through the negative underside of the times.

Acknowledgement

First and foremost, we are thankful to all our friends and collaborators who offered to tell their stories so eloquently and without any hesitation.

We also sincerely appreciate our long-suffering life-partners, Flora and Nellie for their patience and encouragement.

We are grateful to many other people:

- Richard Carver: formerly of Human Rights Watch and Article 19 now Senior Lecturer in Human Rights and Governance, Centre for Development and Emergency Practice, Oxford Brookes University
- The Royal Norwegian Embassy in Malawi, particularly Ambassador, Asbjørn Eidhammer
- The Copyright Society of Malawi (COSOMA)
- Winston Mwagomba of the Uraha Foundation and Manager of the Cultural and Museum Centre of Karonga.
- Shem Kayira, Kapote's Tireless IT Assistant
- Max and Rachel Munthali for their wonderful and generous hospitality
- Gwen Schulman, translator and activist who was our editor and supporter
- Ceciwa Bwanausi-Khonje (retired) for all her patience and encouragement
- Frank Chipasula, Professor in the Department of Africana Studies, Southern Illinois University (Carbondale) for his encouragement and the typesetting

At the time of this reprint, four of our friends had passed away. We offer our sincerest condolences to the families of Rose Chibambo, Willie Chokani, Lawrence Mwamlima and Machipisa Munthali. May their Souls rest in peace.

List of Acronyms and Vernacular Terms

AAPSO	The Afro-Asian Solidarity Organisation
ADMARC	Agricultural Development and Marketing Organisation
A luta continua	Portuguese for "the struggle continues"
Boma	A term used to describe a livestock enclosure, stockade, small fort or a district government office used in many parts of the African great lakes region, as well as central and southern Africa. (Wikipedia)
CCM	Chama cha Mapunduzi
CCAM	Chitukuko Cha Amayi M'Malawi
Chigawenga	Rebel or traitor. A term used by the Banda regime for any of its opponents or even detainees.
CSR	Congress of the Second Republic
Frelimo	Front for the Liberation Of Mozambique
GDP	Gross Domestic Product
Induna	A chief's advisor
Katundu	Baggage
Legco	Legislative Council
Lesoma	Socialist League of Malawi
MAFREMO	Malawi Freedom Movement
MBC	Malawi Broadcasting Corporation
Mbumba	In the Chewa matrilineal tradition, it represents the lineage of childbearers of the clan or family effectively female relatives for whom a man is responsible.
MCP	Malawi Congress Party
Mzungu / Azungu	A white person / white people
NAC	Nyasaland African Congress
Ngwazi	The title Ngwazi means "chief of chiefs" (more literally, "great lion", or…, "conqueror") in Chichewa. (Wikipedia)
Pangale	Refugee settlement in Tanzania
PDP	PanAfrican Democratic Party
Thangata	Tenant land holding bordering on serfdom
Tikkey, tikki	Chichewa for the tiny three pence coin issued during the Federation

Ujamaa	Swahili word for socialism
Ufulu	Freedom in Chichewa
Uhuru	Freedom in Swahili
Ulendo	Trip in Chichewa
Umodzi	United in Chichewa
UUMA	Ufulu Umodzi Malawi Party
WPC	World Peace Council

Foreword

We asked our old friend and comrade, Frank Chipasula, to write a foreword to introduce our work and asked his permission to use a poem from Lesoma's newsletter, Kuchanzo, which we thought he might have authored during his early years of exile. In reply, he referred us to a more recent poem he has written which we feel stands as a very eloquent foreword.

Manifesto on Ars Poetica | Frank Chipasula

My poetry is exacting a confession
from me: I will not keep the truth from my song.
I will not bar the voice undressed by the bees
from entering the gourd of my bow-harp.
I will not wash the blood off the image
I will let it flow from the gullet
slit by the assassin's dagger through
the run-on line until it rages in the verbs of terror;
And I will distil life into the horrible adjectives;
I will not clean the poem to impress the tyrant
I will not bend my verses into the bow of a praise song.
I will put the symbols of murder hidden in high offices
in the center of my crude lines of accusations.
I will undress our raped land and expose her wounds.
I will pierce the silence around our land with sharp metaphors
And I will point the light of my poems into the dark
nooks where our people are pounded to pulp.
I will not coat my words in lumps of sugar
I will serve them to our people with the bitter quinine:
I will not keep the truth from my heartstringed guitar;
I will thread the voice from the broken lips
through my volatile verbs that burn the lies.
I will ask only that the poem watch the world closely;
I will ask only that the image put a lamp on the dark
ceiling in the dark sky of my land and light the dirt.
Today, my poetry has exacted a confession from me.

Posted by The African Book Review in its Poetry section
http://theafricanbookreview.com/2014/11/27/frank-chipasula/

Chapter One - Introduction

1.1 Introduction
1.2 Radical tradition
1.3 Banda as dictator
1.4 Complicity
1.5 Regionalism - Divide and Rule
1.6 The Promised Land and Democracy Bubble
1.7 Truth and justice
1.8 The book's structure
1.9 Methodology

> *The evil that men do lives after them:*
> *The good is oft interred with their bones.*
> *Julius Caesar Act 3 Scene 2*
> by William Shakespeare
>
> The respected African scholar, George Shepperson knew that Hastings Kamuzu Banda admired Julius Caesar. Shepperson had known Dr Banda for many years and used this quote from Shakespeare in a presentation he made to the Friends of Malawi Society in England shortly after Banda's death. He ended his presentation with these lines and went on to wish it wasn't so*.
>
> In Mark Anthony's funeral oratory for the recently assassinated Caesar, he explains how Caesar was one of those men whose "evil" acts overshadowed the good they were able to achieve, typically because their evil acts were *extremely* evil.
>
> Ironically, Malawi's current leadership classes have made a concerted effort to rehabilitate Kamuzu's legacy by exorcising the evil of his regime and perpetuating the myths about Banda's strength and qualities as a messiah or saviour despite ample evidence of his bloody misrule and the tragic consequences which haunt the country today.
>
> * Shepperson, George (1998) MEMORIES OF DR. BANDA, The Society of Malawi Journal, Vol. 51, No. 1 (1998), pp. 74-84.

1.1 Lost Years?

Time and again in our interviews, our friends and collaborators told us how they felt forsaken and forgotten. It was a loss for the victims who suffered. It was also a loss to the country, because enormous talent and skills were wasted as were human lives. More frustrating for the victims is how the suffering they endured during their years of exile and detention has been lost in the romanticised memories that the country's current rulers are selling of Dr Banda's legacy. This loss of historical memory is unfathomable and unpardonable. By giving voice to what really happened we hope to restore a truthful account of the period and honour their loss.

We interviewed 45 people and spoke with many more who suffered abuse and injustice during the Banda dictatorship. While the people herein tell the story from their vantage point often as educated survivors, no one should lose sight of the way the whole population lost out during the Banda dictatorship. It is commonly acknowledged that all Malawians suffered under the jackboot of the Malawi Congress Party and its enforcement arms – the Malawi Young Pioneers, the Youth League, the Women's League, the Special Branch of the police and the party machine itself. Inside the country, the repression was so intense that everyone maintained a steadfast silence in an effort to survive unnoticed and avoid dire problems with the regime. That memory has not been lost and all Malawians denounce the outright abuse of that dark period.

In its report, *Where Silence Rules: The Suppression of Dissent*, written a mere four years before the downfall of the Banda regime, African Rights Watch pointed out that:

Malawi is proof that repression can work. Decades of one-party rule and restrictions on the free flow of information have ensured that this small Central African nation is familiar to few in the outside world beyond a small circle of specialists.

Malawi does not appear newsworthy because… it is a stable, pro-Western ally. But its stability has been bought at a terrible cost of human lives snuffed out or forced to endure years of detention without trial. Intellectual life can scarcely survive the dead hand of the censor and political life is non-existent outside the omnipotent ruling party. The best and brightest of Malawians are eliminated from the scene. The country's leading poet and only neurosurgeon are detained without charge. A leading journalist was assassinated in exile last year. A prominent economist suffered a similar fate a few years ago. (Page 1)

The author of the report is referring here to Professor Jack Mapanje, the detained head of Chancellor College's English and Literature department and Dr. Nga Mutafu who was a skilled and highly regarded physician. The journalist was Mkwapatira Mhango who died along with seven family members when their house was fire-bombed in Lusaka in 1989. The economist was Attati Mpakati the able and popular leader of Lesoma, the Socialist League of Malawi, who was killed by Banda's agents in Harare in 1983. It was for good reason that, even in exile, Malawians lived in fear of their lives and for how the regime would treat their families inside Malawi if they ever got involved in oppositional politics.

1.2 Radical tradition

Dr Ibbo Mandaza wrote very succinctly in the foreword to the book *Malawi at the Crossroads* (ed. Guy Mhone, SAPES Books, Harare, 1992),

On the political front, it is often forgotten that it was prominent Malawian radicals that heralded modern nationalist politics in Southern Africa: Clements Kadalie, who pioneered the Labour Movement of Southern Africa, and was associated with the Communist Party of Nyasaland (formed in or about 1920), perhaps the first of its kind in Southern Africa; Charles Mzingeli, who constituted a vital factor in the labour struggles of Southern Rhodesia in the 1930s; and such persons as Eliot Kamwana, Thom Nyirenda, Jack Muwamba and Oscar Kambona, all of whom constituted key factors in the independence struggles of Tanzania, Zambia and Zimbabwe.(xii)

From the time of John Chilembwe and his effort to resist colonial misrule until Dr Banda grabbed power, Nyasas and later Malawians were very often involved in organising strikes, political parties and many other forms of resistance to colonialism. There was a strong commitment to the goals of panAfricanism. This included extensive contacts with South Africa and Zimbabwe through Zambia and Congo to Tanzania and Ghana. The activists behind the nationalist movement, known as the Young Turks, many of whom had completed further education beyond secondary school, had travelled abroad and had contact with leaders of the nationalist movements in much of anglophone Africa and further abroad in newly independent India. In fact, relations with Tanzania to the north and Zambia to the West were very close and fraternal and Malawians were respected for the principled discipline of their struggle. They both offered and received pan-Africanist support for struggles against colonialism. Rose Chibambo led the women's section of the Nyasaland African Congress during the 1950's and 1960s. She points out how they received help from Ghana, Tanzania and many others during their struggle and that part of their disquiet with the foreign policy direction of Dr Banda during the years of self-government was their belief that they had an obligation to support the struggle of their "friends" in Mozambique, Rhodesia and South Africa.

Dr Banda himself may very likely have met several strands of this revolutionary and progressive movement during his time in South Africa, where he was exposed both to the liberation philosophy of the African nationalist churches and the union organising around the working class struggle of Clement Kadalie before one of those nationalist churches sponsored his education in America. Richard Carver, another astute observer of the Malawian scene, has written that:

> Banda himself, a keen student of his country's history, was only too aware of how the MCP was the modern manifestation of a radical nationalist tradition going back to 1915 and the first violent stirrings of resistance to colonialism. (Page 8, unpublished manuscript – communication 19 November 2013)

Carver maintains that the repression Banda unleashed upon the country

> ...(W)as necessary not because Malawians were passive, but because of Banda's fear of their radical potential. Nor was this fear misplaced. There was resistance to his rule throughout those 30 years....(page 15)

Malawians had provided a fountain of revolutionary and progressive ideas and leadership throughout Central and Southern Africa. The split that culminated in the 1964 confrontation known as the Cabinet Crisis broke decisively with this tradition and redirected the Malawian government into a dictatorship, firmly planted in the ideology acceptable to the Cold War West and the international financial institutions that firmly backed his regime as a bulwark against "communist" influences in the continuing nationalist struggle in Southern Africa and the neighbouring countries. The radical tradition did not end with the split but lived on into exile and into detention as the testimonies contained in this volume demonstrate. Also implicit in their anti-colonial struggle was the will to detach from the root source of the colonial model - western capitalism, and either undertake a social and economic transformation aimed at moving newly independent societies into some form of people-based development or at least take a non-aligned position between the Cold War titans who both demanded allegiance for their aid.

1.3 Banda as a dictator.

The many years in Britain seemed to have turned Dr Banda into a rabid anti-communist, ultra-conservative pro-Western anglophile. He very opportunistically joined the progressive movement that the Young Turks had built out of their radical connections, and then seizing the opportunity he ousted all the competition and any opposition to impose his total control. Thus ended Malawi's formal involvement in the progressive struggles still being waged in Africa against colonialism and racist white rule. Banda quickly established his trademark authoritarianism which then flourished into full-blown dictatorship. He was a dictator who planned his way to absolute power, sought out his support amongst a variety of collaborators, and was ruthless in rooting out any opposition. And thus began the thirty Lost Years in Malawi which begins and ends with Kamuzu Banda.

No-one should pretend that Dr Banda did not know what was going on anywhere, anytime throughout the country. He was famous for micro-managing every aspect of life in Malawi. All party appointments required his approval, and civil service houses for the lowest ranking clerk or nursing attendant were allocated at his wish. Such daily trivia as the headlines in newspapers, gun licenses and expatriate appointments all crossed over his desk. Right into the last years of his deep senility, he may have been used by others, but they very clearly operated along the lines that he had drawn.

Tragically, Dr Banda's presence in the nationalist scene was at the invitation of the younger generation of energetic, progressive politicians. Whatever faults and differences they may have had, the Young Turks were always collaborative in laying out their strategy for independence and what might follow. They had worked together very effectively throughout the period 1953 to 1958. That included the decision to bring Dr Banda to Malawi as an elder to be the unifying figurehead in the last push to end the federation and move to independence. In all likelihood, they assumed that he would work with them collaboratively in the process. To that end, they built his reputation amongst the people and perhaps even went over the top in building the case for Dr Banda's wisdom, courage, skill, and so on, even before he stepped off the plane that fateful 6 July 1958. Once placed on the hero pedestal, he started to kick away the ladders of any others who might aspire to climb up there with him or challenge his dominant position.

Banda had a plan in which he was the central actor and would brook no questionning, criticism or challenge. Others like Philip Short, in his 1974 biography of Dr Banda, confirmed that he negotiated one on one with his colonial counterparts leaving his own Cabinet members sitting outside the door. He treated them with great disdain. He was also known to have a bad temper and would use his angry outbursts to intimidate people who tried to challenge him. However, they did confront him frequently over his decisions and tendencies, but true to the principle of Cabinet solidarity these debates occurred behind closed doors while they continued to present a united front in public. This was partly imposed by the principled discipline of their struggle through the 1950s and also the British government's insistence that independence would only be granted to a clearly united party with a single leader. The litmus test of their discipline was the way they tried to avert the crisis by proclaiming their loyalty to Dr Banda even as they were being called traitors and evicted from the party and Parliament they had worked so hard to create.

They stuck with the game plan of Cabinet solidarity. However, this did not mean that they could not see or did not realise that Dr Banda was slowly imposing his authoritarian and anti-democratic way. Dunduzu Chisiza was one of the most articulate and far-sighted of the Young Turks and foretold of this tendency in his booklet, *Africa What Lies Ahead* (African-American Institute, New York, 1962).

The seventh danger is that of dictatorship. Three things will bring about a dictatorship in Africa: (1) too much trust, (2) too little trust, and (3) neurotic ambition. Of the three causes, the third presents the least problem. A man who makes up his mind to be another Napoleon, Hitler, or Mussolini in these changed times, can be certain that resurgent Africa will deal with him the way Europe dealt with the European misanthropes. People cannot heave off the yoke of colonialism and then fail to pulverize under their feet a demented individual who wants to sit on their necks.

The real problem is posed by those leaders who will lapse into dictatorial tendencies either because their countrymen trust them too much or because they trust them too little. When too much trust is reposed in a leader (sometimes) the thing goes to his head and makes him believe that he is infallible. Such a man is not likely to brook criticism or to welcome alternative suggestions. It is his idea or nothing. On the other hand, when a brilliant, self-assured, well-meaning leader is begrudged trust or is dealing with an illiterate populace, he too will tend to force his measures through in a dictatorial manner believing that the masses will appreciate what he is doing later. (page 15)

Banda quickly consolidated a centralised, top-down authoritarianism using whatever means he had at his disposal. This even included backroom deals with the very colonialists they were struggling to dislodge. He was not collaborative by nature and he did not like people second-guessing him. He went into meetings with governors and foreign office officials alone, leaving his senior cabinet members cooling their heels in the corridors. Then he would announce that the deal for independence had been signed, bragging that he had done it alone. Mary Mwale tells the story from her husband of how Banda short-changed independence.

They also lost the battle in June 1964 when Ching'oli and Chiume came back from abroad. They kept the secret of what had happened. They went with Banda to the UK.... They went to Lancaster House in London, where every aspiring African country for independence goes to. But the details only surfaced just before independence that Banda had signed on his own. They didn't know the details (of the instruments of independence).

Banda sought out support that did not depend on the Young Turks. His appeal to the British as well as to the conservative elements of the chiefs and the churches was meant to sap away the leadership support for and temper the ambitions of the Young Turks. The Young Turks had initially decided to invite him back to placate the apprehensions of the chiefs about their apparent youth and radicalism. The majority of the chiefs derived a great deal of power from the way the British used them to administer colonial edicts, collect taxes and in many other ways directly benefit from the British divide and rule policy. Many of them were very wary about the intentions of the younger generation in maintaining the chieftainships and their power in an independent Malawi.

As if being sidelined did not already frustrate the Young Turks, they must have been all the more upset at Banda's condescending treatment of them as "My Boys." Public humiliation was accompanied by personal slights. He would not even allow his ministers to use the main toilet in his house – they had to use the servants' toilet outdoors.

Once he felt he had the balance of power in his favour he was ruthless in removing them from the scene. The phrase, "deal with them" came to be understood as eliminate them. Anyone who criticised Banda became "*chigawenga*," or rebel, and criticism or even questioning Banda and his policies was equated to treason. Widespread anarchy was unleashed upon the country with party thugs brought in from regions loyal to Banda and his coterie to undermine the structures of the party in the North and South that might remain sympathetic to the ousted ministers. Brutal beatings and planned assassinations were common. Many of our friends and collaborators tell horrific tales of how they and their families were abused.

All orders flowed downward from Banda and his style set the tone for the methods used by his supporters and collaborators. Carson Kayuni tells how his friend was at a meeting of the Malawi Congress Party in Karonga in which they drew up the list of names of people to be eliminated that night and reported how his was on it.

Not everyone collaborated whole-heartedly in the repression that Banda unleashed. There were people at all levels of society wiling to help their friends escape the pogrom of violence Dr Banda unleashed upon the people of the country. The Young Turks had built considerable support and were very popular as leaders. Sympathetic police covered some people's escape, while family and friends provided cover and support. Rose Chibambo tells of the Malawi Young Pioneers in Chiradzulu who were sent to "deal with her." They told her, "We knew you before we knew Banda" and refused to mistreat her.

If there are still lingering doubts that Banda was a dictator that only the exiles and detainees despise, here is what a present-day Malawian journalist had to say in protest to President Joyce Banda's recent praise of Dr Banda. We quote in full.

Give Malawians a break on Kamuzu Banda

By George Kasakula

NATION OPINION

Going through statements from various quarters, including one President Joyce Banda made in Kasungu, canonising Kamuzu Banda as a holy patron saint of development and women liberation, you would think that this is not the same man who for over 30 years ruled Malawi with an iron fist.

Kamuzu's legacy might have one positive thing or two, but those that try to paint him as the most virtuous thing that ever happened to this country should give Malawians who suffered under this man some break.

Those who want to use Kamuzu's name for their own selfish political agenda should know that Malawians will not forget that this is the man whose government agents killed the Mwanza four, Aaron Gadama, Dick Matenje, Twaibu Sangala and David Chiwanga as well as Attati Mpakati, among others, in cold blood for merely opposing his selfish policies that were meant to benefit a clique at the expense of the majority of Malawians.

This is the man who sent scores of innocent Malawians into exile and many only returned after 1994, spending the best part of their lives away from their own home.

Many came back old and broken, finding it very difficult to cope and ended up in graves.

Then, there are those that were not lucky enough to run away from Kamuzu's vindictive ire and ended up being locked away without trial.

I can go on and on, wasting scarce newspaper space, mentioning this group or that group which suffered under Kamuzu's reign of terror, but to cut an otherwise long story short, those that speak of this man in these unprecedented glowing terms are simply throwing a torrent of insults at those who paid the ultimate price with their blood for opposing the despot.

Let us face facts, Malawi was one hell of a place to live in.

Those who oppose this were either part of that evil system and, therefore, benefitted from it or were born dishonest enough not to accept the simple truth that the old autocrat's terror permeated every single Malawian society and its agents such as Youth Leaguers or Malawi Young Pioneers were at hand to pounce on anybody making even the faintest sound, crying for freedom.

I am not a dunderhead not to appreciate the fact that the past belongs to the past and that, as a nation, we should move on, but I also refuse to accept that this past should be painted white for mere political exigencies and conveniences of today, as the President is trying to do, when I know for a fact that it was pitch black.

This is like giving political leaders a blank cheque to kill, maim and imprison innocent citizens knowing that Malawians will forget and might even start praising them in due course.

Kamuzu can never be venerated when Malawians were only saved from State brutality after the fall of the Soviet Union which led to a paradigm shift among Western nations that saw them insist on human rights as a condition for their aid and the bravery of Catholic bishops with their 1992 Pastoral Letter that called for freedom to Malawians.

As for the assertion that Kamuzu developed Malawi, give us a break, will you? Which development is this? Is Malawi developed when a vast majority in rural areas cannot even afford the proverbial pinch of salt?

In any case, did Kamuzu build the infrastructure we wax lyrical about using his personal money? Was it not from donors or taxes?

This habit of personalising development is trifle and partly responsible for the fact that Malawi is still poor 50 years after independence.

Kamuzu is not a hero, but a tinpot dictator, who for 31 years, terrorised his own people to serve his overgrown ego and those close to him.

This is his legacy and the rest is immaterial. No one should cheat Malawians.

(Malawi Nation, May 14, 2013)

The people who provided their stories for this book as well as a broad spectrum of Malawians of all stripes would agree with Kasakula's argument. We cannot sweep this history under the carpet and glorify the man as though he did not know what was happening around him. His supporters were acting according to the procedures that he had set in place, which depended on oral commands, nuanced meanings and opaque explanations if at all. These are not the qualities we ascribe to heroes.

1.4 Complicity

Dr Banda alone could never have imposed his iron will without support from many others, nor continued so long in power. He depended on many others to establish himself over and above the Young Turks who had brought him to power. In that struggle, he quietly built his links behind closed doors with local British officials, the chiefs, the Central Region politicians and conservative elements in the Church. Each of them was rallied to support him with different appeals.

Machipisa Munthali says it quite succinctly, *Banda wanted it, not only Banda, because in a way I look at it, the one party state, it is not only the head of state, because everybody is taking a chance to do that.* In his view, the chance they were taking was that by throwing their lot in with the regime they were hoping to profit and were thus complicit in and responsible for condoning if not committing the many injustices that occurred.

As a dictator, he was firmly at the head, but there were power manipulators behind, beside and all around the throne. There was the trusted inner circle which evolved through the years as the occupants jockeyed and battled for a position closest to Banda's chair. Tembo, Msonthi, Kadzamira, Muwalo, Gwede – the names are well known and as much as they were feared they were envied for their power and the wealth they accumulated through access to land, credit, and business opportunities, in short wealth accumulation. In addition, the elements of the State entrusted to enforce a state of law and to rein in abuse simply gave in and became part of the system that inflicted horrible punishment on real and imagined enemies. The police, military, and the civil service were all complicit for not just allowing, but aiding and abetting the injustices. Even at the village level, Malawi Congress Party favourites, the Youth and Women's League received favours and were feared. They benefitted by promoting his dictatorship and regardless of their status, high or low, they were part of the abuses that were unleashed on the people of the country.

Colonial complicity

The complicity of the British and their Western allies was also key to Dr Banda's rise to power and the sidelining of the Young Turks. By the time Malawi was about to receive its independence, the British had gained a great deal of insight into how to manipulate the process of decolonisation in order to maintain their effective control. The lessons had been learned from Ghana, Kenya, Uganda and Tanzania. Long after self-government in 1962, Banda relied on the British colonial infrastructure to maintain his position and to undermine anyone who might challenge him. At the State level, it was clear that the British far preferred a solid, conservative, anglophile like Dr Hastings Banda, to the hotheaded Young Turks, like Chipembere, the Chisiza brothers and Chiume who spoke openly about panAfricanism and relations with the communist world. The senior civil service remained solidly white until the late 1960s and as several of our interviewees confirm, British police officers seconded to Malawi took part in some of the most brutal interrogation activities meant to root out opposition and intimidate the population. Superintendent John Savage, a British officer in charge of the Northern region exemplified the savagery and brutality of the regime. This included training a generation of Malawian officers in being particularly cruel to those identified as enemies of Dr Banda.

This is an indictment of the British government, which shares the guilt of complicity in human rights violations. A number of British officials enjoyed high rank within the central government including Peter Youens who was the Chief Secretary of the government and had Banda's ear on a daily basis. Colonel Peter Lewis was the head of the army. Peter Long was commissioner of the Malawi Police Force. They clearly knew what was happening and thus were complicit in the installation of and consolidation of dictatorial rule.

1.5 Regionalism - Divide and Rule

The colonial system depended on divide and rule. Ethnic, gender and regional differences were exploited to weaken resistance to colonial authority. Throughout the period of the nationalist struggle, Malawians identified as Nyasas both inside and outside of the country, worked effectively together, and strove for unity. In contrast, Dr Banda unabashedly used regionalism and ethnicity to build a power base to contest the perceived dominance of the South and the North. An early manifestation of Banda's ethnic tendencies helps provide an insight into his later behaviour....

George Shepperson recounts how he, *asked Mark Hanna Watkins what Banda was like when he knew him in Chicago in the early 1930's. Watkins' reply came immediately, in a staccato statement which I have never forgotten. "Banda," Watkins said quickly, was "very tribal." I asked Watkins what he meant by this. He gave me an anecdote to illustrate what he meant by calling Banda in Chicago "very tribal". Watkins used to visit Banda in his Chicago lodgings to get information from him on the Chewa language for his doctoral thesis. At lunch time, one day, Watkins took up a couple of what Americans call "brown-bag lunches": one for himself and one for Banda. Watkins started on his own lunch and began putting linguistic questions to Banda. Banda replied; but Watkins noted that he was not eating his lunch. Watkins asked him why not, several times; until Banda finally asserted, "The Chewa do not eat with strangers."* (Page 76 MEMORIES OF DR. BANDA, The Society of Malawi Journal, Vol. 51, No. 1 (1998), pp. 74-84)

Regionalism was reinforced and entrenched by the events of 1964 Parliamentary Crisis. The ensuing rift between Banda and the Young Turks was exacerbated by the machinations of the parliamentarians of the Centre aided by Chidzanja Nkhoma, John Tembo and Richard Katengeza, who polarised the issues around a Centre versus the South and North. Aleke Banda and Gwanda Chakumba stood out from their Northern and Southern peers to side with Banda. The Centre succumbed to Banda's appeal to tribalism and with the Malawi Young Pioneers (MYP), the conservative chiefs and the support of the British, it gave Banda what he needed to turn the tide in his favour.

1.6 The Promised Land and Democracy Bubble

The end of the Kamuzu Banda era should have created space for a new beginning in Malawian development. Open, participatory democracy should have allowed for a fresh approach based on people-centred development from the bottom up. Such an approach would have addressed issues as urgent and tragic as inequitable land holding, tenancy, poverty, health care, education, housing, gender abuse, equity and corruption. However, the structures of cronyism and self-enrichment established under Kamuzu Banda have unfortunately continued on into what should have been a new and democratic era. Access to power is equated with access to wealth for the few at the expense of the many. In most cases, the same people who profited under the Banda regime are still in positions of power and influence under structures he developed and put in place.

They carry with them the spirit and style of his form of governance and romanticise his rule as a golden era. The relentless, venal wealth accumulation by today's rulers is firmly in the mold of the economic and political direction set by Banda. By virtue of control of state power, it becomes the right of political incumbents to acquire whatever and as much as possible. Guy Mhone in "The Political Economy of Malawi – An Overview" describes an iron triangle of control instituted under Banda (1992. in *Malawi at the Crossroads: The Post-Colonial Economy* ed. Guy Mhone, Sapes Books, Harare). The peak of the triangle was the "iron triumvirate" of Kamuzu, Tembo, and Kadzamira ensuring peace and stability through fear and the threat of punishment. They formulated policy, issued decrees, dispensed favours and initiated reprisals for non-compliance perceived or real. Below them was one corner of the triangle made up of the structures of government, parastatals and civil society which were obedient and beholding to the carrot they were offered and the stick wielded over them. The other corner was the class of agricultural and commercial entrepreneurs who benefited by the profit they made. The whole system was based on the cheap labour of the Malawian underclasses and the profit was always at their expense. The brutal repression was intended to keep these people submissive and afraid to speak out let alone act against their exploitation.

Dr Banda's Press Group of companies still features as one of the Top 500 companies on the African continent, no mean feat for such a tiny country. Banda used his access to land, resources, and finance capital to acquire control over an enormous share of the national economy. This included vast tracts of land turned into estates for producing tobacco and other cash crops using tenant labour (*thangata*). By involving his senior political leaders and civil servants, police and military in the process, they became beholden to him for their welfare and wealth accumulation, but more important, it gave them a stake in upholding the system that offered them these benefits.

Changing the head but leaving in place the structures beneath meant that a whole group of people beholden to Dr Banda were still sitting in the places they had comfortably filled for as many as 30 years. They had no interest in giving up what they had gained. Any new directions in policy and priorities for development were a threat to them. In addition, they were now free to take over the apex and glean riches beyond their previous hopes with the 'iron triumvirate' out of the way. Each successive government has retained this lesson and very quickly embarked on self-enrichment virtually from the day it takes power. In this way, there was no end in sight to the dependency on cheap labour. The poorest groups continued to be forced into tenancy and suffer all the consequences of the maldevelopment practices facing the people of Malawi. In this scenario, there would always be a poor class in Malawi fated to toil for less than subsistence to add to the astonishing wealth of a small clique of rulers.

Similar privileges were accorded to the acolytes of the other two corners of the triangle who toed the party line and pledged total unquestioning obedience to His Excellency. Low interest bank loans with favourable conditions were made available, large tracts of land alienated and great wealth accumulated by a very select group of people. If a business class arose at all, it was within and came out of these groupings. Any route to wealth was acceptable among the ruling classes. Kamuzu, following the dictates of the World Bank and International Monetary Fund, condemned the nationalisation of private interests. Even today, bank managers are reported to receive instructions from people in high positions, who insist that their cronies or relatives be given almost free loans to acquire land, buy houses, or take over businesses without the regular rigour of banking protocols for such loans and advances. As a result, civil servants and politicians with jobs of modest salaries accumulate wealth rapidly upon entering office using the connections and back-scratching techniques evolved over 30 years when this was the way to self-advancement.

In addition, many structures from the Malawi Congress Party/Kamuzu Banda period remain in place. The new parties expropriated these for themselves with little or no reflection on what they represent in terms of gender equity, class relations, the problems of hero worship, and so on. Old habits remained intact. Parties formed youth wings and bused dancing women around to functions, which blurred the line between government business and party politics. Heroic names, and hero worship of the leader were just part of maintaining many of the symbols of Kamuzu's presidency and regrettably perpetuate many undemocratic practices such as threats against political opponents and control of the national broadcaster by the party in power.

The emphasis on peace, order and stability vaunted by Dr Banda has been maintained into the democratic dispensation. The emphasis on peace and peaceful elections has been used to subvert the need to deal with the lack of social justice and equality. International donors as well as much of civil society and the churches preached the need to move on and plan for the future without reflecting on the past and its problems. They feared social disruption so much that they discouraged any form of protest. As a result, the people lack the fora to discuss their malaise and deal with their issues. When they do seek to express themselves it can lead to the kind of violent confrontation of July 2011 when urban protests became very rough and police resorted to lethal force. Under Joyce Banda, the police reaction was more tempered, but was still explosive in January and February 2013 when student protests rocked Blantyre and Lilongwe. Rather than seek routes to deal with the problems, the politicians at the time spoke in very Kamuzu terms about "dealing with enemies."

The election of May 2014 epitomised this failure to change from the old habits of exploitation of the past. Four candidates stood for election, each one representing the previous four regimes and the consistent inequities of self-enrichment and failure to serve the people. None of them presented an alternative to the present structure and in no way broke with the past. If anything, the hypocrisy of hauling out Kamuzu's memory to justify their election rose to new heights and simply promised more of the same. In addition, dynastic rule has been added to the methods of retaining power and wealth.

One of the most egregious examples of the failure of our current leaders to act as guardians and keepers of the national trust is what has happened to the country's forest reserves, especially the Chikangawa Forest. This rich forest resource offered a perfect opportunity for transition and development in the Second Liberation after the fall of the one-party dictatorship. The unbroken stand of trees stretched across the horizon and was arguably one positive residue of the last days of colonialism, as the biggest man-made forest in Africa. However, under the corruption of the so-called democratic dispensation, it has been pillaged for the profit of the greedy few who mismanage the country. The forest has been turned into a wasteland with no economic benefit to the people and the country at large. The nation has been left with an environmental and economic disaster which has jeopardised future development and left the masses to reap the negative consequences of a heavily mortgaged inheritance. The political leaders and civil servants continue to line their pockets by issuing fraudulent and illegal cutting licenses, and endless queues of trucks lumber their way up the highways and across the borders for points as far away as Dar es Salaam and Botswana.

1.7 Truth and justice

When dramatic regime change occurs in any given country a number of different reactions can occur. In the Czech Republic, after the fall of communism, the new government passed a law forbidding members of the secret police and the old Communist Party from being members of the civil service and its related bodies such as the police. In South Africa, a Truth and Reconciliation Commission was established to allow people who had been wronged to recount the injustice they had faced and call to account the person or organisation who had wronged them. Wrongdoers could acknowledge their crimes and not face prosecution. In Sierra Leone, a blanket amnesty was issued to all parties to the brutal civil war with the exception of some of the major actors who were brought to trial before a special international tribunal set up to deal with them. This meant victims of atrocities often returned to their homes and found themselves living side by side with neighbours who had caused them great personal harm.

The Romanian, Malawian and Northern Ireland examples point to what happens when the same people who were highly placed members of a previous regime remain in power after the transition. In her documentary *State Secrets – Part Two*, Wana Iechskeui (BBC World Service Documentaries Broadcast on Friday, 18 December 2009) interviews people about why Romania is facing so many problems many years after the fall of the Ceausescu regime. One of her interview subjects says, "The problem is the communists are very strong. They still control the economy and more important the property. They had the money. They had the vested interests, they had the relations. In effect they remain. A lot of the same people are still around. There is a lot of political infighting and people are more involved with the current struggles than with the past." The point was that after decades of oppressive rule under the Ceausescu regime the interviewee felt that there was "still a little bit of Ceausescu in all of us" and that it would take some time to change the bad old habits of the past that had been so firmly ingrained throughout the society.

The Kamuzu regime was accountable to no one and there was absolutely no transparency when it came to the ruling cabal's decisions and transgressions. His successors in the President's office have adopted or inherited many of the practices he established. As an example, Joyce Banda and her husband learned their politics serving in Dr Banda's government as politicians and civil servants. Upon becoming President in 2012, she refused to account for her personal wealth, using the rationale that she didn't need to because her predecessors didn't have to. The people, who built up resources under the Banda regime, had local and international networks and clambered into the drivers seat as the dictatorship came to an end. They have simply picked up where Kamuzu left off rather than working to transform the system and correcting the injustices inherent in the structure Banda set up.

1.8 The book's structure

A number of our respondents were active participants in the nationalist struggle and we use their stories to set the scene for Dr Banda's rise to absolute power.

Chapter Two carries the title *The Gathering Storm* to provide an element of historical context. Chapters Three to Six give voice to the former detainees, the exiles and those who lived and suffered under the regime's state of terror once he had ensconced himself in power. Contrary to the regime's propaganda, there was popular opposition to Dr Banda which is told through the stories of those who were activists in Chapter Seven, *Organised Resistance*. Chapter Eight: *Living with the Pain* tells the stories of the exiles return and the post-prison reality of the former detainees, their individual disappointment, alienation, dispossession, and bitterness. Chapter Nine, *The Promised Land and Democracy Bubble* provides insights and reflections on the state of affairs in Malawi today from the respondents' point of view. Judging from the critical newspaper columnists and the interest shown in this book, they are not alone in their negative assessment of where today's leaders have taken Malawi.

1.9 Methodology

We were very limited by the very small personal resources we could draw on as two retirees on very modest fixed incomes. We are two amateur historians with passion. We know that many others have written about their experiences and we do not attempt to retell what has been better told by them. There are books about the life of Henry Masauko Chipembere and Vera Chirwa's tale is well told in her autobiography. We envy the craftsmanship of the master story teller, Jack Mapanje in his many poems, articles and, of course, his prison memoir *And Crocodiles are Hungry Tonight* (Ayebia Clarke Publishing, Oxfordshire, 2011). Many other heroes have yet to get their stories told more fully. While Peter Mackay has written about Yatuta Chisiza in his book, *We Have Tomorrow: Stirrings in Africa, 1959 – 1967* (Michael Russell Publishing Ltd, Norwich, 2008), this great hero does not, to our knowledge, have his place fully enough recognised and valued in the pantheon of Malawi heroes and deserves a book of his own.

We also read Jack Mapanje's and Reuben Chirambo's analysis of how orality was an integral part of the dictator's hold over the country. Mapanje describes how after his arrest: *... the public houses will be full of stale jokes: another one bites the dust; another has met his 'orality justice' of our 'orality politics'; and many others. The truth, of course, is that Banda, his coterie, his security officers have been destroying whatever written traditions the British might have left behind. They've been creating a kind of oral culture where documentary evidence for the crimes that their death squads commit* *against innocent people are carefully erased from files and memory. So that when they are brought to book in the distant future – should political changes happen with the grace of God – there should be no concrete evidence to incriminate them for their wrongs.* (page 19, *And Crocodiles are Hungry at Night*, Ayebia Clarke Publishing Company, Oxfordshire, 2011)

Chirambo goes on to argue that, *in the context of a dictatorship that relies heavily on orality, Mapanje's recourse to the same orality is probably the only viable means in the quest for answers and is an effort to hold psychos accountable for atrocities, even if poetically projected.* (Vipers who minute our twitches: Psychopath's that served Banda's Malawian dictatorship in Jack Mapanje's Prison Poetry, quoted in *Spheres Public and Private: Western Genres in African Literature*, ed. Gordon Collier *Matatu* 39; Amsterdam & New York: Editions Rodopi, 2011)

Like Mapanje, we hope that our effort here helps to expose the truth behind the opaque mask of respectability currently being accorded to Kamuzu Banda by the current crop of political leaders. In our view, this is a very dangerous direction, and promoting these myths risks returning the country back to those bad old days and immoral ways.

This book is not what we had originally set out to do. We thought we would do our own personal reminiscences and perhaps something of a polemic. That it has evolved into this type of oral history is a reflection of many factors at work. First, we found so many people who were willing to tell their stories and they were all so fascinating and compelling that it would have been a shame to not give their voices an opportunity to be heard. We found ourselves impressed by the wealth of experience and the depth of their passion. Another factor was Doug's introduction to the Centre for Oral History and Digital Storytelling at Concordia University in Montreal, Canada which explained a great deal about oral history, its practices, methods and possibilities.

Oral history democratises history by giving it back to the people who lived it. True oral history would be the digital recordings of people in their own voices with all the nuance and feeling that that entails. By transcribing their words, we have already diluted their stories and converted them from the original verbal form into another media. We have carefully archived the interviews with our collaborators and hope to find a home for them in a publicly available database. The goal would be to continue the work of collecting this history from as many victims of the regime as possible and archiving it for future purposes. We would appreciate if others were able to extend this history to inform the world about people as worthy as the ones we spoke to in order to help draw a much more complete history of the terror of the time.

Ours is a very small sample. The National Compensation Tribunal which was set up with the 1994 democracy Constitution recorded over three thousand cases of verified abuse that warranted compensation. These were all documented as part of the process embarked on by the Tribunal, but where are these records? They seem to have fallen into Mapanje's opaque void fulfilling the concept of erasing history. We have had reports that over 20,000 claims were submitted and that 3,000 had been verified before the work of the Tribunal was summarily terminated.

In addition, immediately after the fall of the dictatorship, academics from a variety of disciplines came together to carry out a re-examination of the 30 previous years as part of the Malawi History Project. The goal was to address the many gaps in Malawian history created by Kamuzu's orality with its myths, lies and omissions. It is our understanding that the new government and university leadership were not keen to see such a deep examination since many people could easily have been implicated in wrongdoing or still occupied positions that had been acquired with the complicity we wrote about earlier. In addition, the funding from foreign donors that would have been needed to undertake this work was refused on the premise that no good point could be served by picking at the scabs of the past. Healing would occur by building for the future. Nonetheless, the material that was collected and manuscripts written seem to have disappeared from sight.

We certainly do not claim to have written a comprehensive and complete history of the stories we want to tell. In fact, we regret that we could not simply publish the full interviews of all our respondents, and apologise to them for leaving out so much of their compelling stories, but it would have created a unwieldy book. We also acknowledge our particular place in the history and slant on it. Our wish list of interviewees was very long, and yet by the time we had covered the 40 plus people we managed to see, we felt we had come a long way towards exposing this history, even if it is partial. The political climate in the country also drove us to want to get the story out sooner rather than later in order to counter the terrible revision of the truth about Hastings Kamuzu Banda that is being foisted on the people of Malawi and the world.

As part of our methodology we sought out deep background into the inner workings and insights into the thinking of Dr Banda. Justin Malewezi rose to a very prominent position as the Secretary to the President and Cabinet, Malawi's most senior civil servant working directly with Dr Banda. One might question how one who was in such an influential position would be included as a victim, but his story of the dread with which he faced each day is a telling indicator of the nature of the regime.

A note on language

As oral history, it would have been much more revealing to interview everyone in their mother tongue as we did with S.K. Mpango, Chief Mwase's *induna*. That would have allowed an even freer expression of people's feelings and deeper insight into details of their experience. However, even in English, many people without a significant educational background were able to describe what they saw and felt in great detail. Machipisa Munthali is a case in point. He never hesitated, beyond his natural stutter, to find the words to describe his ideas and the pain inflicted on him. We found a wonderful elegance in the simplicity of his English. We have kept the syntax of their language as close to what we believe we heard them say and have signified any modifications to their verbal text with our edited text in brackets either as information or for clarity.

Chapter Two – The Gathering Storm

2.1 Rose Chibambo

2.2 Radical tradition

2.3 Move to dictatorship

2.4 British complicity

2.5 The Cabinet Crisis

2.6 Regionalism - divide and rule

2.7 Popular support

The colonialists always considered Nyasaland an economic backwater. Its only value was strategic and the goal was to keep it out of the hands of their colonial competitors. Its unique shape resulted from the Conference of Berlin in 1885 where the British, Germans, French and Portuguese drew lines based on what little they knew of the geography of the watersheds and river systems. Shortly after that, the British moved in and set up a very basic administrative structure meant to minimise costs to the mother country. The criteria to be a full colony was based on what profit could be derived from the country's resources and people. Nyasaland was valued so little that it was made a mere protectorate. As such the British did not feel obliged to invest in the administrative and economic infrastructure of the country. And so it remained for the next 70 years.

Nyasas were valued as cheap labour for the local settler estates based on a tenancy system known as *thangata* which made serfs out of the people who had been dispossessed of their land by the same estates. They also provided cheap labour for the mines and estate plantations of Rhodesia and South Africa. At independence, the British had built pitifully few government run hospitals and schools and left a seriously underdeveloped power, transport and communications infrastructure.

Missionaries and settlers contributed more than the colonial government by setting up their missions with churches, schools and medical facilities in the Shire highlands around Blantyre where they found the climate to their liking. Others, following in the footsteps of David Livingstone, moved along the lakeshore northward leaving a string of missions equally equipped, and set up more major infrastructure at Bandawe and, finally, a large complex called Livingstonia on the Nyika escarpment overlooking the lake.

The earliest converts took up the educational opportunities the missions provided and migrated throughout East, Central and Southern Africa where they worked as low-level civil servants in the colonial infrastructure. There they became involved in the life of these communities, pursued higher education and brought back to Nyasaland their experience. It was many of these who evolved into the leadership of the nationalist movement.

Many Nyasas joined the Kings African Rifles (KAR), a battalion of rank and file African troops with British officers and fought in both world wars. In both cases, their involvement led to heightened awareness of their status as second class citizens. The uprising in 1915 led by John Chilembwe was in large part a protest against wartime conscription and the serf-like conditions facing the landless peasants. How could Africans be asked to defend the very empire that was treating them like slaves, taxing them and dispossessing them of their land? The KAR also served in Burma during the Second World War. The British thought that the African troops would be immune to malaria, however, the strain in Burma was different than that in Malawi. The post-war treatment of these veterans by the British was shameful and added to the radicalisation of the nationalist movement.

Resistance took shape amongst the Nyasa people to a proposal that had been on the table from Salisbury and London to federate the three central African colonies – Southern Rhodesia, Northern Rhodesia and Nyasaland. Once again the British colonial office was looking to download administrative costs for economic motives. There was also pressure from the large settler population in Southern Rhodesia to secure its dominant position in the region. One of independent Malawi's first cabinet ministers Willie Chokani points out, "... *it was to be a partnership of horse and rider...*" and everyone knew who the rider would be. This was a major concern for the independent-minded Nyasas, who feared the installation of the apartheid style colonialism they experienced when they were in South Africa or Southern Rhodesia. The imposition of the Federation crystallised the nationalist opposition and made the political climate much hotter after 1953. Rose Chibambo, another early cabinet minister, explains the issues.

2.1 Rose Chibambo

Rose Chibambo is one of the living legends of the Malawian independence movement, and made an invaluable contribution throughout the 1950s up until the Cabinet Crisis. She very graciously invited us into her home in Mzuzu and spoke to us with an open heart about the period of the nationalist struggles, being forced out of power, driven out of the country, and her years in exile. Much of it is sad and yet she tells everything, even the personal, as part of the struggle and sacrifice for independence and democracy. Rose Chibambo was in the thick of the nationalist struggle long before Banda made his appearance in the country, yet Banda quite figuratively erased her contribution from the history books. However, the reality of people's memory runs much deeper than that. She was, in fact, never forgotten and immediately after the fall of the Banda regime, she came home to a hero's welcome and the honour she so rightly deserved. She is the only woman featured on any Malawian currency.

Rose Chibambo (2013)

Rose's story provides a wonderful overview and insight into that time and we open with her version of events, which was also corroborated by others like Willie Chokani, Thengo Maloya and Molly Dzabala who are of the same generation. We are using her story to set the scene for the important role of many young nationalist leaders who struggled to end colonial rule only to find themselves sidelined by the rise of the dictatorship and early manifestations of the ruthless cruelty Banda unleashed to eliminate his enemies.

Born Rose Ziba in the Mzimba district on September 8, 1928, she married after Standard 5 and moved to Zomba in the late 1940s with her husband, Edwin Chibambo, a teacher turned civil servant. In Zomba, she completed her primary school by studying for Standard 6 at night. In those days, Standard 6 opened the door to many possibilities and would easily be equivalent to the current Form 2 or Junior Certificate. That made her a well educated woman.

She tells the story from a very human point of view and even though she was treated very badly, remains very objective and analytical about what went on when she was being removed from the scene. Both her effectiveness and her modesty are apparent when she describes her role organising the women during the difficult part of the nationalist struggle in the early 1950s. It also reveals her selflessness and that of almost all the early leaders before Kamuzu arrived and began to subvert the struggle.

A younger Rose, as a nationalist leader, appears on the K200 note

I organised the women. The beginning that started it all was Federation. The Federation of Rhodesia and Nyasaland was imposed on the three colonies in 1953). I only came to know about politics when our men started talking about Federation. That was in the fifties. And then much more what triggered it was at one time my husband was coming home late. So I wondered why he was coming home late. Not that I was suspicious of his life, but it was getting more than late. So he said it was because they are organising meetings to discuss about the Federation. Our poor country is about to be taken over. So I said how? How can a country be taken over?... They want to federate the two Rhodesias and Nyasaland, so that they can rule us, but what we want is to be independent. So I asked him if women attend these meeting? He said no. I haven't seen any women attending such meetings. I said, What about if I come to attend? He said, It's okay if you arrange for it. I have no problem.

She was a natural and effective organiser and quickly appreciated how to gather support and build a movement.

Then... I decided that instead of me going there alone, let me ask my fellow women. I literally went from house to house, near our location where we were living in Zomba.... I went around in the evenings when their husbands were back from work, so that it would not be just a caucus of women, in case the men might think I was trying to coax the women into something they don't know about. So we discussed (how) ... our country is to be federated together with Northern Rhodesia and Southern Rhodesia and I was giving them an example of South Africa where indigenous people are not regarded as anything. Most of our men used to go to South Africa to work, but each time they would come back, they would never come back with anything.... They were just being used as labourers and slaves without being paid anything much. This was quite known. And the women said, Oh yes, If that is the case let us get on with it."

(Some)time after I had organised enough groups, I said, instead of going to meet our men, let's get together ourselves. Then we went into ...Recreation Hall. We gathered there. We had an election. Before the election, I explained to them once again what it is all about and that it is a political group. This is the women now. What do we call it? Because we had Nyasaland African Congress, we decided it would be Nyasaland African Women's League.... That was 1952. Then we made an election and the women said, "It is you that knows all about this... therefore you are the chairman," and I was elected. My sister-in-law in marriage was elected treasurer, the wife of Gabaniso Chibambo nee Phiri, then Mrs. Kachingwe, nee Nkhata was elected Secretary. She came from Kasungu. That's how the Women's League started.

The move from organising to political action took a very practical approach to dealing with colonial attitudes to Africans and directly addressed the issues of concern to women.

We caused havoc. We said now that we are organised we must do something. So in those days whenever the women went for ante-natal clinic, at Zomba clinic, we would get into an open hall... with about four beds. And all the women are gathered, expectant mothers. Then four would be lying on these beds ready to be examined. And the.... examiners (would come) while all your friends are watching. No screen. And that never amused us, because in our tradition, although we are all women, a young girl who is only starting *cannot see a mother who has already had three or four children, because that is an elderly person to you. You are not supposed to watch her. Then we took it up with the director of medical services at that time. We discussed with them that this is what we don't like. I became unpopular with those hospital people.*

Contrary to the image of the passive African woman promulgated by the racist colonial authorities, Rose and those she helped mobilise were extremely courageous. She took on a senior role in the structure of the Nyasaland African Congress organisation and the women would often speak out and act on colonial injustices.

1953 the Federation was imposed and people were almost paralysed. Mikeka Mkandawire was very strong. He tried very hard to reorganise Blantyre District. At one time he called a meeting so that they could choose a leader for the Blantyre District. I attended that meeting and most of them found it a bit strange. They were looking at me as the only woman among many men. Came election time and Mikeka Mkandawire was chosen as chairman for Blantyre district, and Hartwell Solomon from Chiradzulu was the Secretary, and I was elected the Treasurer....

The main body (of the NAC) - up to 1952 James Chinyama had been the president of the Nyasaland African Congress and he retired. That was when we elected Frederick James Sangala president. At one time, he organised a public meeting in Ndirande. TDT Banda was his Secretary General. After that meeting they were arrested. They were accused of inciting the people. This was either 1953 or 54... By that time, I had started politics again in Blantyre and I organised the women. The case was in Zomba and we managed to hire a bus, for all the women to go and attend this case. And with all the singing, we invaded the court and people went around. Instead of sending them to prison, they were just fined and the fines were paid right then and we came back.

By the middle of the 1950s, Rose was one of the high profile leaders of the NAC and involved at the national level, including discussions around the need to find an older leader to figurehead the struggle.

Kanyama (Chiume) and (Henry) Chipembere were chosen to be in the Legislative Council and they were members of the executive of the NAC along with Dunduzu (Chisiza), Yatuta (Chisiza) and I was there also... It was a very difficult battle, because now (we were under the) Federation, and all the laws governing this country are the Federal ones....

We (Executive of the NAC) asked Manoah and TDT Banda to resign and they refused. After that meeting, that's when the idea of calling Dr Banda came up. That would be round about 1955 or 56[1]. I don't remember very well. Du had gone for studies, Chipembere and Kanyama were in the

---
1 Dunduzu Chisiza went to England in 1957.

Legislative Council and we called a meeting of all the regional leaders in the country at Ramsey Hall in Blantyre. We invited quite a number of people. Manoah was there, TDT Banda was there. Manoah had refused to resign and we had assessed that TDT Banda was not strong enough to lead the country. We felt it was important to invite Dr Banda, who had shown himself to be interested in politics and he was always with our people whenever they went overseas. He was anti-Federation... People were very convinced that this man could lead us, that is how we decided to call Dr Banda to come and lead the country...it was a difficult battle, because we had to remove Manoah and TDT Banda who had their own people too, but they were not strong enough to influence the majority of the people.

...We decided that someone has to go and talk to Dr Banda and tell him that the country needs him to come and lead. The way I looked at it, after we removed Manoah and TDT Banda, the majority of those of us on the Executive, strong as we were, we were still young people. The chiefs wouldn't trust us to lead the country.[2] We felt that if we got someone who was elderly, we could convince them. That's how we called Dr Banda back. An arrangement was made for Chipembere to go meet him in London, Dunduzu was already in England. So it was decided that Dunduzu should join Chipembere to meet Dr Banda to discuss with him. This is how we decided to invite him back.

She was an integral part of the senior membership of the organisation that set the stage for Dr Banda's triumphant return. They were very effective at mobilising the population, so that by the time he stepped out of the plane at Chileka airport in 1958 a new energy gripped the country and the anti-Federation independence movement really took off.

When he arrived, that was now the beginning of our struggle. We felt that now we are seeing the way to our independence. We felt that it was a good move. We went along with him organising meetings, of course we had to sell him around to the people.... Yatuta was the person in charge and he worked very hard. In fact, the life of Dr Banda was in the hands of Yatuta. There were so many visitors who had come and Yatuta looked after Dr Banda very well. He organised his welfare, through and through, his political welfare as well as his general welfare.

Rose describes the controversial 'bush' meeting behind Colby Hall. As the people became more politically aware of the issues and mobilised to support the NAC, they wanted to meet to discuss the next strategies. However, the authorities were becoming upset by the state of unrest in the country and refused a permit to meet in the usual Ramsey Hall. A police informer, James Kalua, was present with a camera, as she said, "almost a movie camera." He reported to the police that the meeting had discussed an assault on or

---

2 See the testimony of S.K. Mpango who was a senior induna or counsellor of Chief Mwase for the chiefs' perspective that confirms Rose's version of this motive.

a massacre of all the Europeans and Indians in the country. This was the basis upon which Governor Armitage conspired with the Federal authorities to impose a State of Emergency, ban the NAC, and arrest all the party's key figures. Rose shows her strength of character and determination, when she describes how she dealt with the betrayal by James Kalua. It is important to note that almost of all her NAC comrades were locked away in detention in Southern Rhodesia.

After that meeting - it was the 2nd of January 1959 - we started to hear rumours that the leaders of the NAC were going to be arrested. We felt they were just rumours so we continued. They had said that at that meeting we had plotted to kill all the Indians and all the Europeans. Come 3rd March, they had brought in all the forces and the security forces were full in the whole country and all the leaders were rounded up and arrested. Strangely enough, I was not arrested on that particular day, because I was then expecting my baby. She was supposed to be born that month. They had investigated everything. People were flocking to our house.... I was still out but it was not easy to be outside, because each time I moved out, security forces were round about. If they saw that I had gone out, they would invade the house terrifying everyone, tearing up everything, mixing up ufa[3]. The children were miserable, they would throw them out. It kept on like that.

...After two weeks James Kalua was released to be a state witness. When people saw he had been released, especially the government drivers, they came to me and asked, "How has he come out? It means he has sold the others out..." I was still in my final month (of pregnancy), it was a Wednesday... so I jumped into a bus and went to Zomba to look for Kalua. I dropped off the bus and walked straight to the police camp and straight to the inspector's house, Sweetman Kumwenda was the inspector. Everyone was looking at me. He asked what had brought me there and I told him I was looking for James Kalua, and indeed, he the inspector was the one keeping him in his house. Kalua couldn't believe that I would come there. He came out and the inspector walked away and left us to talk.

I said I have come to find out how you have come out. He told me the story of what had happened to the others. Kalua was very shaky, but he did not hide. He said, "I have been asked to be a state witness. The fact that you are here now, I am worried. They promised to fly me out once I have given all the evidence about the massacre plot, but I will denounce them, that I have been forced to give this evidence." I told him that if that is the case he must put it in writing for me... (at first he refused.) I told him what would happen, that we will all be killed because of him. He agreed to do it, but said, "I cannot give it to you now, because you might be searched and they would shoot me. Go to the bus and I will find you." It was now in the evening and I left. The

---

3 *Ufa* is the white maize flour used to cook the staple food of Malawi, *nsima*.

bus was at 5 and I waited for Kalua and he didn't come and I didn't go. I had to sleep in Zomba. He thought I had gone. In the morning, I went back to the police camp. I went to the same place and told him I am not going. I have come for that letter. Now he was more worried.

He promised to bring me the note to the bus before it left at 1 o'clock.... I waited at the bus stop and indeed he came, but without the letter. He said, "It is very dangerous. I cannot write the note now, because anything can happen. They can search you, so it is better not to carry it. I will bring it to Blantyre before I leave the country...." This was Thursday and I waited, Friday, Saturday... Sunday he arrived very early at our house... We went in his car to our (Nyasaland African Congress) office. There was an anthill behind our office covered with bushes. We went in there and he took out that letter he had written.... I read it in front of him and found it was a good note.... [Then he went straight to the airport and flew out of the country.]

It was Sunday 22nd of March... We found somebody with a typewriter and had it typed... we took it to one of our missionary friends, to make sure it would be given to one of the journalists who can take it overseas or publish it.

At this point she begins to laugh, "I got on the bus for Malamulo Hospital and arrived there late at night and on Monday my baby was born."

She tells a tale of police paranoia reminiscent of the Gestapo as the security forces picked her up barely 24 hours after she had delivered her baby. Through subterfuge she was befriended by a white couple she did not know and they offered to drive her home. Her senses were already on high alert since she could not contact her husband nor her missionary friends. Concerned for her children at home, she accepted the lift and the trap closed in on her.

Then I went into their car and sat.... As we drove out of the hospital compound we got onto the road, in front of us were five jeeps with security forces with their guns in the air. I looked behind, there were jeeps there too with security forces with their guns in the air and our car was in the middle. I said yes this is it. When we reached Blantyre I told them I had a basin of fruits for my children... "You can leave them with the police. There is a Mr Soko who will take them to the house." Then we drove straight to Zomba and we were flying straight to Zomba Prison at the gate of the prison. Now they said you can come out and the prison warders were there. I was not myself, coming from the hospital... they said you come out. There was no friendship now, literally as if they had arrested a thief... They led me into a room.. so they searched me. The lady having seen my situation and the way I was, she said this woman must go to the hospital otherwise she is going to collapse. The captain said, "No, the doctor would have to see her." So the doctor was called and that woman being a woman was touched... she rushed *to the doctor and said please recommend that she should go to the hospital. The doctor examined me, examined the baby...He said, "I think she should go to the hospital." The captain said, "No, she is the most wanted person in Nyasaland. We can't send her to the hospital." The doctor said, "If you want to get something out of her you must send her to the hospital or else she is going to collapse...." (The captain again refused) ... and we were sent to a place like a verandah... and that is where we were sleeping. I stayed there at the prison two weeks before I was sent to the hospital.*

She was not cowed by prison and although she was quite sick, she was carried to the Devlin Commission hearings to testify. Rose and many of the other leaders appreciated how they were helped by friendly whites especially the missionaries. She had regular visits from her white friends who brought her food and other supplies for the baby.

My baby grew up in prison with their food.... Edwin [her husband] was picked up the same day he had seen me at Malamulo Hospital. They picked him (up) as he reached the house. The children were left alone. The children were just crying.... the eldest was 11 years old. We had Gabaniso's sons, Zililo and Kondwani. After their father was arrested and they had been told that I had been arrested, they were left alone and crying. People would not get near. They were all afraid now to be known to associate with us. So Zililo had to go to a certain European friend, an elderly man... he came and tried to comfort them. He went to the government, to the DC's [District Commissioner's] office and scolded everybody. How can you arrest all the parents and these children are left all alone? They have nothing to eat.... After a week or two they arranged to send them home to the north.

Rose was released in April of the following year (1960) and resumed her political involvement from where she left off. With the founding of the Malawi Congress Party at the Nkhotakota convention, she also resumed her party post. She continued to organise the women in the first election campaign for the 1962 parliament and then stood as an MP for Mzimba South at the independence election of 1964. It was an exciting time and she was a key part of the organisation of the independence celebrations.

We were there. We organised the whole independence. I was chairman of the decoration committee.... We had to choose a song for our national anthem.... so many people composed songs... A committee was formed to choose a song. I was in that committee... so many people presented their songs, but this national music from a Malawian [Michael-Frederick Paul Sauka], was very very fitting with our cause....

However, there were warning signs that trouble was brewing. Nonetheless, she stayed a loyal party activist even though she disagreed with Banda's proposed hospital user fee of a tickey (three pence).

I told Dr. Banda that the women are more affected by this fee..., and therefore, I should go around the country to sensitise women... so that they are aware of what to expect when they have to go to the hospital. He said that it was a good idea.... We started in Karonga. We had a meeting and that evening (George) Kanyanya came and said that Parliament is meeting tomorrow.... we had just finished a sitting and this is an emergency one. We had to leave that night and drove all night arriving in Blantyre in the early hours of the morning....

....The speaker of the house, Mr (Alex) Nyasulu, came and told me that I need to go and see Dr. Banda... There was something happening. He needs to know that the people of the North are behind him. While you were away, there were discussions with the ministers and they have not agreed on some things... I said no, I'm not going... I have to hear from my friends first. I can't just go there and say the whole north is behind you without knowing the reasons.... I said those are my friends and we have been together through thick and thin. I have no doubt that they have all the respect for Dr. Banda, as much as I do. If they have disagreed, there must be something... I must see my friends and know what the disagreement was... He reported that I was not coming...

Then the news came that we were being denounced. I was expelled from the Executive of the MCP, I was expelled from the Cabinet. Chingoli Chirwa was expelled from the Cabinet, Kanyama Chiume expelled from Cabinet, Augustine Bwanausi expelled from Cabinet.... When I got home, one of my daughters, she was very young, started crying... we have heard from the radio that you have been expelled...what they had in mind was what had happened during the State of Emergency....

The next day we went to Parliament and we had to sit as backbenchers. The whole Cabinet that had brought about self-government, is now at the back.... and he has organised all the new people. They are the ones sitting with him at the front. Chidzanja and some of the people not even known. They were all around him, castigating us left and right.

Her analysis of the underlying causes of the rupture goes well beyond the standard list of issues aggravating relations between Dr Banda and the Young Turks. The tickey user fee, recognition of the Peoples Republic of China and Africanisation of the civil service are usually cited as the major problems. But for Rose, the betrayal of the pan-African struggle and forsaking the solidarity with the on-going nationalist struggles in the region, were major factors.

These are the main things, but he also wanted us to have diplomatic relations with the Portuguese and South Africa. We felt that we have our friends who are fighting for their independence in South Africa and Mozambique and Angola. They need our help. If Ghana helped us and it is far away from us and yet we have these people who are our neighbours.... Now that we have our independence, then we must assist them."

That is when Dr Banda's authoritarian leadership style became totally clear as did his strategy of sowing doubt and dissension among his ministers to keep them distrustful of each other and off balance. From the way the crisis played out it was clear that he was planning a coup from above.

...He did not like that. In fact, he didn't want anybody to question him. What he had decided must just be accepted... that was the time when they challenged him. You call us boys. We are not boys. We fought for this country and we brought you in. That was the beginning. That was what infuriated him. It was just a question of discussion. Trying to bring some sense in him to understand (that) our friends need our help.

... He had something in mind, only that we didn't know.... I believe that he had been organising this long before we knew. Among us were some he had planted as his spies, working with him and influencing others and promising that they would take over from this one.... So all those people were for him. John Msonthi was dismissed before us and that was one of the questions we were asking him. "Why has John Msonthi been dismissed without the full cabinet knowing the reason?" That was enough...(to make Banda angry) why were we challenging him.

Strangely enough, when we were dismissed, Msonthi was re-instated and was sitting there as a Cabinet minister. I think that Dr. Banda had a feeling that one day we might take over from him in some sort of coup.... He didn't believe himself that he was sitting there as leader and didn't believe that all the respect we were giving him was genuine. Before the Crisis, he had started divide and rule... he would call you and say that you better be careful with so and so... at one time he was showing me a letter, that he said was from my mother-in-law against me.... I said my mother-in-law cannot write such a letter. I know her. Sometimes you would come and he would say there are some letters from Cholo and Mlanje saying that the women there are talking against you.... He was not doing such things only to me but to all the men as well. So he wasn't very much sure of himself.

2.2 Radical tradition

The period following Second World War was full of political excitement and energy. The Young Turks brought with them education, experience in other countries and a commitment to the struggle for independence. They were from all parts of the country and easily and readily worked together for the common purpose of national liberation.

The Bwanausi family was prominent in Blantyre African circles. Ceciwa Bwanausi Khonje, following in the footsteps of her siblings, pursued her education, participated in the nationalist politics, married and started her career in broadcasting. Her whole family was eventually forced into exile after the September 1964 Cabinet Crisis. Over a 30 year span of exile, she followed an exciting career path that led her to senior posts in the United Nations before returning home after the democratic dispensation of 1994.

Ceciwa Khonje

She writes about how her parent's home was a crossroads and meeting place for the Young Turks and other young educated people passing through their household.

I was born and grew up in Malawi's commercial capital, Blantyre, at Nsili estate, the home of a nuclear family composed of the Chisuses, the Bwanausis and the Jumas. Very early on as a child, I was exposed to politics; mostly through my brothers, Dr Harry Bwanausi, Augustine Bwanausi and cousin, Moir Chisuse. The three were attending universities outside Nyasaland and used to bring their friends for holidays at Nsili, very popular for the friends because it was in an urban area. That was how I got to know people like Henry Masauko Chipembere, Mikeka Mkandawire, Manoa Chirwa, Kanyama Chiume, Vincent Gondwe, Mwasi and many others. Apart from this group, a cousin, Ednah Mlenga, was married to James Frederick "Pyagusi" Sangala, the founder of the Nyasaland African National Congress [the nickname Pyagusi meaning one who perseveres.] Surrounded by such a community, I subconsciously grew up to become a political activist.

Her political education at home manifested itself in protest through the annual school concert, with swift repercussions.

My last years at high school, the late 1950s, were when the fight for the break-up of the Federation of Rhodesia and Nyasaland was gaining momentum. I was in a group of six political activists who used to secretly hold meetings at night with representatives of the Nyasaland African Congress, amongst them Yatuta Chisiza. We used to tell them what was going on at school whose teachers were almost 100% British. One student in the school who had grown up in Zambia taught us a Bemba song titled, 'Tatulefwaya Federation' [We don't want federation] for our weekend concert. As soon as the word 'Federation' was heard, the Headmaster stopped the concert immediately. That event led to the six political activists being expelled from school and I had to sit my final school exams, Cambridge School Certificate, as an external candidate. None of the British teachers understood what the song said because they did not understand Bemba, but because the whole of Malawi was dead against the Federation of Rhodesia and Nyasaland, they assumed it was a 'liberation' song against the Federation.

Because of her political activism and family connections, none of the local British employers would hire her, so she worked together with another young activist to promote the struggle in the absence of the leadership of the Nyasaland African Congress, who had all been detained in the sweeping State of Emergency arrests of 3 March 1959.

The fruitless hunt [for employment] *ended when I went to the District Commissioner's office where I got a whisper in my ear from Mr Dick Kangulu. He told me to forget looking for a job because I was on the blacklist of political activists never to be employed by anyone! I ended up struggling to sell* Malawi News, *started by a bright young man called Aleke Banda, on the streets of Blantyre Central, which most people did not want to be seen buying for fear of being arrested....*

Aleke Banda, a young man who grew up in Southern Rhodesia [now Zimbabwe,] had been detained with the other Malawi detainees for political activism, even as a high school student at the time. The graduates among the detainees, the Bwanausi brothers, David Rubadiri, and others, took the opportunity to tutor Aleke in preparation for when he would sit his school certificate exams. Immediately upon his release from detention, Aleke was deported to his father's country of origin, Nyasaland, and Shad Khonje recruited him into the Malawi Congress Party. He became a very active member of the party and was among the people willing to continue the struggle despite the security risks at the time.

Ceciwa describes how the nationalist militants who escaped detention were not fazed by the arrest of their leadership. They continued the work of organising to resist the Federation despite the banning of the Nyasaland African Congress and draconian measures put in place to prevent political organisation. This also explains why the MCP took off so quickly after the leadership came out and resumed political activities.

Early in 1959, following the almost thorough sweeping into detention of the leading campaigners for independence, Shadrack Khonje and Augustine Munthambara were surprised they were not swept in as well. Most university graduates were arrested, except the two. While still puzzled, they decided to use the opportunity of not being incarcerated to continue the struggle. They felt that if after the mass detentions there was no agitation in the country, the Government of the Federation of Rhodesia and Nyasaland and the colonial power, Britain, would conclude that the detainees were a small bunch of rabble rousers who had been tamed by the detention and that the country had now been pacified. The two men formed a party to demonstrate that it was not just the detainees who wanted independence but the whole country wanted freedom from colonial rule.

It was during the state of emergency from 3rd March 1959 when the situation was very tense and dangerous in Malawi that the two friends,

Augustine Mnthambara and Shadrick Khonje, met clandestinely and formed the Malawi Congress Party to succeed the Nyasaland African Congress, which had been banned. The party was to continue agitation *"until Dr Hastings Kamuzu Banda and other leaders came out of detention to resume leadership."*

In those days practically everybody believed that only Dr Banda could lead the country to independence. Even when we now know better and however embarrassing that belief is today, I must admit my part in the folly that at the time I too thought he was the only one capable of leading us to independence.

As a consequence, when Khonje and Mnthambara formed the new Party, they regarded themselves as caretakers who would hand over the leadership to Kamuzu. In addition to having no leadership ambitions, they saw only one man as the leader to hand over their party to; Kamuzu Banda.

Rose Chibambo confirms this commitment to the spirit of the struggle and the leadership provided during the State of Emergency by Konje and Mnthambara:

Before Ching'ole [Orton Ching'ole Chirwa] *was released there was an underground revival of politics. This was done by Shadrick Khonje and Munthambara. These were secondary school teachers in Blantyre. They felt that surely people are now just moving around as if they are lost without parents, so they sort of revived the spirit through underground. Shadrick with his fiancé, Ceciwa Bwanausi, they revived the politics underground. People their spirits were up. So when Ching'ole was released and Vera* [Orton Ching'ole Chirwa's wife] *was also released. Vera was brought to Zomba Prison. We were only together for two weeks... then she was released. So when they were released, Shadrick and Munthambara had to give the Party movement to Ching'ole. They said, "We are civil servants. We have been doing this as underground to keep on the spirit with the people. Now you, since you have come out, you can continue...."*

Thengo Maloya and Kapote

Thengo Maloya was the son of teachers from the Zomba district. By the early 1950s, when he was still a student, he became active in nationalist politics. As he pursued his studies, he maintained his links to the Nyasaland African Congress and was a dedicated Chipembere supporter. He eventually became a Member of Parliament in the Republic elections of 1964. He describes how many young people were swept up in the nationalist fervour and were even prepared to disobey their elders and risk imprisonment.

I would consider myself a bit colonised, because I had an uncle there, a Yao... who told me that immediately after Dr Banda came that this man will send you to prison. You will be arrested.... But I was a young man and I did not fear to go to prison.... and Dr Banda started saying, "Let's go to prison in the thousands." That was his theme. If you want us to be free, we must go to prison. Even if they can exile me to Saint Helena Island. If they kill me. My spirit will fight against them.... This was a very exciting period for us young people. We were ready to go to prison. We wanted to be free. We wanted to be bwanas and donnas[4] in our own country.

Perhaps the event that best reflects the sagacity and political acumen of the Young Turks was the International Economic Symposium, chiefly organised by the highly respected Dunduzu Chisiza. Jay Jacobson writes of how,

Du had been the guiding spirit behind an International Economic Symposium held in Malawi in June [ed. It took place in September] 1962. It brought internationally prominent economists to Zomba and to Blantyre for a week of discussion and sharing of insights and ideas. That a country that was so small and of such slight importance to the world economy could organize and host such a gathering of prestigious world thinkers on the subject was a tribute to the great respect with which Du was held in the field of economic development. Well outside Nyasaland's ability to afford, the costs of the Symposium had been met by grants from the Ford Foundation in New York. One of the outstanding international economists who came to the Symposium was Walt Rostow. His book, published in 1960, The Stages of Economic Growth: A Non-Communist Manifesto, proposed Rostow's theory of the stages through which a developing economy had to move in order to get to fully developed status. Rostow and Chisiza had corresponded... while Du was in Kanjedza Prison (ed. Du was held in Gwelo Prison in Southern Rhodesia) during the State of Emergency of 1959. At the time of the Symposium, Rostow was the head of the Policy Planning Council at the United States State Department. At the Symposium, Chisiza's keynote speech was highly significant. His philosophy of government and society in Africa had its roots both in modern social democracy (of the type being developed in the Scandinavian countries of northern Europe) and the African tradition of 'mlandu'. Dr. Banda may have been envious of the international prestige that was accruing to Chisiza by reason of the Symposium. We recall no significant participation by Banda in the meetings of the Symposium itself, nor do we recall any discussion of the Symposium by Kamuzu outside of the event.

Willie Chokani was another of the early Cabinet ministers to come from a prominent Blantyre family that had settled in Chirimba. He was sent to India to get his degree and returned in time to get involved in the nationalist

---

4 *Bwana* is Swahili for mister and *donna* is the Portuguese title for a married woman. The colonialists imported these terms for their Malawian servants to use in place of "master" or "madam." During the nationalist struggle, Dr Banda used these words to entice the populace with the higher status they would attain after independence.

fervour as Dr Banda came onto the scene. He also reflects the commitment of the Young Turks to serve the people and take the action required to promote the just cause. At the height of the conflict between Dr Banda and his ministers immediately after the celebration of independence in July, they boldly moved to thwart the imposition of the *tickey tax,* the three pence user fee that Dr Banda wanted to charge for access to services at government health facilities.

Willie Chokani

It was nothing personal against Dr Banda.... (he) wanted to charge the people for this and that. For example, I got my own salary cut by 50% and so did my other Cabinet colleagues in order to contribute to avoid the tickey. We were prepared to sacrifice, to show everybody that we were serious about solving the money issue.

Willie Chokani also points out that Dr Banda was quite isolated because the Young Turks had established a considerable power base and had strong leadership qualities of their own.

You see Chipembere was very, very, very, very popular among the people, but most hated by Dr Banda (and the whites). In fact Chipembere was a better leader for us than Dr Banda... because of his forthright nature, and the fact that he was able to consult. [Because he treated people with respect.] *He was a grassroots man.*

The strength of conviction of the Young Turks and their supporters, led them to immediately begin armed resistance to the political coup that Dr Banda had orchestrated to instal himself unchallenged as the President. They were ready to take up arms despite the lack of experience or preparation. Thengo Maloya went into the bush with Chipembere and fought to destabilise Banda's control around the Malindi/Mangochi area. They had widespread support among the people, police and armed forces. This aspect of the struggle is explored in Chapter Seven, *Organised Resistance.*

2.3 Move to dictatorship

Rose Chibambo reflected on how Dr Banda reacted to the International Economic Symposium Du had organised in September 1962. By then Dunduzu had a premonition about the the direction Dr Banda was taking the country and the fate of his opponents.

It [the symposium] *was very, very successful. Now things being in the way they are (were), to me it appeared at that time, perhaps Dr Banda had cold feet. Later we felt that he felt that Dunduzu was trying to popularise himself and yet he was actually doing it for the nation and the fame was to go to the Prime Minister. After the symposium, Dunduzu was invited now* and again, he was meeting Dr Banda... for discussion or whatever it was. I remember one of the days, he came from there, he came to our house and as usual the house was ever full with people discussing politics. So he came in and he found me there, so we chatted together.

It was a bit late in the evening. Then he said "Alright. I am going." He went out and he called me, "Can you come with me?" Because we had so many people in the house, I followed him outside, so he said to me,"Rose. I am sorry for you people." ...I said, "Why?" He said,"As soon is this country is independent, all of you people are going to be locked up." I said, "Why?" He said,"I am saying this to you, because we have worked together for this country, through and through. We have struggled together... to see that Malawi is independent. And here we are now, we are in self-government leading to independence and I am just telling you this. I feel I should tell you. You are all going to be locked up." So I said, "What about you?" He said, "I don't know whether I will be in this country or outside this country."

Jay Jacobson picks up the story and at the same time shows how even the radicalism of the Young Turks had been boxed in by the principle of nationalist solidarity as well as their own role in selling the idea of Dr Banda as a savior and messiah to the nation.

> Within a few weeks after the Symposium ended, Du was dead. The published reason was an automobile accident when his car apparently missed the bridge which spans the Namadzi River on the main road from Zomba to Blantyre. The story about the "accident" was not widely believed. People commented to us that the accident was "unlikely," that Du was careful in his driving, that the police inquiry into the matter could not be relied on for an accurate description of what transpired. So much skepticism abounded that, at the next meeting of the Legislative Council (for that was the name of the legislative body before Nyasaland had extricated itself from the Federation), Du's brother, Yatuta Chisiza, rose to speak and to deny that Du had in any way been disloyal to Dr. Banda. The "disloyalty" rumours were coming out of reports in foreign media about differences in opinion between Du and Dr. Banda, arising out of some approaches at the International Economic Symposium. The late Andrew Ross has written that Yatuta's speech was one of the markers of change in the country; loyalty was no longer measured in terms of adherence to an ideal or to the nation but rather, in terms of obedience to Dr. Banda.

Thengo Maloya declares very forcefully the continuing belief that Du had been "accidentalised" to eliminate him as a potential challenger to Dr Banda. He went in person to the accident scene where Dunduzu had lost his life.

> There was the time of the symposium organised by the late Dunduzu Chisiza... That is why he was killed. Why? Because Dunduzu Chisiza said he would never allow a dictator to rule the country, to rule Malawi.... He

was killed at Ntondwe. I went there myself. I went to the place where the vehicle is supposed to hit the thing the rock. One would have expected blood splashed all over... but there were no blood stains. Now what could have happened.... When we were taking his body home.....I was there. He went with a bandage around his head. We believe that he might have been shot. It was a man-made accident.... We removed him to Blantyre, Chileka and the body was flown to Karonga but Dr Banda didn't go.

Ceciwa Khonje relates a very telling story about Dr Banda's reaction to the death of a political opponent. Banda's attitude may explain his apparent disinterest in Dunduzu's fate.

Malawians used to view political opponents as sellouts and ridiculed them, but nobody ever thought of beating or even killing them. When one such opponent, Pondeponde, died mysteriously, Augustine Bwanausi, talking to Kamuzu, expressed sadness at the sudden loss of the man and Kamuzu told him not to worry about it, "accidents do happen!" Instead of ordering an investigation into the death, he wanted people not to talk about it but forget it and just move on in life. That began to reveal the true 'colours' of Kamuzu.

The nationalist movement was a radical and very progressive movement and they accepted and even manufactured the deception of bringing Banda back as a leader to cover for their lack of age. They promoted the deception and then got caught in the trap Banda and the British had set. Banda, an ultra-conservative and tribalist, took over a progressive movement and slowly but surely undermined all the progressive tendencies and drove Malawi into tribalist rivalry. As Kapote said of his involvement, *"We all participated in the deception, singing the praises of Dr Banda."*

Jay Jacobson provides a tidy synthesis of the problems that were dividing the Cabinet barely a month after the independence ceremonies.

On the nights of August 5th and 6th, the Cabinet (without the Prime Minister and without Colin Cameron) met and compared notes on what had been transpiring throughout the country. Even though Kanyama Chiume, Masauko Chipembere, Yatuta Chisiza, Orton Chirwa and Augustine Bwanausi were eager young men, ambitious for the success of their country, each had areas that were of particular interest to him. But as they met, they found that there were more issues that they had in common than there were issues which divided them. The complaints that they had ranged from the personal to the political. In the former category, Banda had told each Minister where he could live; Banda continued to berate and demean them in public; when they met at Banda's official residence, they were not permitted to use the washrooms but were sent to use the servant latrines out in the yard; Banda had personally posted each of 17 young newly trained African stenographers; no explanation had been given for the Msonthi dismissal; public land had been given as private gifts to both Aleke Banda and Father Tobias Banda (neither of whom was related to Dr. Banda).

And, in the category of political complaints, Banda had appointed a former deputy leader of the opposition settler party both as Chairman of the Board of the Malawi Development Corporation and to a seat on the Board of the new Reserve Bank of Malawi; senior expatriate civil servants had more power than ever before (including power, given to the Permanent Secretaries by Banda at a secret meeting, to recommend civil service promotions in their Ministries direct to Dr. Banda without approval of the responsible Minister); the Kadzimira-Tembo family was consistently winning the choicest overseas scholarships (Miss Kadzimira was publicly listed as Dr. Banda's secretary-nurse); Dr. Banda alone was receiving security information; so many extra-parliamentary bodies were being created that dictatorship was becoming a real risk; and Banda was acting in the jurisdictional areas of other Ministers without telling them.

For the next three weeks, until August 26th, tensions in Zomba seemed to ease. Although the Preventive Detention Bill had not been withdrawn, the inquiries about progress on it from the Prime Minister's office were not a daily feature of Jay's work. But as the members of the Cabinet traveled through the country, complaints met them at every turn: hospital charges, the loss of take-home pay from the Skinner report, the rate of Africanization, and then, also, relations with Portugal.

The problem with Portugal was practical. Malawi is landlocked. Her best access to the sea is through Mozambique through the port of Beira. Mozambique is a Portuguese territory, and, to keep its route to the sea open – for both exports and imports, Malawi could not antagonize Portugal. But, Portugal had a history of torture and abuse of the Africans in Mozambique. Administradores routinely beat Africans, often rubbing salt into the wounds to make the pain more acute. At a Cabinet meeting at his home in April, 1964, just after the resounding electoral success of the Malawi Congress Party, Banda told the Ministers-designate that he would deal with Portugal in his own way. Although he told the Ministers-designate that they could leave with no hard feelings at that point, none of them walked out. But, to many of the educated African leadership, the way that Banda was dealing with Portugal was embarrassing Malawi among Pan-Africans. They argue that there was no need for an exchange of "state visits" with Mozambique authorities; that Banda need not have praised Salazar, the leader of Portugal, so extensively on Banda's mid 1964 visit to Mozambique; that there was no need to allow Mozambique to have the largest pavilion at the Malawi Independence Trade Fair, and that too much publicity was given to the opening of the Blantyre – Beira air link.

Rose Chibambo confirmed the frustrations and issues that were behind the Cabinet Crisis and goes on to illustrate how the issue of support for the nationalist movements that had not achieved independence was of primary importance. She can see in retrospect that the eventual confrontation had been stage-managed. In response to our question about the discussions in Cabinet that infuriated Dr Banda, the tickey hospital fee, the recognition of communist China, and Africanisation of the civil service she added:

These were the main things. Then he wanted us to have diplomatic relations with (the) Portuguese and South Africa. So we felt that our friends are fighting for their independence in South Africa. We have friends who were fighting for their independence in Mozambique and Angola. They need our help. If Ghana helped us which is far away from us and yet we have these people who are our neighbours. Now that we are independent, why can't we assist them? He didn't like that... and as you know, in fact, he didn't want anybody to question him. What he had decided must be just accepted.... That's what infuriated him. It was just a question of discussion. Trying to bring some sense in him. How we have struggled and how we have also received sympathy from other people. Now why can't we sympathise with others. No. That was enough as far as he was concerned. He had this in mind [a cabinet takeover] and we didn't know. I believe he had been organising this and we didn't know.

Ceciwa introduces the way Kamuzu publicly denounced the ministers and at a very famous speech ratcheted up the antagonism.

Kamuzu's introduction of a fee of three pence at out-patient clinics and hospitals in Malawi caused a huge decline in attendance at these health care centres. People could not accept that the colonial regime gave them free treatment at these institutions, and their own government, which they fought for, was now charging them money for treatment. As a poor country, three pence at the time was a lot of money. The ministers resented Kamuzu's tendency to want to run the government alone without consultation as well as his interference in their portfolios. The conflict between him and the ministers was accelerated when on return from an OAU Summit of Heads of State in Cairo in 1964, Kamuzu told the crowd that welcomed him at Chileka airport to spy on the ministers and report them to him.

Thengo Maloya also describes this divide and rule tactic.

You can make a dictator. Dictators can be made. There are people born to be dictators but you can also make a dictator.... We made Dr Banda a dictator. There were times when Dr Banda would say, "You have said something against your friend. Is that so? Is that so? Then he would organise a meeting and he would call that person... and he would tell him, "Would you tell him what you told me? Didn't you say this? Didn't you say that?"

Even before the fateful days in September, Ceciwa Khonje shows how Dr Banda's autocratic tendencies had crept into everyday life and impacted people right in their home life and careers.

Slowly, though, I started getting interference from outside. One day, a lady came to the studio in tears and told me she had been ordered to come and work with us as a broadcaster, but said she was not interested because she wanted to continue with her teaching profession. The lady was Henry Chipembere's sister. She had taught her pupils a song which they sung at a Kamuzu Banda rally. Kamuzu liked the song so much that he decided to 'reward' the teacher by making her a broadcaster. I decided to help her by sending her back with my report which said I had tested her voice and found it not suitable for broadcasting. She was very relieved to go back to her profession.

Kamuzu's control of everything, especially the media, was growing. For me it was when I was given information to broadcast which I knew was untrue and I refused to broadcast it. Immediately after, I went on maternity leave, expecting my second child. One day as I was listening to the radio, I heard Kamuzu denouncing someone who he said was disobedient, full of themselves and never obeying instructions. The description was so clear that my neighbour came and asked me if I had heard the broadcast and if it wasn't me that the Prime Minister was talking about. I told her it was me he was talking about.

Another sign of Dr Banda preparing to give himself autocratic powers was his determination to pass a preventive detention act. In Jay Jacobson's final months in Malawi, he became increasingly concerned as he was asked to frame such a law, a measure almost universally associated with authoritarian regimes. Dr Banda subsequently used it for the many thousands of detention orders he authorised. Jay goes on to explain the circumstances and background to the debate going on just after independence in 1964.

While Dr. Banda was away, Jay received an urgent instruction from the Permanent Secretary to the Office of the Prime Minister. Jay was directed to prepare – on an urgent basis – a Preventive Detention Bill. The minute from the Prime Minister's Office referred to similar statutes in South Africa and in Ghana, and suggested that they would be useful precedents in the preparation of the legislation. The legislation was to be prepared for the first substantive meeting of Parliament, which had been scheduled for September 2nd. (In ordinary course, instructions for preparing legislation came from the Minister of Justice, Orton Chirwa. He was away from Zomba at the time.) Jay confirmed that the instruction had, indeed, come from the Prime Minister's Office; that it was to be treated as an "urgent" matter; and that it was to take precedence over other assignments on which Jay had been working at the time. It did not take much study to realize that the proposed legislation would make a mockery of provisions in the new Malawi Constitution that dealt with individual rights and freedoms. In one very important particular, the Bill sought by the Prime Minister would permit "preventive detention" without the necessity of declaring a State of Emergency.

Preventive detention is the practice of a government imprisoning a person before that person had committed an act that would, if the person were convicted, constitute a crime. It was used by the British throughout Africa as a means of controlling unruly people who were fomenting unease and critical of the colonial officials....

In the spring of 1962, before Pat and Jay had left for Malawi, they had visited with – and sought advice from – distinguished lawyers in the United States. Each of them had said substantially the same thing – "Let me know if there is anything I can do to help." This direction to prepare a preventive detention statute was a circumstance where help was needed. Over the next few days in July, after Jay and Pat thought about what to do in light of the Permanent Secretary's instruction, Jay wrote several long-hand letters to Justice Douglas, Judge Friendly, Dean Warren, Senator Neuberger, the office of Senator Gruening and others. Each of Jay's letters was similar. Each told of the establishment of Malawi's independence on July 6th; each reported on the widespread popularity of Dr. Banda and of the political party he led, the Malawi Congress Party; and each urged the writer to communicate with Dr. Banda to make the point that it would be wise for Malawi not to make the same mistakes that other developing countries were making in adopting preventive detention laws. (In 1964, there was no internet. Malawi communications were very limited; a telephone call to the United States was very expensive and could be made only from a landline in Jay's office in the Ministry of Justice, or from a public land line phone in the Zomba Post Office. Neither location was private. Telegrams were also expensive, and were not a secure means of communication.) Jay sent the letters off by routine "Aerogrammes."

Jay suffered the consequences of challenging the authoritarian direction Dr Banda and his British advisors were taking the government. It did not take long after the Special Parliamentary session September 8 and 9 known as the Cabinet Crisis. Jay concludes his account with the summary way he was dealt with for questioning Dr Banda's wishes.

About two weeks later, Jay was summoned to the office of the Cabinet Secretary, Peter Youens. "Special Branch has determined," Youens said, "that you have been the instigator of correspondence from judges and lawyers in the United States and in the UK against the enactment by the Government of a preventive detention law. You have seventy-two hours to leave the country."

The colonial British civil servants more readily accepted the introduction of the nefarious preventive detention law to support the rising dictator consolidate his power and chased out the young liberal American who had done so much to help craft the new laws of Malawi. Already any criticism was too much criticism.

2.4 British complicity

From the beginning, it was clear that the transition to democracy would be done on British terms. Jay writes in the third person about his role in the negotiations with officers from the British colonial service. Even at the point of crafting the new constitution for a free Malawi, the British ensured that it was going to remain to their advantage. Sovereignty would rest with the British Crown and not the people of Nayasaland:

When the decision was taken in the UK Parliament to transition a colony or protectorate from "colonial" status to independent status, the management of the transition moved from the Colonial Office to the Commonwealth Relations Office (CRO). The CRO organized the formalities of the new country's constitution. The first draft that came to Malawi had been used in Uganda. In the text that Jay saw, the word "Uganda" was stricken out, and the word "Malawi" was substituted. The extensive provisions for the traditional ruler, known as the Kabaka, in the Uganda Constitution of 1962 were part of the draft that came to Zomba, but they were all noted as material to be deleted when the Malawi version would be completed.

The CRO was not preparing an "inspirational" document for the new nations that were being created. Rather, it dealt – in greater detail than might have been warranted – with almost mundane provisions of government. It did not state the source of sovereign power in the new nation. At one point in discussions with CRO lawyers, Jay noted the absence of a statement of sovereign power. "The constitution," he said, "should begin 'We the People of Malawi.'" A CRO lawyer looked at Jay and said, "That was the way you Americans did it two hundred years ago; it is not the way we are doing it now." Orton Chirwa leaned over to Jay and told him, "Don't worry. We'll take care of that later."

Willie Chokani was the Minister of Labour in the first government after Republic status was attained and had a front row seat to this disproportionate influence of the senior British civil servants. Regardless of what was said in Cabinet meetings,

Dr Banda had other ideas... Perhaps (from) some of his friends from abroad. The (British civil servants) were very powerful. They were very polite to Dr Banda, but very, very powerful. In fact they were looked upon as intermediaries between Dr Banda on the one hand and ourselves. We had a man called Youens, for example. He was more powerful than any Minister. After we had left, this man could tell Ministers what Dr Banda wanted. There is the famous case of the late Dick Matenje changing his budget speech overnight in order to suit Dr Banda's whims....

It was our decision to meet Dr Banda on several occasions. We would take our problems and Dr Banda in each and every case, would say, "I'll think about it. I'll let you know." Meanwhile he would go to consult Youens and others....

Q - So he was taking the advice of his white civil servants on how to deal with his African Ministers?

A - Oh yes definitely!

Thengo Maloya describes how these same officers pursued Dr Banda's deposed ministers and their supporters into exile. He describes how police inspector John Savage was ruthless in eliminating the opposition, even in neighbouring countries.

One of the police officers who trained people.... His name was Savage. Mr Savage was arrested at Isoka with a list of our names. The officer in charge who arrested him was Mr Nunkwe.... was someone we knew. Then people found the list of names. Refugees. And this man had a gun. Where are you going? I am going to Lusaka. These are my friends I want to meet them. What is your name. He mentions the wrong name. The name that was on his passport was not the same name. Yes it was a false passport. This is a government it can do anything... I thought you were Mr Savage? The officer in charge had been trained by Savage in Zomba. He was detained, transferred to Lusaka. Dr Banda had to plead for two weeks to get Savage back.... when you saw people come to Zambia with a list of names you were afraid. Afraid of hitmen."

These British officers were on lucrative contracts as part of British "aid" to the new Malawian government. As individuals, they were products of the anti-communist sentiment of the time. It was a short step for them to move from the cold war colonial agenda to supporting Dr Banda and his pro-British ultraconservative directions – even if it involved brutal repression and dictatorship – as long as it buttressed a faithful Western ally.

2.5 The Cabinet Crisis

In response to Ceciwa Khonje's request to tell his story, Jay Jacobson wrote a 28-page narrative describing his experience in Malawi, which corresponds with the period leading up to the Cabinet Crisis. As a young American lawyer activist, he and his wife, Pat, had accepted an appointment with the newly reconstituted Ministry of Justice to: *to take up an appointment as legal draftsman in this Ministry. Both Dr. Banda and the Minister of Justice have been particularly interested in your own interest in this appointment,... The work would involve the preparation of Parliamentary Bills and subsidiary legislation for all Ministries of this Government, working in the Attorney General's Chambers within the Ministry of Justice....*

His position placed him in direct contact with the new Minister of Justice, Orton Chong'ole Chirwa, and gave him a front row seat and deep insight to the events and issues leading up to the Cabinet Crisis. His story is a gripping and detailed account of the events as they unfurled. Jay describes how the final showdown occurred over a very short period.

The August 26th Cabinet Blow-Up

The Cabinet meeting began Wednesday, August 26th at 9:30 AM and lasted over seven hours, in the Cabinet Room adjacent to the PM's office in Zomba. The Meeting started with Dr. Banda introducing legislation for the establishment of a new University of Malawi. This bill had been entirely prepared, and was being presented in the absence of the Minister of Education, Masauko Chipembere. Chip was in Ottawa, attending a meeting of Commonwealth Ministers of Education. One after another -- Augustine Bwanausi, O.E. Ching'oli Chirwa, Yatuta Chisiza, and Kanyuma Chiume -- told Banda what they had learned as they were traveling around the country. As Banda reported to the Parliament at its meeting on September 8th, the Ministers attacked him and turned what should have been a discussion of the university "into a general discussion on my policies since we became self-governing and particularly since we became independent on July 6th."

The Prime Minister said that, at first, he had "tried to be sweet, to be calm." He listened, butting in to the Ministers only briefly to make a point here or there. But, by about 11 AM or noon, Banda began to talk. He told the Cabinet (as Banda reported in Parliament on 8th September) that if he was doing all the wrong things by charging tikkis [three pence] for hospitals, by not Africanizing immediately, by not making every Permanent Secretary an African, by not having all the Directors in the Reserve Bank of Malawi Africans, then it means that he has failed as Prime Minister. "In Britain," Banda said he told the Cabinet, "the only honest, sensible and honourable thing [for] a Prime Minister who is a failure is to resign. I resign now. I am going up to Government House to advise His Excellency the Governor-General, to send for you, Kanyama. If you cannot form a new Government, Kanyama, then I will advise His Excellency to send for you, Ching'oli Chirwa. If you...cannot form a new Government, then Bwanausi or Yatuta Chisiza and on down along the list"

Banda then told the Parliament, that the response from the Ministers at the August 26th meeting was "No, we didn't mean that." In response, Banda said he told the Ministers, "Yes, you did mean that. I take your attack on me as an implied vote of no confidence and, therefore, I have no intention of standing here against anybody's will." He said he would leave Malawi so that his "political ghost" would not haunt his successor.

At shortly before 4:00 PM on the 26th, Chirwa suggested that the Cabinet meeting adjourn to Thursday, the 27th of August at 6:30. The Cabinet reconvened on the 27th, but not at 6:30. Banda had a prior engagement with Sir Glyn Jones, the Governor-General at 6:30, and so the Cabinet meeting was to resume at 8:00 P.M. at the Prime Minister's residence. In the Thursday discussion, the same themes brought up on Wednesday were rehashed. As the evening wore on, Banda told the Ministers to put everything down on paper. He said (according to Banda's statement reported in the Hansard for September 8th) that he would consider the complaints, and that he would "consider concessions, compromises, accommodation, only if [he] could do so with honesty to [him]self, with a clear conscience and with the fullest sense of self respect." Otherwise, said the Prime Minister, "I prefer to go. I prefer to resign."

On Friday, the 28th, Chirwa came again to Dr. Banda's residence at about 4:30 or 5:00 PM. The written list that Banda had asked for on Thursday was not yet complete, but Chirwa gave Banda the part that had been completed. A "Bill of Indictment" was what the Prime Minister called it when he spoke about it to Parliament on September 8th. Not only did it contain the same issues that had been raised in the Wednesday and Thursday meetings, but there were more. Banda said the Ministers accused him of planning the Government "as if it were my personal estate." They accused him of nepotism, and of favoritism. Banda said that he would go and study the document, and that after he had done so, he would ask Chirwa to bring the Ministers to him so that Banda could tell them what his decision was. The Ministers had insisted that the full roster of demands be met by the beginning of the next session of Parliament, then scheduled for September 3rd, just six days away.

At 6:00 P.M. on Saturday, the 29th, Banda had considered the list of demands from the Ministers. He called them again to a meeting at the Prime Minister's residence, and was reported to have acceded to all, but pleaded that they could not be met by September 3rd. Accordingly, the session of Parliament was postponed to October 6th, but the demands were to be met by that date.

By the following Tuesday, September 1, the agreement reached Saturday evening had fallen apart. Dr. Banda had spent much of the intervening time consulting and conferring with friends and supporters who were not part of the Ministerial group. Those persons reported that there was no discontent or unrest in the country. Dr. Banda became convinced that he was being tricked by the Ministers for their selfish ends. He was now determined to have a showdown, and he changed the date for Parliament yet again, from October 6th to September 8th.

On Monday, September 7th, Banda fired Bwanausi, Chirwa, and Chiume, and also Rose Chibambo from their governmental positions. Yatu Chisiza and Willie Chokani (Minister of Labour) resigned in sympathy. Colin Cameron had resigned on August 5th.

<u>The Meeting in Parliament of September 8th and 9th</u>

On the bright and sunny morning of September 8th, crowds had begun to line the road to the Parliament Building. Standing several deep on the beautiful hillside botanical garden that had originally been collected and curated by Sir Harry Johnston, the first Governor of Nyasaland after it became a Protectorate, Malawians had come from many outlying villages and from towns from which there was transport available. Pat and Jennifer were there, along with Anne Hepburn and her son, Kenneth John. The jacarandra trees were coming in to bloom, and soon the whole hillside would be bathed in violet petals. When one looked out from the Zomba Hillside hospital across to Mount Mlanje, it seemed as if the whole forty mile stretch was a field of light purple.

As the discharged Ministers drove up, the assembled crowd of mostly civil servants cheered. When Dr.Banda appeared, not so much of an outburst; indeed, there was some jeering and booing.

Parliament was called to order with the former Ministers sitting as back benchers. (The roster of members in the Hansard listed the former Ministers now merely as "members".) In an unusual move, loudspeakers had been placed in the small square between the Parliament Building and the Government Print Offices so that persons who had gathered there could hear the debate in the Parliament. Banda spoke for about two hours viciously attacking his former colleagues, imputing to them motives of ambition, avarice and greed, and accusing them of having been bribed by the government of Communist China.

The attention to Communist China was unusual. Certainly it was widely known that the Chinese Communist regime had started radio broadcasts into Eastern Africa. But, the programmes that were offered were long on lectures, and short on popular music. So, while it was true that Communist China was increasing its broadcasts into East Africa, it was also true that not many people had listened to the programming.

In January of 1964, Kanyama Chiume in his role as Foreign Minster-designate of the new state, took a trip around Africa. The stated purpose of the trip was to brief other African nations about Malawi's policy once it became independent. Once Chiume was away, he scrapped his itinerary and was "lost" for a while. In fact, he overstayed his itinerary by ten days. When the trip that Chiume actually did take was matched against a trip that Chou en-Lai was taking at the same time, it appeared possible (maybe even "likely"?) that Chiume had been around where Chou En-Lai was for about two weeks. There was no evidence that Chiume met with Chou, but it is possible that Chiume met with one or more persons in Chou En-Lai's party.

Another connection with Communist China involved a heated exchange between Banda and the Chinese Communist delegation over inviting Taiwan China to the Malawi Independence celebrations. It was reported that the Communist delegation went away angry over the brusque treatment that Banda gave their demand that Taiwan be excluded.

One last point. During August, Chiume, Bwanausi and Chisiza had traveled to Tanzania. Ostensibly the trip was to visit game parks to consider how to use the experience of that country in developing Malawi tourism. While in Dar es Salaam, the Chinese Communist Ambassador came to the hotel where the three Malawi Ministers were staying. Also there were Tanzanian leaders Oscar Kambona and Job Lucindi. The Chinese Ambassador made a pitch for recognition of Peking China by Malawi when it became independent, looking to Kambona and Lucindi for back-up on his claim that Communist China had not interfered in internal issues in Tanzania. This, they dutifully gave. Yatu Chisiza, who told this to Jay, said "We just smiled behind our hands." When Yatu, Chiume and Bwanausi returned to Malawi, they reported this approach to Banda. In the September 8th session of Parliament, Banda told the members that Chiume, Chisiza and Bwanausi had been in Dar es Salaam recently, and on returning, demanded the immediate recognition of Peking China. Banda also said that the Chinese Ambassador had promised them that if Malawi recognized Peking China now, then Peking China would give Malawi 18 million pounds. Banda went on to tell Parliament that the Chinese Ambassador to Tanzania had been to Malawi to see Banda, and twice asked Dr. Banda to recognize the Peking Government. Twice, Banda said, he made no substantive reply, merely that he would study the situation. But, in the conversations with Banda, the Peking China Ambassador to Tanzania had offered a gift of only 6 million pounds to Malawi. Banda then asked rhetorically, "Do you blame me if I associate the offer of 18 million pounds and the intransigence, disunity, and disloyalty, indiscipline in the Cabinet [?]"

Banda's speech was concluded at about 11:30 A.M. The members took a brief break, and then resumed sitting at 11:45 A.M. Back benchers, other than those who had been Ministers, began to seek recognition from the Speaker, and when recognized, sang the praises of the Prime Minister.

Soon, the Parliament's only woman member, Rose Chibambo, rose to speak. Mrs. Chibambo had a long and well-known history as a leader of the drive for independence, as the head of the League of Malawi Women (and the person who inducted Jennifer into that organization as its "youngest" member), and as a prisoner at Kanjedza [ed. Rose was held in Zomba Prison] during the Emergency of 1959. She stoutly denied ever having been disloyal to Dr. Banda. She acknowledged that, in the course of her responsibilities, she traveled throughout the country and picked up information from women which information she sought to pass on the Prime Minister. "...If we want to be honest in this country," she said, "if we want to save ourselves, if we want to save this nation, it is better that we give the Prime Minister the true stories that we know. It is better that we ...explain to our Prime Minister what the feelings of the people are." Mrs. Chibambo stated her unwavering loyalty to Dr. Banda, but was subjected to anonymous shouted interruptions. Continuing briefly after the lunch break, she found incredible that Banda could believe anonymous charges that had been levied against her and three other women.

When Parliament resumed at about 4:00 P.M. after a tea break, the member for Port Herald North (G.C. Chakuamba) spoke without normal parliamentary restraint. He casually and consistently referred to the former Ministers as "traitors." When the point was made to the Speaker about the use of the term "traitor" and its particular use with respect to Kanyama Chiume, the Speaker allowed as how "I think you could refer to him at certain stages but not all the time."

Rising to speak at last, Yatuta Chisiza told of his loyal history of support for Malawi independence, and of his dismay at accusations against him and his colleagues that had come to the Prime Minister by anonymous letters. "We are building a nation," said Yatu, and if we really mean what we say, let us build it with honesty and sincerity and dedication." Characterizing the issues that were raised to the Prime Minister as pin-pricks, Yatu went on to say that if bringing these points to the attention of the Prime Minister is treason, then "I am ready to hang this minute". Hansard records "Applause" at the conclusion of Yatu's speech.

The day's final speaker was Kanyama Chiume. He began his remarks by asserting his loyalty to the country, to the Prime Minister and to the Malawi Congress Party. He went on:

> When I told the Prime Minister that ... at least in my Constituency ... the ordinary man, the ordinary women (were) complaining about tickies ...; when I told the Prime Minister that his people were wondering why the pace of Africanization was not as great as it should be; when I told the Prime Minister... that his people were complaining about the Skinner Report because ... it has been reducing the purchasing powers ... of the Civil Servants and ... it is very difficult for the ordinary man [to sell his stuff], I was not being a traitor.
>
> The people who are dividing the Prime Minister from his loyal people – these are the traitors of this country.

Parliament adjourned for the day at 5:30 P.M.

Chipembere had not been present at Parliament on the 8th of September. He returned that evening from the [Commonwealth Education Ministers] conference he had been attending in Ottawa, Canada. In 1964, the trip took two days, with approximately eighteen hours of flying and at least two changes of planes. He listened to the Prime Minister's speech as it was presented on the radio.

On the morning of the 9th of September, Parliament was scheduled to begin again at 9:30 A.M. In a reprise of the conditions on the 8th, crowds lined the road to the Parliament Building, and stood down in the garden where the jacaranda trees and the other glorious Malawi foliage was in bloom. However, the Malawi Congress Party had bused in many supporters to counteract the enthusiasm of the people who had been so vocal in their support of the Ministers on the prior day. At about 9:15 A.M., the Ministerial Humber allocated to the Ministry of Education appeared, and began the climb the few hundred yards up towards the Parliament Building. Supporters of Chip were unsure of what they were seeing, as Chip leaned out of the windows of the car and gave a "thumbs up" signal to the people lining the road. His car pulled up to the steps leading into the Parliament Building, and Chip stepped out to a massive roar from the crowd. As people pushed closer to hear what he had to say, Chip turned to the gathered Malawians (and Pat and Jennifer and Anne Hepburn and Kenneth John):

> You may wonder why I have come to Parliament today in my official Government car. It is because I have one final task for my driver. I have directed him to go to Government House and there to deliver to the Governor-General my resignation from the Cabinet.

There was a sustained roar from the people. It went on and on and on. People were dancing, and crying, and ululating with joy. For Jay who had gone to sit in the officials box in the Parliament, the sound seemed neither to abate nor to end. Chip finally made his way into the Parliament, where in smaller volume, he was greeted by the other Ministers. Forgetting for a moment that he had resigned as a Minister, he went to sit on a front bench, but in a moment, realizing that the other Ministers were no longer "front benchers," he joined them in the back.

Dr. Banda's arrival at the Parliament Building was distinctly anti-climactic. Even with the bused-in supporters, the greeting as he left his official car was much less enthusiastic. When the Prime Minister walked into the Parliament, however, he was given a brisk and sustained welcome by his supporters. He also was courteously applauded by the former Ministers from their back bench positions.

The loudspeakers that had been in place on the 8th were not in place on the 9th.

Professor Colin Baker's indispensable book "Chipembere: The Missing Years" provides a great service in that it includes, in its entirety, Chip's 8000 word speech to the Parliament on September 9th. Jay's memory of that day is the same as reported by Professor Baker: the speech was listened to with careful attention by the entire membership; there were almost no interruptions; Dr. Banda frequently nodded his head in agreement with statements that Chip was making; and the session lasted until well into the evening. In characterizing the speech, Professor Baker said:

He was conscious that this was a major moment in his country's history and he was anxious to place the facts, as he saw them, on record. He repeatedly referred to this: 'Let it be recorded in history, for all posterity.' He was at pains to make a number of points clear: that he took no pleasure in what was happening; that he had not resigned without making serious attempts to bring about an understanding with Banda; that he was at one with the former Ministers; that his colleagues were loyal, competent men acting in the best interests of the country; that he bore no malice or ill-feeling against his detractors; that he had no part in the demonstrations outside the parliament building; that there was widespread sympathy for the stand taken by the former Ministers throughout the country and from people from all walks of life; and that he was taking his stand on grounds of justice of principle.

2.6 Regionalism - Divide and Rule

Regionalism was not just invented during the events of the 1964 Parliamentary and Cabinet Crisis, but it was used critically by Dr Banda to lever his way to power and sideline the popular Young Turks. The ensuing rift and the machinations of Banda with the parliamentarians of the Central Region, such as Chidzanja Nkhoma, John Tembo, and Richard Katengeza, polarised the issue on the basis of the Centre against the South and North. Rose Chibambo speaks of how all the people who led the struggle for independence were relegated to the back benches during the fateful parliamentary session in which Dr Banda had planned to oust the ministers who had stood up to his authoritarianism. Meanwhile she tells of how people who had done little or nothing during the struggle were suddenly being promoted to ministerial posts. As the progressive leadership was being castigated she says: *That was the beginning of regionalism. Actually calling us names and saying, you people from the North we don't know where you are going to pass.*

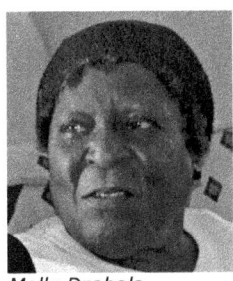
Molly Dzabala

There were a number of underlying tendencies behind the role of the Centre during the nationalist struggle. Molly Dzabala told us about a letter (circular) written to his family by Reverend Zachariah Tembo, the father of John Tembo, just after the 1959 State of Emergency.

…. Lucy Kadzamira was married to a friend of my husband who told us, and oh I shed tears when I was restricted in Zomba then, during the State of Emergency, (she told us that) the father of John Tembo wrote a circular to his family. He was Zachariah Zenus Ungapake Tembo, he was a reverend. To all of the Tembos and the Kadzamiras. The Kadzamiras come from the sister of John Tembo. The Kadzimiras are the children of his sister.... so they are all closely related.... he wrote to them all, warning them not to touch politics, not to go into politics. Because don't fight whites. You will never win. Dr Banda is a madman. He will never come back with all that bunch that went with him. They will rot there. So the Tembos and the Kadzamiras, none of them took part in the struggle for independence, not one of them. None of them. And when we were released we went into exile and they enjoyed the fruits of independence...

Willie Chokani confirmed Rose's analysis that the Cabinet Crisis was the based on regionalism.

John Msonthi and I were the greatest of friends you could ever think of, because he and I, our political feelings on issues were identical. Msonthi and I got into one ministerial car to go to the governor to tender our resignations.... I returned to Blantyre, because I was a Blantyre man to inform my family and my colleagues about what had happened in Zomba. Meanwhile, Chidzanja and the Central Province colleagues got together and put pressure on Msonthi to withdraw his resignation, which he did. And he did that without telling me. It was a pity. Because he was told that this was really a plot by the South (and the North) to undermine the Centre. And that is where it was authored.....

... the Centre was pro, pro, pro Banda and the Mission at Nkhoma became a centre of opposition to these young people... we knew that the church in Nkhoma and South Africa was pro-Banda.

Q - Were they afraid of the young radicals and "communism?"

A - Exactly.... Mind you, their status in this society then was that they were a third rate set up.... They were backward in every way....

The Centre succumbed to Banda's appeal to tribalism, and with the MYP and the support of the British, Banda had what he needed to turn the tide in his favour. It is useful to point out that while Willie denounced the role of the Church at Nkhoma and South Africa, he himself was aided by missionaries at the Blantyre mission to rescue his wife and children from Banda's persecution. Therein lies a significant historical footnote. When the Church of Central Africa Presbyterian (CCAP) was formed, it amalgamated amongst others the Presbyterian Church out of Scotland and the Dutch Reform Church based in South Africa in an effort to reduce competition between the churches and use resources more effectively. In the process, the Scottish church assumed responsibility for the Southern and the Northern Regions of Malawi where its presence in Blantyre and Livingstonia was strong. The Dutch Reform Church had a longer tradition at Nkhoma and hence took responsibility for most of the Central Region. With its roots deeply entrenched in an ever more conservatively apartheid South Africa, the white missionaries of the Dutch Reform Church were firmly anti-communist to which it associated the nationalist movement both in South Africa and Nyasaland. By comparison, a number of Scottish missionaries had a tradition of challenging the colonial authorities by extending education to more and more Africans and offering support and encouragement to the leaders of the nationalist struggle.

Frank Jiya describes how Dr Banda sowed confusion both at a personal level as well as at the regional level, so that people who had once worked harmoniously together, regardless of their origins, were slowly being pitted against each other.

....The story of what happened in those inner circles – I was told by people who were there – Banda deciding to resign and going back to UK. Banda asked them to appoint a Prime Minister and he identified Orton but then started sowing confusion by saying that he doubted if the South and Centre can accept it. He introduced tribal and regional confusion to undermine their unity.

…. They were presenting their grievances and he started confusing them by mentionning them one by one. Then Banda said Chipembere was the number two and was a good leader, but the people wouldn't want him as a Prime Minister. Yatuta, strong and brave, but unfortunately he is from the North. Augustine, very intelligent, the only scientist, but the Centre and the North won't accept him. He was adding all this confusion.

It must be acknowledged that there were some people from the North and South who sided with Dr Banda and supported the MCP putsch. Notable examples are Aleke Banda and Gwanda Chakuamba, who stood out from their Northern and Southern peers in siding with Banda.

2.7 Popular support

Dr Banda won the day in Parliament and lined up the coterie of Central Region MPs to oust the popular Young Turks. Outside on the streets of Blantyre and Zomba, it was a different story as Jay's account recalls.

Willie Chokani confirmed this popular support.

Believe it or not, we were completely with the people, and the people were with us. There were not many who were against the dissidents. Dr Banda, yes, he had a few people. (But) everybody in the army, the police they were with us. They couldn't say it. Everybody. Civil servants... People from Government Printer, to a man they were with us.... in Blantyre. Who allowed us to pass through to get out of the country? It was the police, local leaders, yes. They allowed us to pass through, so we could come back and be with Dr Banda.... The civil service was with us. The police allowed us to pass through and get out of the country. They wanted us to go and come back to deal with Dr Banda.... I left on Sunday evening in my car with Francis Mpepo youth leader. We drove to Lilongwe and then to the border, Khonje, myself.... The police at the border were no problem and let us through freely.... The Zambians organised a party for us when we got to Chipata.

After the Cabinet Crisis, many people remained true to their nationalist ideals and were ready to fight the dictator. The Malawi Congress Party's strong-arm tactics were unleashed on the country in order to rein in this popular support and drive any opposition to Dr Banda underground, out of the country or into silence.

Chapter Three: State Terrorism - Detention and Complicity

3.1 Malawi's Nelson Mandela
3.2 Who is being picked up – regionalism
3.3 Getting picked up
3.4 Torture and brutality
3.5 Conditions
3.6 Getting out

"I lived through the events of that time. It was State terrorism that we were subjected to and I will never live to forget it."

Professor Kings Phiri gave us the title for this chapter. The deep-seated fear of arbitrary detention permeated the entire population of Malawi and throughout the 30-year period was an integral component of the regime's control mechanism. State terrorism was fuelled by the regime's paranoia, which in turn was reinforced by an infrastructure that profited from keeping that paranoia alive. Paid informers and Special Branch police, the Malawi Young Pioneers (MYP), party youth in their red shirts, the Malawi Congress Party (MCP) Women's League and later Cecilia Kadzamira's creature, the Chitikuko Cha Amayi M'Malawi (CCAM)[1], all reinforced their positions, access to power and money by keeping the state of fear alive. Many were trained in the latest techniques of torture and intimidation by Israeli, South African, Rhodesian, Taiwanese and British special operatives.

This paranoia was fueled by some very real earlier threats. Chipembere's armed resistance to Dr Banda's coup, Machipisa Munthali's military training and ideological commitment, and Yatuta Chisiza's brigade of 1967 – all were trained guerrilla fighters, committed to confronting the forces of the dictator who by then was firmly ensconced in power.

However, the majority of the civilian detentions were an outright abuse of power. Many detainees attributed their problems to petty jealousy, job envy, boyfriend/girlfriend problems and regionalism. A victim simply needed to be in the way of someone in the Banda/Kadzamira/Tembo clans or be a relative

---

1 Cecilia Kadzimira became the Official Government Hostess to the unmarried Dr Banda shortly after his return to Malawi. She and her uncle, John Tembo, became the power behind the throne especially in Banda's later years. Her later designation was Mama Tamanda C. Kadzamira, "Mama" to the nation. The creation of CCAM, despite the pre-existing MCP Women's League, provided a power base loyal to her.

of Albert Muwalo[2] who envied your position in a company to be detained. The detentions were all premised on very weak excuses, but underneath was the justification that one's loyalty was suspect and thus a threat to the regime. This was the logic behind the Malawi Congress Party slogan "Unity, Loyalty, Discipline, Obedience" which was used to enforce the State of terror.

Makhumbira Munthali was a discrete, young man and despite his care and caution, Banda denounced him as a public enemy in a speech. To this day he has no idea how or why or who set him up as the target, because he had never done or said what was attributed to him. During the seventies, the University of Malawi was slowly emptied of all its most educated and qualified professors and administrators. In an act of pure irrationality, 18 statisticians in the Bureau of Statistics were picked up in one day. Their detention defies any logic beyond pure and simple tribal jealousy. The Bureau was an exemplary part of the civil service, with a proven track record and its highly qualified and dedicated young statisticians had earned high praise inside and outside the country, including from the World Bank.

Fear was the key element in keeping the population cowed. One never knew who was next and this uncertainty was a daily reality. We interviewed two former Chancellor College professors who lived with the reality of this fear during the period from 1974 to 1976 when many of the University's senior staff were being taken away to detention.

Kings Phiri joined the university at the end of 1975 after completing his PhD in History in United States. He told us:

You see it was a nightmare, because you would go to bed. They usually would arrest the colleagues at night. I do not know why they operated like that. It was only the students they came for during the day. For the lecturers they would come at night. I remember going to bed and every time you heard the sound of a vehicle outside you would say, "Aha aha. My time has come." On going out to check, it would be a friend or colleague passing by. "I just wanted to say hi." What a relief.

Chifipa Gondwe had completed his PhD in Political Science in France and returned to teach at Chancellor College in 1972. Under the Banda regime, Political Science was a forbidden subject at the University of Malawi.

"*We couldn't mention Political Science. I taught Basic International Relations in the Department of Government.*

He described the fear and how frightened they were of a fate worse than prison.

---

[2] Albert Muwalo was the much-feared Secretary-General of the MCP, the second most powerful post in the country after the President throughout much of the 1970s.

Chifipa Gondwe

I was at Zomba Prison for about two months. And one day, the police came and said, "People from the University, lecturers from the University. Out!" We thought we were being released, but we were not sure if we were going to be released, because perhaps either we were going to be released or we were going to be thrown into the Shire River.... because many, many, many people who were said to be opposing the government were from time to time taken from their houses by the police and then thrown into Shire River with stones, big rocks so the bodies shouldn't come up. Many people died that way.

We highly recommend Jack Mapanje's prison memoir, *And Crocodiles are Hungry at Night*, to people interested in a very intimate examination of experience in detention. Mapanje is extremely personal in his anecdotes, referring to people by name and with considerable description of their background and their personalities. This frankness was born of the nothing-to-lose life at the prison. Prison conditions are described in minute detail right down to some of the goriest parts of the latrine and the solitary confinement cells. The cruelty of the guards and commanders are contrasted with the bravery of his friends outside and the one guard capable of operating on behalf of the prisoners by carrying in news and supplies and smuggling out letters and manuscripts, using the nom de guerre of Noriega. He shows the frustration of such arbitrary detention with his frequent flashbacks to reflect on what he might have done, who he might have crossed and how he could have warranted the punishment he and his family received. The intimacies of human relations are closely examined. He goes beyond the purely descriptive to reflect on the arbitrary use of power by a control crazy despot and his inner circles using clear examples and analysis.

Prison memoirs are a common enough writing genre, but in the hands of an accomplished linguist and poet this book stands tall in the field.

3.1 Malawi's Nelson Mandela

Kapote and Machipisa Munthali

We have started this series of interviews with the man who came to be known as Malawi's Nelson Mandela – Machipisa Munthali. Eighty-eight years old at the time of his interview in September 2012, he still stood tall and walked strongly. The abuse he suffered and the lengths to which the regime went to try to eliminate him is instructive of almost all the themes outlined in Chapter One. His story is one of sacrifice and suffering. It is also one of steadfast resolve, determination and courage.

He had been in South Africa during the 1950s and came home after the State of Emergency was lifted in 1960 and the Malawi Congress Party was campaigning for self-determination and independence. He quickly immersed himself in the campaign and became a stalwart of Kanyama Chiume. When Dr Banda used the Cabinet Crisis to force the Young Turks and their supporters to flee the country, Banda unleashed a campaign of terror upon the people of Malawi with the full complicity of the British. Several detainees retained vividly clear memories of the brutal beatings they received at the hands John Savage, a British police officer seconded to work for the Malawi government,. He stands as a representative of a network of British officers, civil servants and agents who were seconded to reinforce and stabilise the regime during the transfer from colonial status to a self-governing country.

Machipisa began his story at the Cabinet Crisis in September 1964.

I stayed here and started campaigning against Banda. Some police came and warned me to escape, because they were handing over political people to MYP to dispose of. In October 1964, I went [fled] to Tanzania. In December, I was sent to Communist China for training.... I was 7 months there. I came back with weapons and training and did not need to use them.

After receiving training in guerrilla warfare, Machipisa returned to Tanzania and was sent to carry out reconnaissance and sabotage on one of many sorties organised by the former ministers into different parts of the country. Since he was a supporter of Kanyama Chiume, he was sent to Rumpi and Mlowe. However, he came to doubt the utility of armed struggle given the conditions he found inside the country.

When I came [into Malawi] I was welcomed there very fine. My headquarters was at Thimba School in Mlowe. I was talking with the people. I went all over. I had other people I was sending them here and there.... I came in with about 8 and [we were looking for information]. I was with Chisausau Msowoya, and Gondwe, but I have forgotten his first name.... [ed. Kamtekete]

As we were coming back I sat down with them and said the first thing we must find out is what people are saying. So they found out and sent me [reports], so I decided not war. It would not pay us you see.... I looked at the situation and I said, "No, I will not accept war. People don't want Banda but they were afraid. So why would I make war? Doctor Banda is a dictator and if we do this we will become dictators..." and I could not do this.

This country, we already got without any war and it is in our hands. So it is no use to have war. However [long] it takes us until God he will tell us.

He later told us that this same philosophy sustained him during his time in prison. His guerrilla training is evident from his account of how he tried to escape arrest.

In 1965, I was arrested at Mlare [in Karonga District]. When they came here [Mlowe], they found out where I was. I told my people, one of the women, that if the enemy come to make a [pounding] sound [as a signal]. So we got out.... I used a canoe to run away to Mlowe River. I found that way I was going the police were using search lights. I saw how they were using it, so I was paddling near to the shore so they couldn't see me. I went like that all the way Chiweta, Chombe until Uliwa. That is why they came up with that Chilembwe thing, the police boat from Karonga coming this way.... They were searching... So I was giving some jobs to other people... (He laughed at his own joke.)

I took my gun and pushed it into the sand. And they didn't know that I had a gun. I knew if it went to a case [in court] there will be no case. I was too clever for them.

.... So that was the time, I was arrested. They suspected that I was Yatuta Chisiza. I was taken to the MCP district chairman and finally an MYP man confirmed that I was Machipisa Munthali. I told them I was here for peace. If you want peace, stop what you are talking about.

In the morning we went.... by road to the police in Karonga. They took my statement and after that they locked me up in a cell. At 10 o'clock they announced I had been arrested. "Chigawenga chachikulu." The big guerrilla has been arrested.

It was almost as if the police were inviting people to come to the station to see him in his cell. Until that point, Machipisa says his police captors treated him politely if not respectfully. He was certainly not abused. That changed dramatically on the first night with the arrival of the very appropriately named John Savage, a British police inspector responsible for security in the Northern Region.

When John Savage came that was the time. He was terrible. That one was savage. They came 10 other people with him and they beat me all night. When they got tired, they asked the electrician to shock me. That man said, "I was not trained to do that. If you want to do that you can do it yourself." So they failed. After that they took me to a place where the sun was too hot and they took away my shoes.... After some time I could not walk.... They had to carry me to the vehicle.... they took me to Mzuzu prison for 6 months. For 3½ months I could not walk. I had to be carried all the time when I went for treatment.

Other detainees were treated in a very similar fashion. Mordecai Gondwe still carries the scars received from beatings administered by John Savage and Thomas Nyirenda allowed us to photograph how he and fellow prisoners were shackled for torture. That picture appears later in this chapter. Nyirenda was arrested almost 20 years after the Cabinet Crisis and although Savage had left the country by then, his treatment was just as brutal and was clearly embedded in the regime's methods of control.

Machipisa continues his story.

They did not know I had a gun. I showed them the gun later. When the gun has been in the sand you cannot use it. It will kill you. The gun we were carrying was that short one, an automatic. After six months the police took me back to Songwe to show them how I had crossed. At that time there were too many crocodiles.

While he was treated as severely and cruelly as others, it was clear from the way he was transported and how they mistreated him that he was already designated as a special risk to the regime.

After six months, I was better and they transferred me to Zomba Prison, the headquarters for the prisons and the police.... They used seven vehicles to take me there. In each vehicle there were seven police ready for action.... The man who received me was a white man. In those days all the top men were white men. They took me to the cell at gunpoint. They locked me up. I was tied here. I was tied there.... I was there [shackled like that] for three days. I was not allowed to see anybody.

He tells a revealing story of how the regime tried to use the legal system to convict him. The law was manipulated retroactively and two cases against him were dismissed before he was convicted of carrying an illegal weapon.

They charged me with high treason. So we went to the court. The statement I gave to them the judge did not accept it. There was not enough to charge me with so I could not be tried. So they went to Parliament and passed another law that anyone found with guns should be sentenced to life in prison....

The first judge threw out his case of treason. The government then wanted to try him with a law passed after his arrest and the high court sent it to a magistrate's court where he was sentenced to five years hard labour instead of the life sentence the government was seeking. Once again, it is clear that Machipisa inspired special paranoia and hatred among the Banda authorities.

I was working within the prison and one day a Special Branch man was going to see Banda and he saw me working there. So they reported to the headquarters of the police. One officer of prison came to see me. They took me back to prison.... they gave instructions to prison warders. "From this day this man should not see anyone. Nothing to read...." They wanted me not to get any information... to isolate me....

Despite the state of terror designed to frighten the nation, brave people stood up and confronted the system.

So I had my cousin, Msonda, father to Kennedy Msonda. That man was very brave. He went to the head of the Special Branch. He said, "I have come to see Machipisa. If you do not allow me to see Machipisa, it means that he is dead. According to the Detention Act when a detainee is dead, his body must go back to his home. Show me where you have buried him. I will take that body home."

So that head of Special Branch was very shaken. He went to Dr Banda... who ordered that Msonda was the only man to be allowed to see me. All my children and anybody else was not allowed to see me.

Msonda was detained at different times but otherwise escaped lightly for his temerity. His son, Kennedy Msonda, was the dynamic and enthusiastic headmaster of Mitundu Day Secondary School in 1968 when Doug taught there. His detention in 1975 was one of the factors that motivated Doug and family to move into exile the following year.

After Machipisa had served his five-year sentence, he was about to be released but once again, he was subjected to special treatment.

Then they re-arrested me with Preventive Detention Act for 11 years. So after that then I was sent to Dzaleka where I found Chakufwa Chihana and many others. [When it was] *time to transfer us to Mikuyu Detention Centre within Zomba District, all my friends were transferred to Mikuyu. I was the last one. So when they came for me, my feet were tied and my hands ... When we were entering that Mikuyu Detention Centre, they were ready. One police on that side and one on the other side right up to A Section. They were ready* [armed], *and I was locked up there. I did not know where my friends were. After one week, one warder whispered to me that your friends are in B section like Chakufwa Chihana, Dr Nkwazi and Augustine Munthali. Luckily people were passing that side.* (The bath was close to A Section and people could whisper hurried messages to him when they went there.)

Mikuyu Detention Centre was almost exclusively for political detainees. But even these were segregated according to the degree of risk the regime ascribed to them. A Section was where the most dangerous prisoners were held whether the danger was real from a man trained militarily like Machipisa or imagined enemies who were simply outspoken and articulate. Conditions were terrible.

…. In Mikuyu Detention Centre, my cell was three feet by six feet. [He was over six feet tall.] *Sometimes they take me out and some time they kept me in. From 1973 up to 1992. It was very hard.... I was alone there in solitary confinement until the end of 1974, when they brought Chakufwa Chihana, Dr Nkwazi and Augustine Munthali. So we are four there now and so we discussed politics. My friends were interested in how I was brave.*

I told them you have to be brave. It is no good to allow a dictator in a country.... everybody will die. Why should we worry about that. We should not be suffering when we know this thing is bad. Better I die from what I believe.

It is a testament to the prisoners' courage, that they still had the determination and resourcefulness to foment resistance, despite their harsh treatment.

So we were discussing how we can hunger strike – the food was very bad. So we chose Chakufwa Chihana and Dennis Nkwazi to speak to our friends. I was given the chance to convince the prison guards. I did it until I convinced them and we started. So I said the first job is to convince these people. When we were at Dzaleka Prison Camp our cooks were the detainees. Why now do criminals cook at this camp? My idea was doing things and it worked very well. Then we started asking friends. They were in C Section, B Section and D 1 to 4 and ... the top A Section. We were writing with soap like this... do so, so so and so.... D1 means there was one block with one wing D1 to 4 and B Section was the same thing B 1 to 4. C Section were the people from Mangochi.

"The people from Mangochi" refers to the supporters of Henry Masauko Chipembere, who carried on an armed struggle for many months after the Cabinet Crisis. Those who were captured and who were not executed right away were isolated in the C Section of Mikuyu. We have included a drawing by Kirby Mwambetania of the layout of D Section of the camp.

So the Commissioner of Prisons came. The people chased him away. They said we don't want you. We want to speak to the Inspector General who arrested us. Not you. So he went. The Inspector General spoke to the Special Branch head, so Gwede went everywhere (in the Centre).... Then I heard his voice..... So I told my friends to not worry about him. He is rough but you hit him back. So after he finished (talking to) all the people he came to our side. So he came to our lawyer first and he said, "You Mister Munthali, You are telling lies. You are telling lies." [Munthali] said I am the one who lives here. Who is telling lies? He was rough to Nkwazi. He was rough to Chakufwa and so I told him what I wanted is the truth. Gwede said, "I know the thing [the hunger strike] came from here (He was accusing them in A Section of being the ringleaders). And what you said is true. So today I will go to the Commissioner and tell him to give you food. Of course, that day the food started coming good.

Time dragged on until 1977, when the most abusive elements of the ministers and Special Branch were caught in their own plot. Albert Muwalo was the Secretary General of the Malawi Congress Party and held enormous power, which he used as a major instrument enforcing the State of terror. He was arrested along with many prominent members of the regime for allegedly having plotted to oust Dr Banda. When he fell, it seemed like many things would change and a general amnesty would be offered to the political prisoners. Dr Banda used the release of prisoners to appease the international community. Even Machipisa was given some hope, albeit short-lived.

Then we stayed and stayed until the time Muwalo wanted to overthrow the government of Ngwazi Dr Kamuzu Banda. They were having some secret meetings in the North. So they wanted Dr Banda assassinated there. So the police knew that... the Special Branch starting with the top. They were all arrested and they came to Mikuyu. At that time Banda was very happy, so he gave the chance to the Inspector General to release other people who he thought should be released. Those people were released. The first person from A Section they released was Dr Nkwazi. We stayed, we stayed. Then they came back.... They took me and Chakufwa, but when we got there [police headquarters] *the Special Branch saw me. They asked the officer, "Why is Machipisa here? You were supposed to release Munthali* [meaning Augustine] *not Machipisa." They told him to put me back and Augustine was released. So they were releasing people all the time.... Only I was* [still] *there in 1977.*

[From 1977 to 1992] *We stayed. We stayed. We stayed. Things were really tough. I really suffered a lot. The Commissioner of Prisons came to see me. He said, "Mr Machipisa you have really been suffering a long time, so I will take you out and put you in D section by the side of the kitchen so you can walk about." I told him that I don't agree with him but that I will go. You do not have the power to make this move.* [Later Banda ordered him back to A Section.] *A Section was the section for the people who were of top importance. To Banda they were dangerous people..... It is more isolation. There was no contact with the other prisoners. I could talk with some who would sympathise with me. They would come and say this and this and this. Later people* [prison guards] *hated Banda. He thought they were still with him, when they were not, so that is why I had a chance to communicate.*

By the 1980s, he was an elder and while nonetheless a prisoner, he commanded respect from his guards. Jack Mapanje tells how even the warden respected his wishes. When Machipisa asked to take English lessons from the professor, he was allowed visits from Mapanje. Mapanje was escorted from D Section to A Section and Machipisa literally, "dismisses the commander and his guard who brought me to him and tells them to squat at the far end of the courtyard as we deliberate on matters of value." (Page 229, *And Crocodiles are Hungry at Night*)

[It was] *11 June 1992, I called a warder. My gate was number 4. I told him I wanted to know who was in numbers 1 to 3. He came back and told me. Then I told him to tell Chakufwa that today we must meet. It was Sunday and the officer in charge does not come to there. So Chakufwa came there.*

They talked about politics including what they would name their political parties. Chihana was once again in Mukuyu after returning from exile and attending the United Front for Multiparty Democracy (UFMD) Conference in Lusaka in April 1992. It was Machipisa who reassured him that their freedom was imminent. His resolute determination after 27 years of confinement was unparallelled.

I told him that we will be released there is no doubt, because the great Mandela is out. That government in South Africa released Mandela [which means] *they have given up. So we are going to get out with no doubt. We got that news. When you stay a* [long time] *in a place we can know how to get news.*

His faith was confirmed by the fast moving events in Malawi in that period. The story of his release speaks volumes about how people felt about the oppression they had been living under.

Next day, in the morning when I went to bath, the Commissioner of Prison came and told me to leave everything and follow him. So I followed him outside. He put me in his car. He picked up other detainees. He took us to headquarters in Zomba. He addressed us. .... "I have been instructed by the Inspector General to take you to him. When the Inspector General says something - don't answer, because you may lose your chance to be released...." The Inspector General was Lunguzi.... We got to him and they first took the old body guard of Dr Banda, James Chikwenga. The Inspector General said I want Machipisa first. He gave me a salute and gave me a chair. He said, "Mr Machipisa, at the time they arrested you I was just a constable, but today I am the top. I want to tell you that we also knew Dr Banda was a dictator, but what can we do?"

Such an admission from the most senior police officer reveals that the system of rule under the Banda dictatorship was seriously questioned by all levels of society. For decades, the police, military and civil service respected and enforced the rules of the government almost without question. Now the man who reported directly to the Life President was paying homage to Malawi's longest living detainee.

Machipisa was uncowed and unrepentant. He knew he was about to be released but rather than show any gratitude he immediately made a demand.

So I said to him, I have nothing to put on. My house has been set on fire. I've got nothing. What I have got is this [his prison uniform]. *So if I meet a news reporter I will tell him what I am at.... So he rang a man to come. He told him to look at me and go get a blazer – an expensive one – I will pay. So he gave me so many things.*

But old habits die hard and the Inspector General felt he should give Machipisa a warning on how to avoid trouble now that he was a free man again.

He asked me where I was going to. I told him, I am going to Blantyre to Mr Msonda. He said,"Do not go to Blantyre.... You know it is dangerous there. Don't go there. He [meaning Msonda] organised the trouble that was in Blantyre and Mulanje. I [the Inspector General] warned Kennedy that if he would come [back to Malawi from RSA] he would be killed." I told him I will go back there. I cannot leave this. People know I am still alive because of that man so I cannot leave him. So he finished with me and sent me back to Mikuyu to take some of my things and I took a bus to Blantyre.

The return to his people in Blantyre is more evidence of how the temper of the times had changed. In a few short months, the climate of fear was evaporating and people openly celebrated his release.

I got there very late. I found a taxi to Mr Msonda at Zingwangwa. I found his house and there were people. I wondered why there were so many. They know something. So we danced there. They said, "Let's dance malipenga," because I was the best one in those days. When I sat down there was a phone call from the BBC... Msonda called me to the phone... They asked why I had been arrested. I said I was against the one party system. Can you tell us some prison stories? So I told them the whole story. The police were very bad. This government is very bad. So I went on talking about this and that. The last question was, Now that you are released what is your plan? My plan is I want a multiparty system. I am not afraid. Why should I be afraid? That was the end. We finished that.

For the regime and its structure, the old habits resurfaced nonetheless.

The police were not happy about that. After two days they came to see me to say that the Inspector General wants to see me, but they didn't come [to get me].... The following day there was an announcement that Nelson Mandela from South Africa was there to visit Dr Banda. At that time, I was nicknamed the second Mandela of Malawi. After Mandela left they came to pick me. They took me there and put me in a office where there are files. Everyone wanted to see me and they came so many. The Inspector General didn't come himself, but he sent somebody. He found those people and he was very angry and chased them away. He questioned me. Mr Machipisa, why did you tell lies about the people of Malawi? You told a lot of lies. Lastly what you should not have done is to speak about multiparty. You should wait for the government to (announce) then you can start.

By now Machipisa was in his element and was not about to take orders from anyone. He defied the senior officer and as one would expect of a person with such deep conviction became seriously involved in the transition away from dictatorship.

Just because a person doesn't want multiparty, why should I wait for them? He called me munthu wovuta - troublemaker. He told his police to take me back home. Now I was free. I was addressing meetings in every district.

There was no district that I have not been there. Everywhere. And I was very brave at that time.

We were already overwhelmed by his amazing story of courage and determination. However, his place in our esteem rose even higher when he told us how his family fared during his imprisonment. As if being detained for 27 years is not bad enough, his family was left penniless. He used the clandestine prison telegraph system to send a message to his wife.

My family – they were here [in Mlowe]. *Nobody was helping them. They were not beaten, but they had no help. It was a duty of my relatives to help them but they didn't have anything. There was no chance. My wife was still in Tanzania when I was arrested. She came back in 1970 and she was arrested. She was six months in prison. She was released. So I wrote her. I smuggled a letter to her. You are very brave. This woman has suffered a lot. I released her from marriage so she could marry someone else, because I knew I was going to be in for a long time. She married in Chilumba.*

He ends his interview with a very touching story of love, compassion and generosity, which also stands as a testament to his principled and determined character. He clearly loved her dearly and never gave up hope of re-uniting with her. After his release, when he was travelling around the country promoting multiparty democracy, he came to the Karonga district and someone told him that his wife's new husband was at one of the meetings.

If I can be released I can do something. So I went to see her husband. We didn't divorce each other, so he discussed with his relatives about Machipisa returning. He sent me a message, I went there, so he handed over my wife and we are together again after 27 years.... I am with her here. She suffered, I had a little bit of money so I had a guilty conscience, so I felt it better that she be looked after. She was in prison in Tanzania. She came back and she was put in prison here in Malawi. I owed a duty to her.

Despite his own dire condition, he sympathised with his wife's suffering and released her from her marital obligations in a gesture of magnanimous generosity. That they could manage to be re-united to spend their elder years together is a very fitting end to this part of his story.

We hope the testimony we have published serves as an epitaph for this brave man. Our respects to the widow and his family.

3.2 Who is being picked up – regionalism

The State of terror was the way the regime reinforced a pernicious regionalism. The Cabinet coup engineered by Dr Banda introduced an element of ethnic divide and rule that had been noticeably absent in Nyasa communities throughout the region and previously inside the country. The unity fostered through the nationalist struggle was shattered by the introduction of this disruptive and divisive practice designed to destabilise entire groups of people and pit them against each other rather than against the true source of their problems – the regime itself.

Kings Phiri lived the reality as his regional compatriots were picked up one by one.

.... *The police were being tipped off by colleagues from the Central part within the university.... It was colleagues and students from the Central part, particularly those from the Chewa ethnic background. I think those were being recruited to serve as eyes and ears of the regime that was Chewa based. Banda's regime was in many ways Central Region based.... They had a hand in all these arrests.*

You have to look at it this way...in the early days of the development of the University. Those who were educated came from the North and they took the positions from the expatriates as their posts were given over to Malawians. The colleagues from the Central part did not have a matching academic record. The regime reassured them that once the Northerners are cleared then you will be the ones to take up these positions of responsibility.

Alex Kalindawalo was our registrar at that time, 1975-76.... Alex Kalindawalo was typical of these people in academia from the Chewa background from the Central Region and for some reason he had a pathological hatred of Northerners. He was one of those people from the Central Region who was aspiring to senior positions. John Banda [a northerner] had been groomed by the expatriates to be university registrar and Alex Kalindawalo was eyeing that position. Peter Mwanza was being groomed up to be Principal of Chancellor College. Somehow Kalindawalo had the impression that the Northerners were being moved into positions that were not being equitably shared with the rest of the colleagues from other parts of the country, particularly the Central part.

Chifipa Gondwe confirms this insight into the situation at the University.

The situation was bad. The problem was that most lecturers were from Northern Region... they were dominant. We could see that the few others were not happy with us.

In the country basically the atmosphere was tense. It was the time the government was removing senior civil servants from top posts. Those who had very high posts in the government were being removed or retired.... We could see that there was a little bit of tension, that something was going to happen. At Chancellor College, we could see that our colleagues from the Centre and South were not happy with us. Even in the Senior Lecturer's Common Room people from the Northern Region would sit together somewhere and others elsewhere... We could see that the Vice-Chancellor being a Northerner, they were not happy with that.

Kings Phiri tells how a group around Zimani Kadzamira and Alex Kalindiwalo would gather in the Senior Lecturers Common Room to celebrate every time another Northerner was detained and thus removed from blocking their career paths. By October 1976, only he and another Northerner left at the University, had not been taken for detention, when Albert Muwalo, the politician, and Focus Gwede, the Special Branch head, were arrested and the detentions of University staff ceased. Colleagues remarked at how lucky he was not to have been taken.

When we asked if his colleagues from the North, Centre or South, who made those remarks had any sense of remorse, he responded:

It was a sense of relief, especially colleagues from the Southern part of the country. They seemed to sympathise with those of us from the North, but I wouldn't say the same with those from the Centre....

The link was so obvious because Mr Kalindawalo even appointed some of the college drivers to be directing the Special Branch whenever they wanted to arrest these people. He was Registrar. He knew where everyone was accommodated....

Who were these people from the Central Region who had a vested interest in the rustication of academics from the North? David Zimani Kadzamira was one of them. He proved to be overly anxious. It is amazing how soon after qualifying for his PhD, the way was literally cleared for him to rise up. Not only to be the Principal of Chancellor College, but they were clearing the way for him to be Vice-Chancellor. The other one from the Central Region was this former Minister, Louis Chimango... and Isaac Lamba. In the library, Raf Masinjika from Mchinji. In fact, there is evidence that Raf Masinjika was responsible for the arrest of Augustine Msiska because they were in the same department of the University and Raf Masinjika saw that Augustine Msiska had been better trained and if he could be removed then room would be created... How did we come to know that they had a vested interest in this? Because apparently every time a key northern academic was arrested these would somehow find an excuse to come together and drink, play chess and rejoice, literally rejoice, that another one has gone down. Apparently those who knew, we would hear this through the grapevine, every time a key northern academic was arrested that very same night Kalindawalo, David Zimani Kadzamira, Isaac Lamba, Raf Masinjika would be having a party of some sort - a get together.... Sometimes they would meet at Gymkhana Club or sometimes right there on campus at the senior commons room. They would arrange with the steward to make the bar to remain open to late. It is only the next day we would be hearing that so and so had been taken and that the Chewa fraternity were together celebrating. They would have known in advance through Alex Kalindawalo.

....This went on for a year. By the end of that period, they had arrested everyone who had experience of what it meant to work in the university....

We kept joking about this, the few of us remaining. What exactly is the Ngwazi doing? Mikuyu, the Detention Prison, from Chancellor College something like 5 kilometres, you could see the flood lights there.... So we would say what is it Dr Banda has on his mind? He is trying to build a new university, the Chancellor College campus in Zomba was brand new at that time. It was opened in September 1973 so in 1976 it was a brand new campus, in fact, it was amazing. Everything was new. Vehicles were new. The classrooms smelled of fresh paint. So we said, what is on Dr Banda's mind? Here he is building a university... and yet he seems to be building another kind of university because Mikuyu then boasted the highest concentration of trained educated Malawians at that time. This country did not have that many graduates, not to talk about those who had been trained at the post-graduate level, doctoral level. They crowded them there.... We woke up one day in Zomba to find that they had arrested all the graduates at the National Statistics Office. There were 18 graduates, because of the nature of statistics it was the one area after the university with such a concentration of graduates. They came and arrested all 18 of them. All of them were from the Northern Region. So it gives you an idea of the kind of concentration camp it was.

It is fitting that Kings Phiri ends with the reference to a concentration camp, because it brings to mind the persecution of minorities and the awful consequences of pogroms like the one carried out during the reign of Dr Banda.

One of the most scandalous examples of the blind, crude regionalism behind the detentions was the famous case of the National Statistics Office (NSO), when the Special Branch Police arrived in force and collected 18 statisticians in one fell swoop. Dickson Mzumara had risen to be Deputy Director of the NSO and knew that it was a sensitive situation.

After 1964, you knew your location in the map of Malawi. I was offered a teaching post at the University but the offer was working with a guy from Rumphi and so I said, "No, I am going to work elsewhere."

That took him to the NSO. He describes how he warned his European Director about the problem of the recent hirings all being people from the North.

Colin Greenfield... While I was at the National Statistics Office, we had several vacancies. Colin said I am going to interview people for these posts. He interviewed several young men. [Colin said,] "I had a great time, I met several brilliant young

Dickson Mzumara

men." He gives me the list. I begin to read the list, Nkosi, Mwenifumbo, Ngomba. Colin do you know what you have done? You have put us in trouble. They will accuse me. They will claim that I recruited them. They will say I have selected them. Eventually the recruitment process continued and they all came to the NSO and everyone was saying this place is full of Tumbukas. I received anonymous phone calls and was told that I am hiring only my tribesmen.

3.3 Getting picked up

Some, like Margaret Khonje, said, "We could smell it coming," and managed to flee into exile before the the police could pounce on them. Chifipa Gondwe knew it was coming and got his wife to make plans for that eventuality. Others had no idea why they were picked up and were taken without warning, like Mathews Kalambo, James Mwagomba, Makhumbira Munthali. Still others, like Senior Chief Mwase, knew he was in trouble and was duped into arrest even as he tried to make amends for his "crime."

Chifipa Gondwe had read the signs at the University and so it was no surprise to him when it happened.

So we actually saw it coming. I told my wife, she was expectant with our second child. She was seven months pregnant. I told her anything could happen anytime. That we were going to be detained... quite a number had already been detained. My uncle-in-law, Mr Gondwe, my brother-in-law, Alan Mthegha had already been detained. And we were also told that a few other relatives of mine had been detained.... my younger brother, Christopher had been detained. I told my wife to be getting ready to come back home... I am going to be detained anytime. On that same day I told her I was going to be detained... I had moved from my house and went to my office about three o'clock. I met the wife of Zimani Kadzamira. I waved at her, but she didn't wave back, so I knew the situation was not good. I went back home and since it was 14 November, we were sitting outside and I was taking a green, a Carlsberg. We were discussing what my wife would do if she were to go home and I was detained. Before we could finish our discussion we could see a police vehicle moving, going past our house. I said, I think those people are looking for me. And indeed they were... they came back... I said bye, bye my wife. This is the end.

Makhumbira and Rachel Munthali

Makhumbira "Max" Munthali's story is indicative of the temper of the times. He was part of the first generation of educated Malawians to pass through the brand new university system and looked forward to a promising career.

In December 1969, Max had the good fortune to get the job as understudy to the British expatriate who ran the National Archives. This was part of Dr Banda's go slow Africanisation. By July 1973, he had achieved the position of civil service archivist supernumerary and would have replaced the expatriate at the end of his next contract. He had been sent to Ottawa for an in-house training programme in Canada's national archive and was due to depart in August for England to get a Masters Degree in Library Science. Married, and with his wife Rachel expecting their first child, life was turned upside down without any warning.

On 5th July 1973, I was supposed to attend the Republic dinner dance in Blantyre... I was representing the department. My wife was expecting and I was speaking to her friend who would go to dinner with me. They (Special Branch) came to pick me up from the office at that time during the day... they did not give me any reason.... [However], during the day of 4th July, President Banda had addressed a meeting at Nkula Falls... where he was talking about a young man living in Zomba driving a big car, living in a big house and coming from the North. The young man was criticising Banda that there was no development in the North and that there would only be development in the North if Banda allowed communist help. During the evening news of 4th July, I had heard that, so I was picked up the next day on the 5th of July... During the meeting of 4th of July when Banda was talking about a young man from the North in Zomba, I didn't know it was me, because I didn't fit that description.

For Mathews Kalambo his arrest was also an unexpected surprise. He had resigned his post, applied for a British work permit and was at the airport when he was picked up without any explanation or warning.

I obtained a work permit through the British High Commission. The permit came. I was ready to go to the UK. [At] Chileka Airport then on 8th October the police landed on me saying that the Commissioner of Police wants to see you. I was at Chileka Airport so the Commissioner wants to see you in Zomba so I am taking you back to Zomba, but since it is evening now we are keeping you at Chileka Prison. I was at Chileka Prison up to the morning. On the ninth, they took me to Zomba Prison and locked me there. But you said the Commissioner wanted to see me. What's happening? He said yes but now that you have arrived here we will tell him that you are here and he will tell us when to come and pick you. He never returned..... I finished one year there. No interrogation, nothing. I talked to the wardens there to get out to see the Commissioner of Police. They wouldn't do that. They wouldn't allow me.... [I was] with political prisoners. I can remember Nkanga, a lawyer, Dr Chifipa Gondwe, a political scientist, and Chipasula who was also a political scientist, Dr Harawa from Rumphi was also at Chancellor College. There were many of us.... I stayed two years and three months. No one told me why I was detained.*

James Mwagomba grew up in Zimbabwe where he did most of his schooling. He worked in the private sector for a British-based company and had only recently returned to Malawi on assignment from his company. As a newcomer to Malawi, James Mwagomba learned a very hard lesson about the political culture of fear and paid a terrible price because of another person's jealousy.

1971, I was then posted to Malawi to work here in Malawi, and ... I was welcomed by the Leopard Match Company in Blantyre where I was posted to work.... Later on, that was 1972, 28 January, I was detained and then I was posted to Zomba Detention Yard. From there I stayed for a year. I was reposted to the prison in Lilongwe, they call it Maula Prison but in the Detention Yard.

They didn't tell me why I was detained. I asked the police Special Branch why are you detaining me? They said this has been authorised by the authority of the Minister of State, at that time it was Mr Muwalo. He instructed to detain me....

I had to discover later that people were not detained particularly on political grounds, but from jealousy. If you are a Northerner doing a very good job, the Southerners don't become happy. They had to create lies against you. Oh that man. He is so and so and so.... particularly me. I arrived there. I only worked three months. Everything was okay. The job was going on well, but then there was detention. Did I participate in politics, speaking Malawi politics? A bit. I was from Zimbabwe. So I was just seeing and learning.

That is all. But I did not have friends to discuss with. Never! But I discovered that if this man is a Northerner - there is hatred. Some were against other people because of girlfriends. Some were detained because of jobs, particularly jobs. Many people finished because of hatred not politics. Each one I was discussing with in detention, I would ask the question, Why were you detained? Akuti [exclamation], I don't know. I was employed. I was a manager in import and exports. That was the reason.

How did my release come about? Those Europeans [a fact finding team was examining prison conditions in Malawi] *who came to talk to me, they asked me, you work under which company? Leopard Match Company.... The proprietor of this company is in London. I'll talk to him.... Off he went. We stayed about another three months.... then I had to see Kamwana* [Inspector-General of the Police] *coming. After my release, I went to the company. Come and get your little money. They gave me my little. Do you want to come to work. No I can't because Muwalo had a cousin who was working in the same company.... He was going to take that position. Instead they had to send me from Zimbabwe to take that position, so he was very annoyed. He told Mr Muwalo who asked Special Branch Mankambo to detain me.*

James Mwagomba was never charged and never did get an official reason for his detention.

3.4 Torture and Brutality

Opponents, real or imagined, were treated with special brutality which was meant to dehumanise them. The police and prison warders involved were particularly cruel. Torture was a common practice, widespread and ruthless. The minions embraced the practice and participated in it with energy and enthusiasm. At the same time, the torturers were reduced to savagery and in the process lost touch with their own humanity.

Machipisa has already described the brutality of his treatment.

When John Savage came that was the time. He was terrible. That one was savage. They came 10 other people with him and they beat me all night.... After that they took me to a place where the sun was too hot and they took away my shoes.... After some time I could not walk.... They had to carry me to the vehicle....

Mordecai Gondwe also was on the receiving end of Inspector Savage's brutal methods. Right from his midnight arrest, intimidation was the objective.

Mordecai Gondwe

I found behind the back door a big bang - "Come and open the door" .... Bang!! The door got broken. I thought I was dreaming again about bringing back the old State of Emergency. What have I done? I asked. "You here, are you, Mordecai Gondwe?" Yes I am. "If you tell us the truth you will be safe, but if not you will suffer, you will be beaten.... Open the shop. Come outside." When I went outside as they instructed, I found somebody sitting down – askaris [Swahili for African policemen] around him. It was Machipisa Munthali. "Do you know this man?" I said, I didn't know this man, but I have known him just this afternoon. I went to the police [station] where I [saw] him. "Tell us the truth - is there any connection between you and him?" I don't know him. How can I be connected, I don't know him. "If you don't tell us the truth you will have it."

"We are going to take you to tell us exactly about Machipisa Munthali." Machipisa said in front of me, "I have been forced to say that I know you, but otherwise I don't know you. I have been forced to say so." Anyway, I was taken to the police station and there I found my friends the late Dishon Malema, late Nelson Mbuye, late Chewe Ndovi and another boy again.... In the morning Savage came to me. He pulled me out of that room and took me to that wing of the CID section.... So there he started telling me, "If you tell us the truth you will be released just now."

"…. Do you know George Kanyanya? You met Kanyama Chiume at Kyela. Then Kanyama told this Machipisa Munthali that if you go to Karonga go get money you can get anything he wanted from this Mordecai Gondwe." I said no I have never been to Kanyama Chiume and I have never met anybody. First of all I was entirely refusing… So he started to beat me with his hands and he kicked me and sometimes he knocked me with his small pistol…. In most cases we were seated, chained….I refused and I was beaten and the beating was very heavy and I was crying as a small kid. Anyhow, anywhere, mostly the head. I tell you I am [lucky] to be alive. I have this scar. This scar was very alive then. [He parts his hair and shows a wide scar extending from front to back.] It was very wide then. It was over 1 inch wide. I lost the sight of this eye which I only got to know later on…. There I talked to my friend, Ndovi who was beaten, beaten, he was crying…

That was 1965…. Malema was beaten already I found him. He was two nights there. The next day that is when I was taken to Mzuzu. This scar was swollen with a lot of pain and puss…. The following night that thing was still swollen and I was feeling a lot of pain, too much….

His persecutors tried to recruit him to return to Tanzania and spy on his countrymen. He was intimidated into one unsuccessful effort, returned and reported to his handlers, Lomox and Savage, and then released.

After staying some months, I was re-arrested by this one, Chibambo [Regional Minister for the Northern Region]. *I hear that Mordecai has been released. Don't you know, Mordecai is very dangerous…. pick him and tie him with a stone here and a stone here and throw him [in the lake]….*

The police found I was not safe. They came. They arrested me. "You are in… just to safeguard. Please we are advising you that [in prison] *you will be meeting some informers who will be speaking very much against Kamuzu. Don't join them." This time straight away to Dzaleka…. In Welensky's time* [The Federal Prime Minister during the State of Emergency] *when we were in detention we were given tea…. This time I thought it was going to be the same…. Just arriving at the gate [it started] I was taken to the office. They were very happy, they had a new recruit and they enjoyed beating. Beating again! My God. I took off my clothes, just remaining trousers and shirt. The place is cold…. After that they took me to their small, small cell built by malata [corrugated iron sheets]. There I found only a broken bucket to sit on. I found there was some excreta on all the walls there. When people were being beaten it would fly to the top [of the wall]. In the morning, I found a wheelbarrow coming there full of sisal. Sisal is a good stick… because…. they start beating and it gets broken it cut, cut, cuts. Then the water [juice] goes [into the wound]. They came. They advised me to take off my clothes. I was naked and they started…. three of them* [he uses graphic sound effects to describe the beating.] *On the head here…. I was crying there…"*

When Mordecai Gondwe was finally released, he was very much a broken man, physically, emotionally and financially. Simple imprisonment was not considered enough to break the spirit of people like Mordecai, they had to be brutalised.

Tom Chabwino Nyirenda had been sacked from school because he was a cousin of Kapote. Eventually he went to Tanzania.

Coming back in 1984 April, the Malawi Police and MYP caught me at Kiwe between the border and town. I was detained from 9 April 1984 to 13 November 1987. Three years, 8 months, 13 days. First I was kept at Karonga cells in the prison. From there I was transferred to Mzuzu prison. I was there for almost one and a half years and they sent me to the hospital in Nkhata Bay...

I was beaten severely with an axe handle. They were saying I was one of the Lesoma members who was opposing the government here. They used the axe handle and sharp knives and they used hot pepper in my eyes. You see my eyes? I was not born like this. [He shows his scarred eyes.] *It was because of pepper that has made my eyes brown and burnt...*

It was the Malawi Police Force. I know them all. They are retired now, but Chinkopole Banda, Nkowani. I was arrested by a Mr Mbaki a Special Branch Policeman....

They started beating me here, right away with those hose pipes. I was full of cuts at my back. In Mzuzu, I was received by Mbeza, this man from Kasungu. He became Inspector General, by then he was regional officer. He was just telling his young boys to beat me.

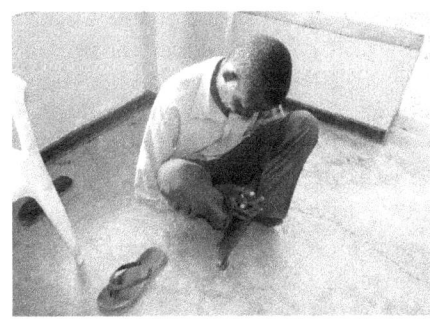

Tom Nyirenda demonstrates how prisoners were shackled.

Nyirenda demonstrated how he and other prisoners had been chained to the floor. His wrists were cuffed and then a short chain attached the cuffs to a ring on the floor in such a manner that he could not free his legs. He had to feed himself from this position and it was in this position that they beat him for most of a month. In KyaNgonde he described how he was fed.

I was given food to eat every day at 2:00. Given a piece of nsima cut into 4 pieces. They would take one quarter and put it on the plate with cold beans at 2 o'clock lunch. The same nsima they cooked the day before, and then the next quarter the next day for 4 days. [He demonstrates how he had to eat.]

Even today I don't eat easily, because of the broken ribs. The beatings lasted for just a matter of a month. They were through with me within a month. The beating it was only a month - each and every day. Naked, not even a pant, no underwear. [He crouches to demonstrate how they were shackled in the sitting position with the arms through the legs.] *For seven months like this, but it was only one month we were beaten.... they took me to the hospital after the seventh month when I fainted. The leg got infected. Five months in Nkhata Bay to heal. Worms had formed in the wound and were coming out...*

I beat up a policeman in Mzuzu prison when they were beating me and that is why they beat me even harder. They heated an iron rod and burnt me on the back.

This was in 1984, twenty years into the dictatorship, and the torture and abuse continued unabated. Senior policemen who were supposed to protect people were the ones ordering and leading the abuse, only to retire into old age with pensions while the people who suffered their torture were left broken and forsaken.

3.5 Conditions

Makhumbira Munthali provides a good description of Mikuyu Prison and overall conditions facing the prisoners.

Mikuyu Detention Camp was divided into three areas, Section A, Section B and Section C. Section A was supposed to house what they called the most dangerous detainees. These were dangerous in terms of influencing people. They thought these were influential people in society and could influence even other detainees, so they were separated from the rest of the detainees. In this group, you had Machipisa Munthali, you had Chakufwa Chihana, you had Augustine Munthali, you had [Michael] Mwambande [from the Chisiza incursion of 1967], you had Arthur Chipembere. I can remember those five, but they were eleven in all. They were treated differently. Each one of these had his own cell and when they woke up in the morning they were given a number of hours to sit together, otherwise they were supposed to stay in their own cells, not outside. So this area was supposed to have 11 cells and you had these dangerous inmates as they called them.

Then you had Section B. Section B was supposed to house people who had been arrested when entering the country. So people who had visited Zambia or were visiting Malawi from Zambia. People who were coming from visiting Tanzania or coming from Tanzania visiting Malawi or people who had been to Zimbabwe or were coming to visit from Zimbabwe or people who were visiting South Africa of coming from South Africa to visit Malawi. If they were detained they were sent to that section.... They were still political, so they were supposed to be kept separate from the rest of the detainees who had no knowledge of what was happening outside. This is Section B.

So Section C, this is the section where I was. It had two sections. The sections were split up by virtue of the cells. There were two cells. One area was for people who were detainees but who were cooking for everybody. So these were in a separate section. So the rest of Section C was housed on the other side. Detainees in Section C were either political detainees as such or they were political detainees who were arrested because of the Chilobwe[3] incident in Blantyre. If they had been picked up at night going to work or coming back from work, those were detained in Section C with us. So you had two groups of people - those who were picked up in Blantyre because of the curfews imposed because of Chilobwe and those who had been picked up for political activities, faked or otherwise, alleged or otherwise. So I was in this section, Section C. ....B was more than 150 (people). C was more than 300 ... in common cells.... you had two rooms. These rooms were supposed to house about 48 detainees in each cell. But that was not the case. You had over 100 in each cell, in each room.

Now the Chiperone blanket is 60 inches wide. So each person was entitled to a space which if you fold the blanket which was 60 inches, if you folded it twice - that is the space that you are entitled to and that makes 15 inches. What happens is once you spread your blanket, when sleeping, you had to sleep [so that] every other person on the line had to face the other way... head to foot. So if I face north [with] my feet facing the south meant that the next person, his head was facing south and his feet north. In each cell.... there was only one toilet. It was water borne, a flush toilet. One toilet for over 100 people.

You had to learn to accommodate other people's tempers, because some people were sort of obnoxious, but when you have lived with them for an unknown time you have to learn to accommodate people's tempers.

When asked about access to reading materials, Makhumbira replied:

Only during Christmas. During Christmas you were given a Bible to read... and they would come and remove it away soon after New Years Day.

The food we were eating was ngaiwa which is flour made from unthreshed corn and with pigeon peas. That was it. We were not allowed to go out, so we were not working. In fact, they had built Mikuyu Detention Camp because Amnesty International used to take pictures of detainees working in fields in Lilongwe in Dowa where there was Dzaleka. Detainees were going out to farm and Amnesty International was publishing pictures of detainees being used

---

3 Chilobwe and other suburbs in Blantyre experienced a series of murders, over a period of several months starting in 1968. In the culture of fear, orality and silence, a number of rumours circulated in the place of real news. Many blamed the killings on Banda and withchcraft or to repay South African Government loans in human blood or by the enslavement of Malawians to work in South Africa. Banda treated these acts as political subversion, blamed the former Ministers and reformed the justice system to ensure perceived opponents were punished despite the lack of evidence.

on the detention farm. That's what led Banda to decide to transfer everybody from Dzaleka to Mikuyu for closed detention.

Most people at Mikuyu in my group at least they had high school education.... What we used to do to keep ourselves busy, we decided that those people who couldn't read or write and they wanted to learn... so what we used to do, we used to cut soap into chalk.... to use soap on a blanket or on the cement to write what we wanted to teach to the people who couldn't read or write.... we had a lot of people, old and young from Mangochi or the South in most cases, because every detainee who came from the North was able to read and write. So we were teaching them how to read and write using soap as chalk and a blanket as a blackboard. That was one activity.

Those who wanted to have a bit of exercise as a group we used to use the cells and do exercises, say every morning we would wake up and do exercises in the room while everybody [else] sat against the wall outside.

We decided that we were going to organise discussions. So we would ask individuals who had worked in the civil service in whatever capacity, to give a talk. Say somebody had worked in the Young Pioneers, we would ask him to talk to us about Young Pioneer activities and we would ask him questions. So we learned more about Young Pioneer activities that way. Or if somebody was a DC we would ask him to tell us about how they managed the district as a District Commissioner. What sort of problems did they face? How he was interacting with politicians and things of that sort. We had a lot of people who had skills and we wanted to learn from them their skills, from their field. So that kept us going.

No books. No newspapers. Nothing. No radio.

We used to talk about Kamuzu Banda or our experiences in the civil service in whatever capacity we had been involved with government, then the activities of Banda as President of the country. In fact, that was the only place that we felt safe to talk about Banda. (We were) very critical of Banda's activities. We knew that there was no way we could move to something worse than what we were going through. Even if there were spies amongst us, it didn't make any difference to us. We were already detained....

Usually the guards were polite if you didn't insult them. In most cases the guards at Mikuyu knew that the people who were in detention had done nothing wrong. So they were sort of sympathetic with what we were going through. So unless you did something that was against the prison rules you were safe. You didn't come into contact with the guards most of the time. The cells were divided in such a way that you were cut off from the areas where the guards were most of the time. So you were amongst yourselves. In most cases, you came across guards when you were going to the clinic or when you had a visitor, because a guard would come and call your name and pick you up to go and visit with your visitor. Or when you are going to have a bath, when you were going to have a shower, they would come and pick a given number at a time and take you to have a bath and come back and take another load like that. If you are not involved in those activities then you are not involved with the guards.

There was no need [for structure]. We were not organising ourselves against government, so there was no need for leadership. The only roles that came up were those for volunteers. There were people who volunteered to keep the place clean, so they would sweep the place everyday. There were those who volunteered to cook, so they went to cook for us. Apart from that there were no hierarchies.

If you broke prison rules, you were taken to the officer-in-charge and the officer-in-charge would decide how you would be punished. Either, you were put in seclusion, so you are put in a dark room. You would stay there possibly two days without a meal. Or you would go into a cell and they would pour water in before they put you in so it is all wet and it means that you can't sleep, you can't lie down. Or they would put you in a cell and they would chain you up and pour water on you. You are chained so that your feet and legs are sitting down and you are sitting in water... for two to three days."

Augustine Msiska was held at the Mpyupyu Minimum Security Prison Farm near Mikuyu and although conditions were supposed to be better than in the detention camp, his story shows how miserable life could be.

Malaria was very common at Mpyupyu, at Domasi, there is a lake there, Lake Chirwa, mosquitoes, open windows. It was hell. I remember another night... I was bitten by a scorpion. It was darkness, I just grabbed it, but I suspected. I have lived at Mlowe and Chitimba and never been bitten by a scorpion. I just threw it against the wall. In the morning I found it dead there.

I had problems with my health. I had piles - terrible. Another time I had problems with my stomach. There was a medical doctor, Dr Mwale. He was assigned to visit detainees once in a week. He recommended that I should get rice and milk. Mwanza too ended up doing that.

No reading material. We never had a haircut. Even to have our fingernails cut, we had to ask for permission. They said if you keep razor blades, you can commit suicide. You can cut yourselves.

We had a routine there. In the morning, the ordinary prisoners brought in water from some well. They came to drop the water before they opened for us. That was our water for drinking and also for bathing.

One thing I should mention. We ate food below our dignity, whatever. I remember in Central Prison they said, "Oh there is fish today." So the fish came. It was utaka. This utaka is dried by the sun and they don't even sieve to sort the utaka, so you find crabs, you find feces of birds, you find there rotten bits, what, what, what. So they just take the bag and empty it in the drum. Boiled them for maybe ten minutes and then you ate that. I remember the same stuff.... I got a very big dog. What am I going to do to feed this dog? My salary is very meagre. So I went to the market and bought this utaka. You know what the dog did? It was just smelling it.... So when my friends said there is fish today, I said, I can't eat this. My own dog refused. I am not going to sink so low.

And I remember when I went to Mpyupyu, it was Peter Mwanza encouraging me. "No there are some proteins here. You have to eat" ... If we ate meat, it meant they had hanged somebody... that was the tradition. If they were hanging tomorrow, then today that person must get some meat for dinner. But the meat that entered Mpyupyu was always rotten. I stayed there only two years but I think it was only three times that I ate some beef and it was rotten, so we were used to that. Oh and these beans with weevils.

Kirby Mwambetania's testimony covers his arrest as well as providing a detailed and vivid description the conditions the political prisoners were subjected to.

Doug's Note: Kirby was one of my oldest and most faithful friends from the time I arrived in Malawi in 1968. We had been introduced by a letter by common friend of ours that I met at university in Ottawa. They had been childhood friends in Tukuyu where both their fathers worked in the hospital. They had become separated by the political iron curtain that descended between Tanzania and Malawi after 1964. Kirby involved me in his family life very intimately and taught me a great deal about the life and culture of Malawi.

In the course of our research, we managed to contact Kirby's first born son, Lwitiko, with the intention of interviewing him for his own memories of life when his father was in detention. Instead, he willingly offered us what we presume is a draft of what Kirby's lawyers submitted to the National Compensation Tribunal.

It is in honour of the lives tragically and wastefully lost by the excesses of the Banda dictatorship that we reprint verbatim his testimony here.

Written testimony begins.

INTRODUCTION

Whilst working as a lecturer in the University of Malawi since 1970 I was arrested and detained in 1974. I was detained on 26th of September 1974 and released in February 1977 (I cannot remember the exact date).

During the first month of my detention I was interrogated by Special Branch Officers on two occasions only. On both occasions I was asked questions related to my past school life. I was asked where I went to primary, secondary and University Education.

(ed. note - The following two paragraphs were circled for removal by the author.)

<u>Zomba Prison and Special Branch Headquarters:</u> The interrogations were simple and I experienced no torture during both occasions which lasted approximately ten minutes each session. However, on both days I was collected from Zomba prison at approximately 7:30 A.M. and taken to the Special Branch Headquarters in Zomba and would wait for the interview which took place late in the evening at approximately 4:30 P.M. to 4:40 P.M. On both occasions the suspense from 7:30 A.M. to 4:30 P.M. was extremely traumatic. I had heard before about police brutality and torture chambers and feared for the worst on my life.

On my first day of interrogation, I was interviewed by some Special Branch Junior Officers and on the second and last day I was interviewed by Mr Focus Gwede who was Head of the Special Branch.

HISTORY:

The sequence on my arrest were dramatic. It was on a weekend prior to commencement of the first term and I was preparing for classes at Chancellor College when I was confronted by two Special Branch men in the corridor leading to the Chancellor College Principal. I identified one Mr Ngwata, who in later years became Inspector General of Police and asked if I could help them. To this Mr Ngwata informed me that he had been sent by his Seniors to collect me for some questioning. I was told not to worry and directed to follow them. When we got to the car park they apologised that I had to leave my car behind and get into their Landrover which was not as comfortable as my car. In later years, I knew this diplomacy was sham.

On our way from Chancellor College I was constantly assured not to worry and that everything would be alright. The matter was simple, I was told. At approximately a kilometre away from Chancellor College I was told that they needed to go to my office which happened to be at Parliament Buildings close to the Parliament Chambers. In my office they searched in very casual terms for letters and documents and said at the end that they could find nothing which was of significance.

Page 2/

MY HOUSE

Then we moved to my house at Kalimbuka Estate near Zomba General Hospital and they stopped in the living room demanding to see my personal letters. Again the searching was very casual and nothing matching my fears of the notorious Special Branch tortures. At the end they informed me that they could find nothing of significant.

ZOMBA PRISON

It was around 4:00 P.M. when we left the house after driving by the Zomba General Hospital that I requested to see a friend, the Chief Matron, to inform my wife about my plight. Mr Ngwata agreed and I informed the Chief Matron of my plight and requested her to inform my wife who was in Lilongwe on that particular day.

From the hospital Mr Ngwata told me in the Landrover that since it was late in the afternoon, the Senior Police Bosses would see me the following day and I had to spend the night in Zomba Prison. Once again, Mr Ngwata assured me that I did not need to worry, I would be treated well and that everything would be alright soon.

When we got to Zomba Prison I was ushered into a room where Mr Ngwata handed me over to a Prison Officer with the instruction that I should be treated well and he would fetch me the following day. After Mr Ngwata left I was instructed to remove my wrist watch and shoes. After the brief ordeal I was ushered to a room called Cell A. Cell A was packed chock a block with detainees whose cases were pending further investigations. In Cell A a detainee received me and ushered me into a room approximately 9 feet by 6 feet. There were approximately six detainees seated in that room, each with a plate containing mgaiwa nsima with cabbage clutched in their laps. They were eating their last evening meal at approximately 5:00 P.M. When I got into the room they all paused eating and greeted me. Before I could narrate my episode of the day a Prison Officer called and asked me to follow him to another pace. I can remember murmurs from detainees saying that I was being taken to a very nasty place. That was my last experience in Cell A.

I was taken to what is commonly known as CC or Condemned Cell in full. CC accommodated convicted criminals who were sentenced to death and awaiting for the day to be executed. There were approximately 15 cubicles in CC with each measuring about 10 feet by 7 feet. If crowded a room would accommodate five persons.

When I got to CC I was ushered into one cubicle and locked in. On looking around the cubicle I saw a bucket for the collection of urine and fecal matter. There was no toilet paper. Hardly had I settled to reflect on my predicament than a Prison Officer, with frightening Nazi type Officialdom, brought in one blanket for my use. It was about 6 P.M.

Page 3/

I had heard of solitary confinement before but never imagined I would experience it one day. The night was long and the mind got lost in wandering. I was convinced something was terribly wrong and that someone had made a gross error. At the end of the following day I hoped Special Branch men would realise that I was innocent and would set me free, I mused. Never did I imagine 26th September 1974 would be the first of hundreds of days in Prison.

It did not take long before I heard church songs being sung from somewhere in the vicinity. It was only in the morning that my cubicle door was opened and in the open quadrangle all except one inmate were gathered to greet one another. Only one inmate was on leg chains. An inmate came to greet me and showed me a water tap at one corner of the quadrangle.

I washed my face without soap and without a tooth brush I gargled some water to freshen my mouth. One inmate noticed my plight and offered some soap which I accepted with reservations. My thoughts were driven to imagine a murderer being a kind man. As I walked past the other inmates who numbered approximately twenty in number I had fear that one or more would pounce on me. The stigma of being a murderer was real and the trauma unbearable.

Porridge was served and one inmate offered some of his sugar to make the porridge drinkable. I thanked him profusedly. It was not proper to be rude especially in CC. I vowed inwardly to be extremely cautious and tactful when dealing with the inmates. Seating in one corner I was approached by literally all inmates to greet me and express their dismay at the evil regime which, they suspected, victimised well to do persons like myself. I did not understand their reasoning and I was confident the day would not last before I would be released.

Page 4/

As I looked around the inmates I saw my colleague Dr Chilivumbo at a distance with clear instructions not to meet me. I was instructed to remain in my cubicle but the other inmates were free to mingle in the quadrangle.

One group came near with a game of Bao and I patiently sat by before someone asked me if I knew and wanted to play. I consented and joined them. As I played the game of 'Bao' I kept on watching the CC gate for someone to summon me to see the Special Branch Officer as promised on the previous day but alas no one came until after several days.

4 P.M. was time for all of us to be locked up in our respective cubicles until 6 A.M. the following morning.

As time went by minutes turned into hours and hours into days the routine was much the sameness. Inmates told many horror stories and sometimes hilarious stories surrounding their predicament. Many confessed to having committed murder and others continued to deny having committed murder. Those who had experienced the previous group being executed told horror episodes leading to the time of execution.

As I had no clue to my fate I suffered with the inmates and many days of false alarms to our fate passed with excruciating psychological pains. One day I decided to wash my shirt and left it at a convenient place in the quadrangle to dry when I was summoned at approximately 7:30 A.M. to go to the Office. I informed the Officer that I had just washed my shirt and I did not have any other to put on. The Prison Officer left without a word and shortly returned with a prisoner's shirt for my use.

I was handcuffed on my way to the Special Branch office. We arrived there at approximately 8:00 A.M. and instructed to wait. At 12:00 Noon I was directed to a police cell where I was given a plate of rice with a revolting dish of pigeon peas for lunch. After the lunch I continued to wait for my first interrogation. It was not until sometime around 4:30 P.M. when I was summoned to an Office to meet two Special Branch Officers. They demanded to know where I did my primary, secondary and University education. The interview took approximately ten minutes and I was taken back to Zomba Prison.

The following day I was once again summoned to go to the Special Branch office for further interrogations. Once again I was collected at around 7:30 A.M. and waited until around 4:30 P.M. before I met Mr Focus Gwede, the head of Special Branch of Police.

Page 5/

The questions were very similar to the ones I was asked the previous day – I was asked where I went for my primary, secondary and university education. The interrogation lasted about 10 minutes and at the end I was told that it was possible someone did not like me. I was taken back to Zomba Prison.

On both days of interrogation no torture was used and I was expecting more interrogations with a charge against me. It did not occur to me that the second interrogation with Mr Focus Gwede was to be my last contact with the Special Branch Officers until my day of release in February 1977.

I spent approximately 2 months in all at Zomba Prison in the Condemned Cell (CC) before I was transferred to Mikuyu detention Camp.

MIKUYU DETENTION CAMP

On the day to Mikuyu Detention Camp I was given what was known as a Full Detention Certificate signed by the State President Dr H Kamuzu Banda. For the purposes of public SECURITY I was to be incarcerated and kept at a detention camp. The time period was not stated. The certificate was taken away from me and kept by the prison Officers.

I was chained and handcuffed on my way to Mikuyu. On arrival at Mikuyu at about 6:00 P.M. I was ushered into a corridor where I was given prison uniform and ordered to undress there and then into prison attire. A harsh voice commanded me not to be proud and dress up quickly. I was told to forget all formalities and obey orders without question. No underwear, no shoes, no wrist watch, except the prison shirt and shorts were allowed into the cell. I was next ushered into Cell B.

Cell B was approximately 30 feet by 16 feet. The room was full of people. They were all seated and one man whom I later learned was a Nyapala (equivalent to a headboy at school) welcomed me on the door and ushered me to a place to sit down with the rest of the group. The smell and the stench in the room was revolting.

Page 6/

In the cell, I met Dr Chilivumbo and a few other familiar faces. Before they explained cell etiquette they wanted to know how Dr Banda and outside world was thinking about their plight.

Life in c   rous.
[THE] F   ISTRATE THE
STRUCT

CELL B – ITEMS PERMITTED, SLEEPING ARRANGEMENTS – VISITORS
ITEMS ALLOWED IN CELL B WERE   1 Toilet paper
                                  2 Tooth brush
                                  3 Tooth paste

The above items were the only items allowed into cell B. They were not supplied but a visitor was allowed to give it to you.

Page 7/

In subsequent months none of us was allowed to see a visitor so toilet paper and tooth paste was not available.

A TYPICAL DAY

A typical day started at about 6.00 A.M. when a Prison Officer would open gate B (see diagram one and two) for inmates to be able to spread out in the open quadrangle (see diagram two). The quadrangle was surrounded by very high walls and although there was no roof it was covered with security wire so that attempts to escape from the quadrangle would prove futile.

Water would be brought in pails and each inmate would take turns to wash the face and brush teeth (for those with tooth brushes) with a couple of cups of water. The water came in limited quantities and inmates had to be considerate in its usage.

FOOD

Porridge would next be served in an aluminium dish without sugar.

Lunch was served at 12:00 noon with mgaiwa as sima and almost at all times khobwe was the relish. Many times the khobwe was rotten if not full of weevils. In order to survive one had to take a piece of sima and dip it in a cup of khobwe to get a feel of the soup but shake off floating weevils. It was sometimes possible that the khobwe was not rotten but each bean would definitely contain one or more weevils. Many times weevils formed a supplementary protein diet for us all. Once in about six months meat would be served and for meat eaters it was a day of great jubilation. Vegetarians had no alternative to meat. Although I was a vegetarian I was forced to eat meat to survive. Meat supplied was one piece the size of one standard peach in Malawi and soup of some juice from boiled meat. Rice was not served. Only once 'bonongwe' a vegetable was served instead of khobwe. The evening meal was similar to lunch and served at about 4:00P.M. We were all locked in the cell at about 4.30 P.M. to stay in until 6.00 A.M. the following day.

SLEEPING ARRANGEMENTS

Sleeping arrangements were inhuman. Only one blanket was supplied. We slept on bare cement. Neither mattress nor a mat was supplied. We used to spread half the blanket on the cement and cover with the other half.

Page 8/

If the room were not congested then definitely one blanket would not be adequate especially during the cold months of June and July. Human heat compensated for the inadequate warm cover.

Sleeping time was traumatic. As shown in the diagram, space for one person was approximately 67 inches by 12½ inches. We formed three rows and covered the entire width of the room. The next row started at 12½ inches from the wall. If one can imagine the congestion, it was necessary that inmates faced sideways in one direction and in the middle of the night all of us would turn in the other direction to avoid breathing into each others or one anothers face. [ed. the author had marked this next for erasure. We decided to include it because it is so instructive.] With hindsight the turning was almost rhythmic. It needed no bell or alarm. It was almost automatic.

TOILET FACILITY

There was one flush toilet for approximately 70 detainees. It was positioned at one corner without an enclosure. Anyone who needed to use it did so in full view of the others. It was not as bad during the day because most inmates stayed outside in the quadrangle. However, use of the toilet at nights had its ups and downs.

When everyone was asleep at night to get to the toilet from one end of the cell was a problem due to the crowded nature of the cell. No matter how careful one got it required an acrobat to miss tramping into an inmates head or feet.

The toilet facility broke down several times during my stay at Mikuyu. If it got blocked at night and the pan was full, a prison warder would be summoned to supply a pail. The attention of the prison warden would be drawn by banging loud enough on the door for him to hear from afar.

Once supplied, fecal matter would be manually transferred into the pail for further use by other inmates. The blockage would usually be fixed on the following day. Sitting on the pan in view of all others had its dehumanising effect. The shy ones, especially newcomers, would take off their shirts and and cover their face to facilitate bowel movement. The old timers grew to be accustomed to sit on the pan and go through all the motions without blinking.

Page 9/

BATHING

We were allowed to get a shower three times a week. On many occasions water would run out whilst one was having a shower. There was no alternative if water run out. If one was unlucky to have applied soap and water run out, there was no alternative but to wait and dry up. There were no bathing towels. To facilitate drying one simply jumped up to shed off excess water.

DRINKING WATER

Drinking water was supplied in a pail with one cup for use by all of us. If one inmate had an ailment such as tonsillitis or a cough no precautions were available. It was survival of the fittest.

VISITORS

Any visitor allowed to see a detainee went through a rigorous procedure. The visitor was physically required to go to the Special Branch Headquarters to apply for permission to see a detainee.

In many cases the visitor would be told to go back and wait for authorisation. Once approval was given the visitor came to Mikuyu and declared any items brought for the detainee. As stated above items permitted were toilet paper, tooth brush and tooth paste only. Not even bathing soap was allowed.

The visitor would then be taken to a cubicle separated by wire mesh to chat with the detainee. Time was of the essence to the Prison guards and only a brief period of approximately 10 minutes was allowed for the whole visit.

From 1974 to early 1976 one visitor was allowed every month but from early 1976 to mid1976 only one visitor was allowed once in 6 months. From mid1976 to the time of my release in February 1977 no visitor was allowed to see a detainee.

As each day passed, prayers were said at varying times for Christians and Moslems. Moslems would usually start praying at about 4.00 A.M. and the Christians at about 5.00 P.M. Evening prayers would be said after 5.00 P.M. lock up. Any non-believer had no choice but to keep quiet and pay respect to others.

Page 10/

No reading materials were allowed. Not even a Bible or Koran was allowed into cell B.

My 2½ years were full of nasty experiences. Mosquitoes, and other insects proved a great nuisance especially during the rainy season. As the windows were not sealed various insects and other animals would invade the room and our lives to be absolutely unbearable.

On a hot day when one does not need to cover with a blanket, I being bald headed, needed to cover the head from mosquitoes. My inmates with hair needed to cover the face from mosquitoes.

Lice also gave us problems. At one time the cell was inundated with lice. It settled mostly in the seams of the shirts or short trousers. So early in the morning we would all undress and cover with blankets to vent our anger at the poor creatures. Each one of us would pluck one louse at a time and crush it with two thumb nails. It was a source of great pleasure to crush lice to death. But the lice proved resilient as even larger numbers were coming by the day.

One day after several complaints, the Prison guards came into cell B to spray chemicals. That saw the first plague destroyed.

During the rainy season other insects came into cell B in abundance. One particular insect called "Nyauhango" was notorious. Its tail resembles that of a scorpion and I was absolutely petrified at the sight of "Nyauhango". But fortunately "Nyauhango" does not sting like a scorpion. It was only the thought of scorpions which sent jitters into my spine.

The cicadas came also in abundance. It was their sting and smell that was repulsive. Millipedes and worms were also coming in their large numbers during the rainy season.

All told Mikuyu was the real den of inequity for the regime of Dr Banda. Inhuman treatment, poor food, unsanitary conditions, crowded environment and psychological torture were characteristics of the physical and mental torture I went through at Mikuyu.

Page 11/

In my last three months before being released, I became very ill and had to be taken to Zomba General Hospital once again but this time in a special cell reserved for detainees who were critically ill. The nature of my illness was that I experienced terrible headaches and as expected lost a lot of weight. Crude medical examinations were conducted with some success.

I was put on traction for approximately one month. The treatment of traction meant that my neck was tied in a special manner to allow heavy weights pull it in order to release tension on my spinal cord. I was told by a visiting medical doctor that they needed to release tension on my vertebral column on the D5 position whatever that was, the treatment gave me a lot of relief.

RELEASE

One day, I cannot remember the exact date in February 1977 I was informed that I was required to go back to Mikuyu. When I got there I found my inmates in a great mood of jubilation for we were almost all of us in cell B including other detainees at Mikuyu from other cells were to be released the following day.

Trucks came to collect us early in the morning to the police Headquarters Zomba. We were gathered in a big hall and told to sit down. Special Branchmen physically touched each one of us to get a head count. The counting was dramatic as several Special Branchmen did the exercise over and over again. That done the Inspector General of Police then came in with full police regalia and addressed us.

The message was short and simple. In essence he told us that all of us were now free men, transport would be arranged to take us to our respective home districts through the regional headquarters of police. The police had apprehended trouble shooters (sic) who had caused our grief. He emphasised that some amongst us were truly subversive but that was then all over. We did not need to worry and that when we got to our respective villages we should report to the nearest police. If in trouble we should always seek police assistance, we were told.

Page 12/

When I got to my village in Karonga I was informed that I had been dismissed from work as a Lecturer in the University of Malawi the day I was arrested by the Police. No reason was given for my dismissal.

Given the political climate I kept quiet from the day of my release until this time when I need to seek compensation for wrongful dismissal from the University and compensation for violating my human rights during the time of my detention and loss of my career as a Lecturer.

The fact that I was never told why I was detained pains me enormously to date. With the advent of the new Multiparty Government I trust that my case shall be appropriately handled by my Lawyers to seek appropriate compensation.

End of written testimony.

Lwitiko also attached a copy of the Detention Order signed by Kirby himself and H. Kamuzu Banda which was a standard procedure and also shows the level of micromanagement of state security that Dr Banda exercised.

3.6 Getting Out

Mathews Kalambo was a self-made medical man. He never sought state sponsorship for his studies and was looking forward to continuing to expand his knowledge in medicine. His detention was totally unexpected. It literally ended his career, and left him and his family financially ruined. His wife was also punished and forced from her job, and MCP hoodlums sacked his father's homestead and set it on fire. Even after his release, he was taken to the Commissioner of Police who said that he had been forgiven, but that was not really the case. Forgiven means his record should have been expunged and he be allowed to pick up his life from where he left off. But in Malawi, ex-detainees continued to be punished for their 'crime' even after their release and pardon.

I don't know about the others, but the time they called me I was alone. They called me on 8th December 1976. We are taking you to see the Commissioner of Police. "Where's your luggage?" I don't know. You should know where my luggage is. So after collecting my luggage they took me to Zomba, that was their main station. So they took me there and we were taken into the Commissioner's office and the Commissioner said, "Now you can go home. Dr Kamuzu Banda has pardoned you. You can go home now." But, how do I go home? "They will give you warrants and you can go home now." I said, but I was supposed to go to the UK. I should have flown to the UK. I've got work permits and things. What am I going to do about that? He said, "You are very lucky that you have come out alive. You should be dead. Just go home to join your wife and family and don't engage yourself in politics." I said, I am not a politician. I am a professional man. I never talk politics. "Give him warrants. Let him go home."

My wife had been a teacher. She was interdicted. They said that if you want to work then you have to divorce your husband. She said "No. If you had told me that he is dead, yes, but since you say he is in detention, then No." We are taking you home, so they took her home. They wanted to take her to her village. She said, "No, I am married. Take me to his (Mathews') home..." So when I came back, I found her at home. I stayed with her from 1976 to 1979 doing nothing.

Following Kalambo's release, he was not even allowed to work.

I found a job in Botswana. I applied, but they refused to allow me to go. I got a job in Ghana, they refused me to go. They said you have not been cleared yet. Although you are at home, you are still in the hands of the police. So I was busy cultivating in the village....

My father died while I was in prison. My brothers came to tell me but they were refused permission to see me. I only learned about his death after I was released. Two years three months no explanation.

It was clearly a very difficult time for a very proud professional man. The fear of re-arrest had literally immobilised him in the village.

Makhumbira Munthali found himself similarly frustrated.

I made applications to various organisations, and whenever I found a job, I was supposed to ask for clearance from the police and they couldn't give me clearance, so I couldn't work. My friends were lucky [some found work] but I was not allowed. I wasn't going to work again in Malawi. I was asked to write an apology letter to the President by the Regional Minister for the North. Malani Lungu.... I refused. I said writing an apology for what? I didn't do anything that I deserved to be detained for. So I am going to apologise for what I had refused to write an apology letter in detention and I am not going to write an apology letter when I am out here.... When I was in detention I knew it was going to be difficult for me to settle down and get a job when I was out, because some people who had been released earlier than myself were not working, so I knew it was going to be rough to find a job.

Many detainees were released in 1977 after the arrest and execution of Focus Gwede and Albert Muwalo. Even after their release, the continuing punishment, stigma and discrimination simply reinforced the state of terror amongst the rest of the population.

Jack Mapanje was detained in 1987, twenty-three years after the Cabinet crisis when the great darkness descended on the country. His compelling prison memoir, *And Crocodiles Are Hungry at Night* is a revealing in-depth look at how the state of terror was maintained. Like many other political detainees, he had no tangible idea what had led to his imprisonment. His release was as inexplicable as his arrest, and it was only a little later after the fall of the dictator and his cabal that he learned he had been picked up at the express order of Dr. Banda and that he was to be left in prison to rot despite the international outcry.

Chapter 4: Exile - The First Generation

4.1 Carson Kayuni
4.2 Escape
4.3 Conditions in Exile
4.4 Divisions in the Exile Community
4.5 The Children of Exile

Introduction

No one ever planned to live a life in exile. They never contemplated leaving their homeland for which they had fought so valiantly. The struggle for national liberation was for all Malawians, but after Banda overthrew his Cabinet they felt that only a select few were being allowed to benefit. Many refugees believed they would return home very soon and, by their presence, coalesce the internal resentment to Dr Banda, thus creating enough pressure to force Dr Banda to leave the country to those who had done the heavy work in the nationalist years. Many of the people who took the places of the deposed Cabinet members had played very minor roles in the nationalist struggle. This doubly frustrated the exiles, many of whom were amongst the most talented and hard-working of the pre-independence leaders. Many suffered in bitterness and lost everything when they left the country. Some stayed jobless and others failed to continue schooling, which had been cut short by fleeing the country.

Exiles were particularly bitter about the way they were portrayed, especially after the democratic dispensation when they were accused of having had it easy in exile while the ones who stayed at home suffered the daily fear and indignity of life under the regime. They were also accused of not working to overthrow the regime or even being cowards.

We call these the first generation who fled into exile as part of the fallout of the Banda Cabinet Coup that subverted the move to a more democratic independence and installed the culture of dictatorship. The days and weeks following the events of September 8 and 9, 1964, were followed by an anarchic situation because there was no central command. The word went out from various power brokers and in the name of the Ngwazi, the MYP, youth leaguers and the police under the likes of John Savage hunted the "traitors" down like animals. One was lucky if the police got to them first, because roaming bands of MYP would descend on houses and families suspected of harbouring sympathisers of the ministers who had been denounced to "deal with them" meaning to eliminate them. The word *chigawenga* was another code for anything goes when "dealing with them."

Harrowing as their experiences were, our interviewees are the survivors. No one knows how many did not escape and suffered the ultimate sacrifice of losing their lives. There is a famous dam named Box 2 in Limbe where the MYP were reputed to have disposed of innumerable bodies. Throwing people to the crocodiles was not a simple metaphor but a reality for many unfortunate victims.

The lucky few who were already out of the country were spared the life threatening circumstances of escaping. David Rubadiri and George Michongwe fled into exile from their diplomatic positions and posh New York offices when they were recalled to face the discordant music in Malawi. They joined the other exiles in Tanzania, Zambia or Uganda, where, in the case of Rubadiri, he moved effortlessly into teaching at Makerere University, his alma mater.

The experience in exile was not all penury and misery. Malawian professionals, who could not get back to their homeland, ended up contributing elsewhere and becoming important actors on the national and international stage. People like Thandika Mkandawire, Guy Mhone, Dr John Lwanda, and Ceciwa Khonje made a great impact on their host countries and further afield. In Tanzania, Professor Michongwe was well respected and his talent was appreciated at the various institutions where he taught. Suzgo Kabuzi Munthali rose to become a judge in the high court of Zambia. Businessmen like Francis Mphepo made a solid success of their career in Zambia.

While success stories appear to outnumber the stories of penury and suffering, the reality was very different for large numbers of refugees. At the Pangale camp for refugees from Malawi and several other African countries life was difficult. It was located in the remote central region of Tanzania, near Tabora. Carson Kayuni, Jomo Chikwakwa and many, many others spent 30 years as refugees, essentially surviving as subsistence farmers. For someone like Mary Mwale camp life was a shock, after moving from a comfortable, urban educated existence to join rural tent dwellers at Pangale.

Whether in a camp or pursuing a career, exile life posed numerous problems. Family life was irrevocably disrupted, families scattered and people could not properly mourn the loss of their loved ones. For those 30 years they could not even enter into direct communication with loved ones whether by letter or phone. Emotional scars from the treatment, the escape and the loss remained forever. Education was disrupted and while some refugee children got a good education in exile, the children who grew up in Pangale reached only the end of primary school when their educational careers ended.

People in senior positions who would have become the first of Malawi's senior officers, or principal secretaries, ended as middle level civil servants in neighbouring countries, blocked from rising further by their status as non-citizens. Other lost opportunities included businessmen and women whose land and properties were forfeited or taken over by MCP vultures.

Perhaps the most tragic are the stories we cannot include in this volume but deserve their own telling. They are the ones lost in exile – lost to the dream that never was. Returning home did not happen in their lifetime. There were heroes like Atati Mpakati and Mkwapatira Muhango brutally hunted down and assassinated by the Banda regime for their outspokenness. Dr Banda even crowed about eliminating them in Parliament. Lesser known heroes are the activist student leader, Tojo Msowoya, and the militant trade union leader, Suzgo Msiska. Suzgo found his way into exile in Dar then in Nairobi and now in Toronto Canada where he has maintained a distance from the Malawians there and has been difficult to contact. Tojo, after a successful student placement in Moscow, also ended up in Canada, where his descent into alcoholism has led to his total disappearance to any of the old friends who knew him there. Mzee Kachingwe was a prominent businessman who stayed in Pangale until Yatuta died and then moved to Zambia where he managed to rebuild his business career and remained very helpful to the struggle until he died in Zambia. We say, "Hamba Kahle" to these gallant fighters and old friends.

The children of exiles also faced enormous complications getting an education and deciding who they were. Uprooted from their homelands, families and culture they often struggled with identity issues and conflicts of cultural values. Were they Malawians or citizens of the countries they lived in? They carried many emotional scars as they grew older and live with the pain even many years later, to say nothing of the difficulty of being raised by parents harbouring trauma themselves.

4.1 Carson Kayuni

We feature, the story of another exceptional person, although not one with the high profile of Machipisa Munthali or Rose Chibambo, to illustrate how exile impacted people from all stations in life. Carson Kayuni was born in 1927 in what today is Chitipa District. He did his early primary school there and was selected to higher primary at Livingstonia Mission. He had *to foot for 6 days* to get to school, a challenge that would have discouraged many students with less determination, but reflects the kind of courage, commitment and perseverance that he was capable of. He had a brief career as a prison officer in Tanganyika and in Posts and Telecommunications before he finally came to Nyasaland and worked as a court clerk.

Carson was politically active during the nationalist struggle and was one of the activists on the ground in Karonga and Deep Bay (now Chilumba). He was district secretary to the MCP and a close associate of Yatuta Chisiza and George Akogo Kanyanya. The details of his harrowing escape from death and the courage of the people who helped him is instructive of how difficult the times were under the mounting repression.

It was on 7th November after Kamuzu had expelled most of his ministers and declared that anyone accommodating or coming into contact with those ex-ministers was to be dealt with. Being dealt with it meant killing. So [among] those who were victim it was me. Yatuta Chisiza and Akogo Kanyanya came to Nyungwe to report to me. By then I was Vice-District Secretary to the Malawi Congress Party.... They came to report to me what had happened in Zomba [and] to say we are expelled and if they are seen with me, then we are in for it. So on Sunday, after meeting me they left for Livingstonia.

Carson Kayuni

Did I know that I had enemies nearby? Young Pioneers had seen Akogo and Yatuta at my house which was just next to the court at Nyungwe.... The following day they sent for me.... I continued working in my office. They sent a second man. I told him that anyone [who] wants to see me can come here to my office. Little did I know that I had angered them. Luckily enough... I owned a shotgun, I kept in my house. I said to myself, these people, I don't know who they are. Let me go hide it outside of the house and took my shotgun. There was a bundle of grass and I hid that shotgun in the bundle of grass.

I went to play bao¹ with Themba Mwilangombe. It was dark then.... As we were playing, those Young Pioneers came to my house and found my wives. I had two wives.... They started beating them and even the children. They were shouting and that is when the wife of Mwilangombe came and said [in Tumbuka] they are beating your wives and children. So I had to leave for the house and as I started moving someone [lit] his torch and said "Ali kuno." [He is here.] They surrounded me and asked me, "Yesterday, Yatuta and Akogo were here, what were you discussing about?" I asked pardon from one of them standing there.... "We came to deal with you." I was rolling down. I was beaten. I was beaten. I was bleeding from my nose.

My wives shouted for help but people who came had to stand very far, watching what was going on. I talked in Chilambya language. I said to my wife go get the bambam [shotgun] from the bundle of grass. While I was being beaten I had three bullets, AA and #3 in my trousers. Yet they had torn my trousers you could hardly believe what they were. I saw as my wife was coming, she held the gun like this [under her skirt.] I could see the end of the gun. It was night and they were still beating me. What I did, I had to crawl to my wife.... I had to throw off the Pioneer who was next to my wife, took hold of the gun, put a bullet in the chamber and fired in the air. They dispersed, all

---

1 Bao is played with stones or seeds on a board or on the ground with 4 rows of 8 shallow holes each.

of them and I took a second one [bullet] and I fired. I didn't aim. If I meant to kill, I could have killed, but I said no.

I was left down bleeding. I said to my wives, please go inside, I am on my way to Karonga. From Nyungwe to Karonga it is about 35 miles. I walked up to Ngara with my injuries.... I knocked at the door of Maxwell [owner of a cotton-ginnery], I knocked and he looked at me and could hardly believe it was Carson Kayuni. [He asked,] "What is wrong?" I said escort me to the hospital.... He drove to Karonga and dropped me near the prison saying, "If they see me there, I will also be in trouble, so please just go."

I had my gun. I took it to the chap who was secretary to the council.... I gave him my shotgun. So I walked to the hospital. After arriving at the hospital, I started crawling and entered. I found the nurse on duty. That nurse after seeing me asked, "Are you Kayuni?" She had to ring to the doctor who was a Boer by then, Dr van de Bich. I remember him very very well. He came and called a second man Mayuni [who cried], "EEE! What is wrong?" I said Young Pioneers beat me. Of course, they started treating me, gave me a bed. "We'll do everything tomorrow." The following morning, Young Pioneers came to the Karonga Hospital looking for me and got me on the bed. They called the doctor in charge and said, "Look here. This man wanted to kill us at Nyungwe. Remove him from here. Take him to an isolated room." The doctor tried to ask why and they accused him of arguing. They called the nurses and moved me.

Crawling into the hospital was a testimony that helped me after that.... After 11h30 the police officer in charge came and said, "Doctor, I want Carson Kayuni. Is he here?".... [the doctor] said, "But he can't walk." He wanted to take my statement.... Nurse Msowaya had heard that I had been beaten... She carried me to a tree, that tree at the old hospital is still there, where the police officer was seated. That police officer asked me his first question. "Why were you beaten?" I answered him, I don't know, but I was only asked one question. "Were Yatuta Chisiza and George Kanyanya accommodated at your house? Now what were the discussions about?" This was the only question and before I answered I found myself crawling on the floor being beaten. In fact they had torches that lit me and it was difficult to know how many they were, but not more than seven.

"Actually did you know these people even by voice?" I said, in fact they were talking in Chichewa so it was not easy for me to know them so I can give you a true story about them. He [the policeman] had chased away the Young Pioneers who were watching me because that room where I was kept they had put four of them guarding me.

Now he said to me, "Kayuni, I am very, very, very, very sorry. You were beaten for no reason and I am releasing the news to you. This was the 9th and on the 11th, Kamuzu was coming to Karonga with instructions that those who are against Kamuzu, get rid of them before Kamuzu comes here." He said, "You are being killed tonight. If you have a means of escaping I would advise you to do so. But in the condition you are, you cannot. They are killing you tonight."

I knew I was dying. He said, "Sign here." I signed a statement that he had written. He left and called Nyausowoya. "Take him back to his room." I was taken back in readiness waiting to be killed. It came to a quarter to seven evening and a certain boy came and called them. James Mwamulima who was district chairman of the Malawi Congress Party, had prepared dinner for them [MYP guards]. So all four of them went to eat leaving me alone. They said, "He can't run away. He can't move."

After leaving the premises, I came down from my bed, crawling to the toilet. The toilet I entered was fenced with grass. I just opened a place where to pass through. Went to that small mbuyu [baobob] running. I left my shoes, I left my shirt. I only had my trousers running to that man where I had left my shotgun. He, too, was at the meeting where they were listing people to be killed and that my name was there. "Are you here? I am weeping, because I am aware that they are killing you tonight." I said give me my gun. He gave me money, ten shillings. He gave me a shirt. He said, "Please don't go straight on the road. Be very careful."

[By the time] I arrived at Baka, they finished eating, they arrived at the hospital, they found only my shoes, only my shirt underneath the bed. I heard [he makes the sound of a siren.] They had galimotos [cars]...going to Ngerenge and this way and that. I knew I could be intercepted. I branched. I crossed Rukuru towards Masoko towards Ngerenge on the way to Misuku. Walking, walking, walking. I came to night fall, I had to stay in the bush. I walked, I walked, I walked.... I came to a village with three houses just surrounded with hills that was the beginning of Misuku.... The wives of that man were harvesting finger millet. I greeted that man. He said, "Madala [old man], where are you from?" I said I am from Karonga. [ed. He made up a story of being cheated by someone who had beaten him and he was returning to his home.] He said, "Look here. Some of those chaps have been here, some Young Pioneers. Somebody has escaped from the hospital and they are looking for him." He did not know it was me. This was an isolated village, very far. He called his wife. They made food for me from finger millet which I had never ate. They made me porridge. I had bruises. I had leaves with a rope tied around my feet as shoes. That old man gave me bananas. I asked him, "Where is Kapoka?"

Kapoka was very far.... It took me four days to reach Kapoka. I was sleeping in the bush. It was a relief when I came to streams from Misuku [the Misuku Hills.] With my legs swollen and bruises, it was somehow a relief.... At Kapoka, I had a step-brother, who was a teacher. I knocked on the window after hearing his voice. It was half-past nine [p.m.].... He opened the door and took me inside. He started weeping. I said escort me to Chinunka.... arriving at Rufita at first cock, kokoriko [he made the sound.] [Carson tells his step-brother,] *Please go back. You will be involved. Leave me.*

I went to a hill... sat there, the sun rising. I could see someone at his premises. I knew him. He was the father of Jackson Mzinza who was an MP of Kamuzu, yet it is me who helped him in his whole lifetime, even paying school fees for him. I knew this one, the father can't betray me. I was hiding in a thick forest, so I had to take stones and throwing [them] ... he saw the stones and he came in a very worried way. Just to see me, he jumped and grabbed me. "You are alive! They say you escaped from the hospital. We knew you couldn't escape in the condition they told us... We thought they were telling lies - that they have killed you and said you have escaped." He took me to his house and went to report to my mother-in-law, Nyanyondo, the mother of my wife.

He did not reveal my presence to her, but told her to come to his house. The same day the police brought my family to Fort Hill for their safety. They were with guards.... That is why Mzinza decided to take my mother-in-law instead of my wife. She came into the room.... She grabbed me as if I wasn't her son-in-law[2], crying, crying. They boiled water and she bathed my whole body and prepared me nsima with chicken. I failed to swallow. I had to take only soup.... In the evening my mother-in-law sacrificed to escort me across to Tanzania. She is the one who took me up to there. She said, "The way I was carrying your wife, is the way I am going to carry you...." I said, no - traditionally... She said, "No."

So we had to move with her. If we saw someone, she had to cough so that I had to branch so that man goes away without knowing I was there until we arrived at Mwakabanga. She went and awoke the uncle of my father just on this side here at Kafora..... It was my father's uncle who took me carrying me on his shoulder taking my gun up to this river Nkhangwa River across to Tanzania. He is the one who brought the shotgun to my father down here [Fort Hill]....

Mother heard that [her] boy has arrived in Tanzania.... so she had to cross the border, to come [and see me]. .... Katoba Msopole was with the MYP and they came to my house to find me. Katoba told the MYP that if he is not here he must be at his aunt's and they found the gun. My father was beaten and they accused him of hiding me. That gun was taken that day. From there they wanted to cross. They [my family] wanted to send the wife of my young brother.... "Warn him that we don't have any security here. Tell

---

2 By tradition, a mother-in-law would never speak directly with or enter the same room as her son-in-law.

him to go away, somewhere farther in there [from the border]." Of course mother was just returning and found father bleeding. They never knew she had come from seeing me..... The TANU [Tanganyika African National Union – governing party of Tanzania] executive assigned these TANU Youth league to protect me.... [Even in Tanzania] the wife of the doctor protested, that if you treat this man we have no way to protect ourselves.... so I was taken at night up to Mbodzi where I had to catch the bus DMT to Dar es Salaam.

I had no transport [fare]. They asked me, "Fare? How have you jumped in?" I said, I am a sick man. [The conductor wanted him to get off the bus.] Luckily enough there was an Indian in that bus going to Dar es Salaam. He... told that conductor to give me a ticket, I will pay for him.... He left his place where he was sitting and joined me. He asked if I had been in Karonga? Yes. "Whom do you know as far as Indians are concerned in Karonga?" [I told him,] Andani and Katharia and others. He asked, "Do you know Chisiza?" I know Chisiza. That's why I am here, because of Chisiza. "Am I wrong to say that you have been District Secretary? Because Andani had a guest at the meeting of Chisiza. And who was allowing people to come into the meeting? It was you. I was the guest of Andani and that is why I remember you."

He sat beside me and gave me tea from his thermos. As I arrived in Dar es Salaam, I was so sick I collapsed.... As they were carrying me out I said, I don't have anyone who knows me here. So they took me to Dar, straight to Police Central Station. They immediately took me to Muhimbili [hospital] and they had to put on the radio that there is a man from Malawi. He has been beaten and almost killed. Chisiza and Kanyanya heard about it and they came to find out. They found me on the floor of the police [station] lying there with no blanket.... They couldn't release me because Ministry of Home Affairs had not cleared me.

Fortunately, Obedi Rugimbana, The Commissioner of Prisons, he was my friend and we were together at the depot prison, and I was the second man to him in exams. He said, "I had a friend of mine from Malawi. He was very argumentative. Let me go find out about him." He came to police and found it was me. [The police refused to release him without clearance.] So he went to see Mr Job Lucinde, Minister of Home Affairs and told him about his friend from Malawi [who] was in a very bad condition. "I want him." He phoned the officer in charge and told him, "I am with the Commissioner of Prisons. Release him [Kayuni]." He took me to Aga Khan Hospital which was very advanced. My collarbone had a crack. It took me two months of treatment.

After he had recovered from his injuries, he joined the other Malawians who were given refugee status at an old Salvation Army camp, before they became too numerous and were resettled to Pangale Refugee Camp in the interior of the country. Like many refugees, he could have found work in Tanzania, but he was determined to return to Malawi and fight for democracy.

You can read more of his contribution to the armed resistance in Chapter Seven entitled, *Organised Opposition*.

4.2 Escape

One of the most vivid aspects of the exile memory is the escape. People found their way out in different ways, but the escape was an important feature of their transition to life in exile. It was often the most dramatic part of their stories. Some were amazed at the ease with which they left. Willie Chokani and a group of his peers essentially had police cover, which allowed them to go safely from Blantyre to the Zambian border almost in style, with their families, cars and some possessions.

On the other hand, Carson Kayuni, John Jando Nkhwazi, Kapote Mwakasungura and many others were under considerable threat to their lives. They faced beatings and death if captured, moved at night to dodge MYP patrols and received heart-warming support from family and often from unexpected quarters. Young people still in school were treated with the same contempt as their adult mentors. Kapote tells of the bands of MYP who came to his hostel at Blantyre Secondary School, surrounded the campus and removed all his belongings – books, bedding, clothing, the whole suitcase. Fortunately, a group of his close friends (all Central Region friends and one a son of a senior MCP Banda loyalist) had warned him of imminent danger and he had already escaped. Even then it was a hair-raising trip to the Tanzanian border with danger arising at every bus stop, police barricade or MYP inspection.

Mary Mwambetania tells two stories of escape – how Banda gave her husband, Mundu, along with Lutengano Mwahimba and Clement Marama, 24 hours to get out of the country; and then her own subterfuge later to join him in exile in Tanzania.

After the Cabinet coup organised by Dr Banda, Rose Chibambo joined her husband in Chiradzulu. However, things went from bad to worse. They stayed as long as they could, hoping for the situation to calm down, but were eventually forced to drive through danger to escape Malawi, then to struggle through hostile Southern Rhodesia and finally, to convince recalcitrant Zambia border guards to let them in. She tells of her harrowing escape:

I was sitting in Chiradzulu and there came the Member of Parliament for Chiradzulu. "I am living under a very difficult situation. The fact that you are here and I am the MP for this constituency, things are not good for me."... I said I am married to this man. Then afterwards they said we were supposed to be transferred to Kasungu of all places. I called the Cabinet office and it was Mr Richards who answered. I said my husband cannot be far from the hospital. He said, "No, Mrs Chibambo. It's not me, I'm only conveying the message. It's not me that wants him to be transferred." I said whoever that is you tell him. While at Chiradzulu, the Young Pioneers came four different days. They came and they would just stand there. I came out on the verandah and they would be standing there looking at me. They said, "Whenever we come, we are being told whenever we see any ex-minister, we should do anything with them and nobody will ask us. So you know it is you who told us about Dr Banda. We didn't know him. You are the one that told us about Dr Banda... We don't know what you have disagreed in Zomba, so for us just to get on and do whatever we want - We are also afraid of God. We can't just jump and do something."... After saying these words, off they go and they came four different times. After that they said we are being transferred to Mwanza. We stayed in Mwanza Inn for two weeks …. So one of the policemen said in secret, "We didn't know that you would last in this area, because the Young Pioneers were told they could do anything and nobody would ask [a question]. We the police were told don't interfere, so we have just been watching." … We were there for a month in Mwanza. The Young Pioneers came and one leader who was at Nasawa with his friends within Mwanza, he said, "There will be no trouble from here in Mwanza but the trouble will come from Blantyre. They came two different times saying the same thing.

And then there was a man, I think he was a district chairman for Mwanza area. He came several times saying Mrs Chibambo, you had better go where others have gone. At that time all our friends [the ex-ministers] had left. It was now January 1965. Then he came and said, "I think it is better that you leave to where others have gone. We do not want to see your blood here."

Then the word came that you are being transferred back to Blantyre. And the senior District Commisioner in Blantyre had come to Mwanza. So in the evening we went to see him. He said,"I have come to see that you are gone." This was a Mr Walker.... So we packed up our katundu and asked our young man, our servant to go ahead with our katundu. I told him to go to the house of Mr Chibambo.... We are following.

We took the little that we had with the two little ones, because we had sent four of our children up here in the North so that they can go to school because in Blantyre the situation was very bad. Little did we know that we were going to leave the country. So we sent the children here to go to school [thinking that] as soon as the dust settles down here in Blantyre, they can come back. So when the time came we wondered how we can travel to the North and get our children. It wasn't easy.

We took our two little children and went into our car. We drove as if we were going to Blantyre, not knowing that the man, Mr Walker, was following us. We came to a junction and we stopped. Should we go to Blantyre? We were asking each other. He [Walker] arrives there and asks why we are stopped there. I said we are wondering whether we should go to Blantyre. "Where do you want to go then," he said, "because it means that if you don't go to

Blantyre then I will lose my job." Can you imagine? So your coming was to see us come to Blantyre.

I said, "Mr Walker, don't allow yourself to share in our blood." He said, "Mrs Chibambo. I feel as if I have no intestines." He said, "Mr Chibambo. Have we ever quarrelled, you and me? We have been working very well [together]." I said, "You know very well what is happening in Blantyre. Then why do you allow us to go?" He said, "Open up your boot so people aren't wondering why we are stopped here."... [ed. He wanted them to precede him but they refused and told him to go ahead.]

He started off in such a rush and we started off and returned to Mwanza. We just passed through Mwanza and got to the border. My husband said, "... We just want to visit your main town, Tete...." They gave us a note to allow us to enter Portuguese territory. We took that note and we drove off. We came to Zambezi. It was late [and] the thing [ferry] had gone off [for the night]. So we had to sleep there....

In morning, we were the first to be on the ferry. We crossed... to Zimbabwe. In Zimbabwe we were afraid to even go into the hotel. Smith here is a friend of Kamuzu. If we go into any of the hotels, I am sure we will be identified. Then we had the address of a Greek doctor whom we knew.... We found him. He said, "So you people are alive." He gave us a place to spend the night. My husband was tired, because he was the one who was driving. We [rested] the day and the next day ...we went and crossed into Zambia. At the Zambia border my children and my husband were allowed. I was not allowed. "Why me?" They said, "You have a federal passport. We don't allow anybody with a federal passport to enter our country." [ed. Ian Smith had just declared Unilateral Declaration of Independence and the boycott and sanctions were about to begin.] They said, "Go back to Malawi and get a Malawian Passport." ...These fellows didn't know who I was. I quarrelled with them. I said, give me the Minister of Home Affairs, I want to talk to him. They said, "Who are you to talk to the Minister of Home Affairs?" Never mind who I am. I know him. Later they went into their room and talked. "Alright, we are giving you this letter, You better report to Immigration within seven days."

That is how we entered Zambia. That is how we left Malawi. It was terrible.

The anarchy Dr Banda unleashed on the country also forced John Jando Nkhwazi to flee for his life. His is a tale of disbelief in which he first thought he could stay inside and work for change, only to realise that he had to run for his life. Jando had grown up in Zambia and was deported from there by the colonial government because of his militancy as a leader of the student movement. Once in Malawi, he became involved in the nationalist politics leading up to independence. He was a talented musician and became widely known for his singing and militancy. He was a Kanyama Chiume loyalist. Like many young educated and talented leaders, he rose quickly within the civil service.

John Jando Nkhwazi and Kapote

During the Cabinet Crisis obviously I was in the good books of all those who were sent out. So I went and attended Parliament.... Suddenly now these people are running away, wanted dead or alive. I was scared. Then one night, Alex Nyasulu was then Speaker came at 2:00 a.m. I saw the Humber there... I thought that since he is from the Northern Region maybe he was coming from Rumphi and carrying a message from my wife... He said "No. I have been sent to you by Dr Banda. He wants to know you are on which side." I told him that I attended Parliament. I said there are no sides here.... As it is now I am very confused. I have no side. He said, "Should I go tell him like that? He thought that ... you could become the Minister of Community Development, because he would like someone from the Northern Region. I said there are so many people, so I cannot... After two days, I got telegramme from my wife saying that she was very sick with malaria, I should send her quinine... I set off to go and check and said I will be back in two weeks.... So I left for the Northern Region not knowing that behind me Aleke Banda was sending people to Magomero for me....

Then I got a telegram at home, saying, "Jando, can you come back to Zomba as quickly as possible?... A few days later a police Humber came hunting for me. "You are supposed to return to Zomba. You are wanted by the Ngwazi."... I went to Mzuzu to see my sister who had been admitted to the hospital. My brother-in-law said, "What are you doing here?... People are hunting for you. They already know that you are on the run and coming to Mzuzu."... I spent the night there. The next morning, I went very early to the hospital. I found my sister. The bus going to Rumphi leaves at one o'clock... so from here I will go straight to the bus stage. The [nursing] sisters there said, "No you can stay here as long as you want."

I went to the bus stop. Before the bus came in, I saw the police officer in charge of Rumphi in his vehicle. He came and spoke to me. "Jando, come with me. I am also going to Rumphi." I jumped in. As we were driving there we a number of roadblocks by then. We will go and hunt ducks before you go. So we went to hunt ducks and he killed 33 wild ducks. When we were driving back to Rumphi, it was already around nine or so, he said, "You know, I am trying to save you, because we already knew that Kanyama Chiume was going to pass through Rumphi so we don't want you to be involved." He was hunting for me before he was rushing to Tanzania, but no one knew where I was. So this man gave me two ducks.

Despite all the signs of danger, he still was not sure if he should flee or stay. He made a fateful decision to return to his post in the Southern Region.

The following day.... that same day Gwamba Chakuamba was beaten badly in Zomba by the civil servants... things were getting worse. Should I go now or wait till things finish? Hassan who had a shop in Rumphi was taking things to Lilongwe where his father's shop was. I said, give me a lift... then he got this young man to give me a lift to Blantyre. I reached at Munthali's place, the one who worked at MBC [Malawi Broadcast Corporation], I knocked and the wife opened... she was startled.... "What is happening? Your name is among the eleven people who are wanted dead or alive.... you were safer staying there [up North]. How are we going to assist you?" I still have to go to Magomero to see the situation.

I left very early in the morning. There was a very early bus from Limbe to Zomba that left every day at 5:00 a.m. One of the [Magomero] drivers went to Zomba very early in the morning to pick up mail, saw me and told me I am going to take you to [brother's] house no other place, because you are a wanted person. Gwanda Chakuamba has come here twice. He is now the Minister of Community Development.... so this driver picked me and dropped me outside Zomba, Machinga, by then there were not as many houses as we have now. While I was there waiting for a vehicle ... another driver I knew was passing. "You! Why are you here? I will take you to Liwonde. You are not supposed to be here." He collected me and dropped me at Liwonde. I went across the ferry to the other side.... I found people waiting for the bus which is going to Lilongwe.... At Ntcheu the bus was stopped. There was a meeting for Dr Banda. All the people on the bus should go and attend the meeting. I saw the one who was the Education Officer at Rumphi [who] was transferred to Ntcheu... I knew by then that he was a member of the Young Pioneers movement. Oh my God!!.... Stayed on the bus with the driver. We stayed there for about 30 minutes and they came back when the meeting was over.

When I reached Lilongwe, I was puzzled. I didn't know where to go. My sister by then was at Likuni being trained as a nurse....I went to Likuni. When my sister saw me, she said, "Hey you! You are here. They came to interrogate me but I didn't know why. I think now I can understand. They are hunting for you, so you are not going to sleep here. Let me arrange for you to sleep in the X-ray room at the hospital it will be safer".... I spent the night there. In the morning a health officer used to go to Mponela and some other places, so there was one who was supposed to leave for Mponela. So she discussed with this officer and he said okay..... At Mponela it was even more exposed... I waited for the bus for the Northern Region. I knew when I jumped on that bus I was going to be safe. The bus came. It was full. Basi [Expression meaning finality or there is nothing more to do.] *I spent the whole day until it was night. There was nobody who could take me. I said there is this night compost going to Mzimba. When it reached there it never even stopped. Let me at least follow it. Maybe some people will have dropped. I took a taxi. I had no money, but I remained with a watch. I said my friend I will give you this watch.... He rushed but the bus didn't even stop. I dropped there. In the morning there was a bus going to Mzimba. I jumped on that bus...*

When I reached Mzimba and I was scared. The bus was carrying mail so it stopped just by the Post Office before it got to the bus stop. Then I saw the officer-in-charge, whom I knew to be the nephew of Dr Banda who was approaching. He was coming to enter the bus. He saw me and said, "Come down." I knew I was trapped..... I got down. "Follow me." I thought that was the end of me. Then he took me to his house. After we entered, he hugged me. "I have been waiting for you to come through here for three days. Don't forget that you assisted me a lot.... When I heard that you were in trouble I thought I should do something about that...." When he was sent to the UK by Dr Banda for some more training... I used to go and just pay a visit to the family, but he was very grateful. He said, "Don't you worry. I will put you on the bus very early tomorrow morning." …. I spent the night at his place.

In the morning, he had already arranged with the bus conductor and so on... I went and entered the bus at the Post Office... When I reached Rumphi... I found my friend Nsaunsau in trouble. He was already sleeping outside.... He was head of Rumphi Council. Nsaunsau was not sleeping in his house. They were hunting for him. What should I do? Should I start sleeping outside? He had heard and he came during the night. I knew the [Indian shopkeeper]. [He said], "The next morning pack your things and wait at my shop. But ask your wife to take a bus and we will find her...." My wife had already gone by bus in the morning. We started walking and we were close to Njakwa. The road was so dusty that nobody could see who was going or whoever jumped into the truck... So he stopped while we jumped on the back.... We reached home and dropped our stuff.... By then my father had shifted from South Mlowe to North Mlowe. So we went there.

We have to catch Ilala so we can go across to Mbomba Bay [and safety in Tanzania]. *My sister went very early in the morning looking for fish.... While she was there, she was told that security men had slept there. They are looking for Jando and Nsaunsau.... We had a visitor, a certain South African lady, and we were afraid she might tell people there were ulendo* [visitors] *so we delayed her until late at night.... When she left, my sister came and told us not to go to Ilala. We just have to go by foot and by night and then go to Chitimba. By then the security people were now at Chiweta where they knew that is where my uncle is. They thought maybe I would be hiding there. They went and raided my uncle's house. We met at Mkanta's place. Mkanta was a local judge.... When the wife saw us she told us to go hide under the bed* because the security men are at the school there.... So we went into hiding, I, Nsaunsau and my sister. While we were there, dogs began to bark. She went to the kitchen and started to prepare food for us. They came. "Why are you here?" My husband has gone to Nchalo. He is coming today and I don't want to cook and he finds the food is too cold.... "Did you see three people going this side?" My dogs bark many times. It is possible people have passed, but I didn't see anyone.... "We are looking for some people who may be running away. So please. Do not allow anybody to pass through here. When you see some people, send some people to tell us...."

We decided to leave as soon as possible, so we started off. We crossed the big river there, but by then it was October so the water was very low... It was a little early in the morning. So we remained in the bush waiting for Ilala [the largest of the Lake Malawi transport ships]. When the Ilala docked, we went to the shore.... The first boat which came from the ship, we saw Stain Msiska and Mwangulu jumping out of the boat even before it reaches the sand.... They warned us both, "Don't go.... After this boat, it [Ilala] is not going to Tanzania. It is returning from here, so please don't go...."

When we reached Chiweta somewhere near the junction to Livingstonia. We found Nyirenda, a teacher who was our friend. Why can't we go and stay at his place.....So we went to that village and we found that mother and sister were there.... they were our relatives. What is happening? We have heard that you people have been killed.... We jumped through the window. When [he] came at about 1, he opened his house just to find us in the house. "What is happening?" We are going to stay until night. We started walking going to Uliwa. So we spent the whole day there. In the evening, we did not really tell him we are starting at what time. We just said we are leaving.... so we started walking. We walked and walked and walked.... Between Chitimba and Uliwa as we were climbing the mountain, those mountains were very popular for the lions. At one time we thought we were seeing a lion. We decided it was better to be eaten by a lion than to be taken by the Young Pioneers. So we moved. Later we discovered it was not a lion.

We walked until we reached Uliwa. That's where the parents of my friend were, the Reverend Msowoya. So we knocked. By then people had already gone to.... So we were put in a store room where they used to keep maize. We stayed there until morning. The old lady made a mistake. She had a friend, a very good friend,... who came to greet her in the morning.... The old lady quite innocently came and showed this lady to us. She greeted us and went away. We asked the old lady, who is this one. "She is a very good friend of mine. She is the wife of the headmaster at this place." We said, then he should be in the Young Pioneers movement....

So we left and went somewhere in the mountains that's where we spent the whole day. While we were there, we began looking for the cousin to my friend who was closer to that place. When he came he said, "Okay, I *will use my bicycle. I shall be escorting you on my bicycle and carry you till we reach Karonga." He picked one and then dropped you and went for the other one. So that is how we started going from Uliwa. That same night the headmaster had gone to report to the Young Pioneers, so that same night the Young Pioneers were in that area. So they came and surrounded that house.... This young man was very good. He went ahead to organise some food somewhere. We would go and eat then on the road. It took us six days and six nights to get to Songwe....*

So this young man³, when we were crossing Karonga, there was a barricade there. Fortunately there were a lot of cattle, so they had to give time for the cattle to pass in the morning before letting people pass. He had known about it. So he brought in these bedsheets that we can tie... so we would look like the people who would pass with their cattle there until we crossed. We took them to where they were meant to go. When there we removed the blankets and he took them back. And he started picking us up again on the bicycle.

When we reached Kaporo closer to Songwe, he said let us stop here. I've got my friends somewhere here. Those friends told him that around about 12 [o'clock] they [The Young Pioneers] *are tired of staying there. They go for food. Because those that remain behind in most cases will find that the food will be finished, so these days they have decided that they will all be going there to eat together. Then after one hour, that is when they come back. So that is the best time for you to get across. So he made sure we reached Songwe at 12 and we found nobody there. So we started crossing. By then the water was this size* [very shallow].

We crossed to freedom. We were received by the area commissioner who came. He said, "We are expecting people from Malawi."... They had food for us. Gave us a letter to take to Mbeya and arranged for East Africa Railways. In Mbeya, we reported to the Commissioner of Police.... so we reached Dar es Salaam very early in the morning where we went to Central Police Station.

The flight out of the country was a life or death event for many of those Dr Banda labelled *chigawanga* [traitor]. Even rising senior civil servants were given short shrift once open season was declared on the opposition. Mary Mwambetania tells how her husband, Mundu, and two of his colleagues were given quite literally 24 hours to get out of the country. Mundu had studied economics to the Masters level in newly independent India in the fifties and came back to Malawi to join the nationalist struggle and contribute to the development of a newly independent Malawi. He, Lutengano Mwahimba and Clement Marama had all trained in India and were among the most senior African civil servants. His sister had married Yatuta and he was a close friend

---
3   ed. A brave hero in his own right.

of Dunduzu, which immediately made him suspect following the cabinet crisis. Mary, his wife, recounts the story of the classic, "Get out of town in 24 hours or else."....

> That time it was really hot water. MCP we were running up and down. People couldn't go to the market and buy anything without a card. When you go to the market you must have an MCP card.

> At the time [of the Cabinet Crisis] he was just a civil servant. They were just running up and down until the day that he got a letter that he must leave the country within 24 hours. The signature on the letter was from Kamuzu himself. We do not know whether or not he wrote it.... When we were in Dar es Salaam we had it, but if it is the house now, I don't know where.

When asked why Kamuzu would tell them to leave the country, Mary replied,

> Actually I don't know, but they said they were threats to the government. That time they chased three - Mundu, Lutengano Mwahimba and Clement Maramba. So they had to leave the same day. In the morning, because I was not feeling well, he took me to the hospital in Zomba. After he left me there, I was admitted and he went to the office. When he got there, he found that letter, that he must leave the country within 24 hours. He had to rush home, pack and come with Lutengano. Marama went to Likoma, I think. They had to rush to Blantyre from Zomba. He only had his suitcase, a small briefcase. In the hospital I just got the message from Mwamlima's sister, the nurse Catherine. She told me that Mundu was here, he said goodbye. I knew that the situation was not good in Malawi. So they have left.... Mundu and Mwahimba drove up to Blantyre. In Blantyre they stayed at home, because our house was at Michiru [the Rubadiri home] which was just near the airport. They went to the airport, but they found that the plane was already gone. They wanted to go through to Zambia. Mother said, "You have to sleep." [They replied,] "Not here." George Carroll from Scotland was a friend of theirs. He took them to his house because the situation was not good at that time. He said anything can happen. So they went there and slept...

> So very early in the morning, they had to go to the airport. They had booked. There was a plane going to Zambia. So there, most of the workers were friends of theirs. They had been together at school... they had to call someone of these friends of theirs and say, "Hey guys we are not in good condition here. We are running away. So we are afraid to sit at the public. Anything can happen. Where can you put us until the time when the plane is leaving?" They said, "Okay come." They went with them to the toilet. "Sit here." They stayed there. After a short time, I think Marama also came in. He said, "Where are my friends? I have heard that they are here." So there were three of them, until the time when the plane was ready. They came and said, "Now come." So from there, straight to the plane.

After the plane has started to go up the LandRover full of Young Pioneers came to the airport. We have heard that some of the rebels are here. "Ah! The plane has already gone." So they had to go back to the Malawi Congress Party to report that they are already gone. The next stop is Lilongwe, so rush to the airport and tell them to stop the plane in Lilongwe. They started again up to the airport. By that time, the plane dropped at Lilongwe and it was already gone.... That was their chance. The place was full of Young Pioneers with their weapons.

So when they reached Zambia, they went to see Peter Mackay. He was a friend of ours.... They rang Peter Mackay.... He went there and welcomed them.... After some days they went to the president, Kaunda. So when they reached there... they asked Kaunda for a place to stay.... "We have run away from Malawi. Can you give us a place to stay?" So Kaunda said, "No, not here. I don't want any quarrels with Kamuzu Banda.".... So they had to ring Yatuta in Tanzania. Yatuta said, "You come over here if Kaunda doesn't want you." So we had to come to Tanzania..

Mary Rubadiri Mwambetania

Meanwhile Mary, young and pregnant and with both her husband and brother on the run from the dictator's wrath, had been left at home with her widowed mother. She tells of their own escape and the dangers they faced.

He left me in the hospital, because I was expecting, and I was vomiting a lot. I was very sick. After some time at the hospital I was alright. They asked me, "Where do you want to go?" I said I will go back home at Michiru in Blantyre... so I went home and packed everything and looked for transport.... My parents had a European friend from Britain. They told me that he was there in Zomba. I said please ring him. I want to see them.... He and the wife came to the hospital, so they found me there. "What's the matter?" At that time, I was just a small girl playing with children. "Are you married? How do you want me to help you?" As you can see my condition now. I want to go to Michiru at home. Mother is there. "Oh Mother is there. I want to see her so I'll take you to Michiru." At that time, all cars, buses at Ntondwe, they had to stop them there. Beat them then "Go whereever you want to go." So it was better if you were in the car of a European. They would say, nanny or a worker. So that was my [good] luck. They took me to [their] house [in Zomba]. I stayed there for three days with them. Then they said, "Today, let's go. We'll take you to Michiru." We had to stop at Ntondwe, but they [MYP] said you can go. So we passed there. So they drove me to Michiru. They were happy to meet with my mother after a long time....

After some time, Mother received a call from Zomba headquarters ... asking Mother, "Where is your son?" That time my brother was ambassador in America. "I don't know. I should ask you, because you sent my son to outside. I don't know where he is now. Me, I know he is in America." On the phone, they said, "We told your son to come back. He replied, 'I am not coming back to Malawi. I want to go and study again.' So we don't know where he has gone. He has just said, I will go to Uganda. At this time, he should come here first and then we can send him to Uganda.... Didn't he come here to visit you first?" Mother said, "I don't know anything about him...."

That time Yatuta was still in Malawi and he heard that they wanted to bring back David here straight to the prison.... He warned David, they were friends. David, if anything happens, if any letter comes telling you to come here to Malawi, don't come. You are in danger. That is why David said, "I must go to Uganda.'....

Now here stayed Mother and me. They wrote a letter. You and mommy must get out of this country and go to your son and tell him to come back as soon as possible. Me, I was already in danger, because my husband has gone out. Now what should we do? We arranged to go to Tanzania. We said, if we go by bus, they will catch us. Let's go by steamer. That time, Ilala was reaching up to Kyera in Tanzania so we started our journey from Limbe with [the] train to Chipoka waiting for the steamer. We slept there two nights and caught the Ilala. In the Ilala, every stage, when Ilala stops, Young Pioneers were coming in looking for rebels. "Where are they?" They didn't know me. They didn't know mother. We were just seated there. "Who are you?" We are just going for a visit to Kyera. When they asked for our names, we just gave them other names. We travelled up to Kyera, Tanzania. When we reached there we were [not] coming out until the last boat, because the weather was not good, so we waited for the last boat. Off we went. My sister-in-law was there. She came to welcome us. This was my first pregnancy. I arrived there 1st of August 1964. At that time, Munda was already in Dar es Salaam with Lutengano Mwahimba, but Clement was still in Zambia. We just rang each other. Okay, you are safe.

But all the katundu we had in our house had to go to Michiru to our house there. Our mother's katundu, they were there. David's katundu were there. So what Mother did [is] she rang the Anglican bishop at Malindi. She said, please can you keep my katundu? You have got a place, because I am going away. I can't leave my katundu in the house with nobody. So the Bishop agreed. He sent a lorry and took all the katundu to the diocese. After that, I don't know how they heard that, the Young Pioneers at the headquarters heard that the katundu of the Rubadiri family was with the Bishop. So now there is a connection there. Some people went to the Bishop, when they heard that the Young Pioneers will come here to search for these katundus. Be careful Bishop. So what the Bishop did is take all the katundu and give it to everybody. So the place was empty... when the Young Pioneers went there. "We have come here. We want to search." "You are free. Come."

"We have heard that you are the keeper of these rebels katundu." "No. I don't have anything. All the doors are open. Come in." So they went in searching each and every corner. They didn't find anything.

David and Gertrude Rubadiri agreed to have us come to their house in Mzuzu for an interview in September 2012. David was a talented degree holder and had just been assigned to be Malawi's first ambassador to the United States and the United Nations. He had grown up in Uganda where he did all his schooling. Gertrude tells the story.

Gertrude and David Rubadiri with Kapote

1964 we were already in New York, in fact Washington, DC. We were based in Washington DC and he used to commute because he was doing two jobs. [We went to the US] in 1964 April. David had gone there earlier in February to be groomed by the Canadians. I think Canadians were among them.... We [she and the children] stayed on [in Malawi] because David's dad was very ill at the time. When he passed away in April, then David brought the whole family, except the old lady - she stayed behind. We didn't stay long, because we left the job and went to Uganda. Apparently Dr Banda used to direct him that at the UN, David was to vote on the side of Britain and the USA. Whatever the topic, Malawi would vote with them. Then there was this issue of the Unilateral Declaration of Independence[4] in Zimbabwe and David was expected to be pro-Smith.

So in the end David said no. I can't be working against my conscience. That is when he decided that we had to leave. So he asked for sabbatical.... He wrote to Banda and said, I would like to go for studies, to go to Makerere to study, but it was really resignation. But when we got there, Yatuta said, "David, you better make yourself clear, because people here think according to Dr Banda's claims that you are pro his policies. But you tell us that you left the job because you couldn't stand it anymore, voting against your conscience." So David had to write to Dr Banda. Unfortunately, he wrote an open letter which was also published in the newspapers. So Banda was livid when he said he had resigned from the job. That is when he sent him a note about feeding him to the crocodiles. That was 1965 when he left the job...

---

4 In November 11, 1965, Prime Minister Ian Smith of the colonial white minority government of Southern Rhodesia announced a Unilateral Declaration of Independence (UDI) in order to prevent Britain and the Zimbabwe nationalist leaders from implementing a majority government. Dr Banda's government defied an Organisation of African Unity declaration that the regime was illegal and refused to respect the economic sanctions imposed on the breakaway colonists.

He was appointed in 1964. We went in April 1964. Officially, of course, he started the job in July after Independence. But in the few months he worked there, he used to come back especially from the UN, really tense and so on, because he wasn't enjoying the job. So in April 1965, we went to Uganda, when Banda allowed him to go for study leave. When he was at Makerere then he wrote this letter to say, "I have resigned from the job." That's when Banda said, "Alright. You come and I will throw you to the crocodiles." David just found the job very stressful.

4.3 Conditions in Exile

The Banda regime punished Rose Chibambo with the worst form of torture. They refused to allow her four children to leave Malawi and join the family in Zambia.

We had four children in the North and we wondered how we could get them. My husband said, "Let us leave. When we are where we will be, we will write home. We will send a word for them. We will get the children." For almost three years, we tried to get our children. It wasn't possible. We appealed to the International Red Cross. Appealed to the International Jurists. Nothing. Nobody was able to convince the government of Malawi to let us have our children. So they all just grew up here [in Malawi without their parents].

There is an element of blackmail in this act, since they were coercing into silence an otherwise outspoken militant by holding the children hostage. It is also a very cruel form of punishment. In exile, Rose and Edwin found work, but it was still very difficult.

By September 1967, my husband started getting sick and his brother, Walter, came to take him home. [The brothers argued.] *He refused to go. We have been forced to be here. We want our children back and you should have brought them to us.... By Jan 1968 our son Roy came. He was found at the bus stop in Lusaka. He was just wandering about. Fortunately, he came across the nephew of one of our friends who had also run away.... He brought him to where I was working. I couldn't recognise my son. He was covered with all the dust. "It's me, mommy." I had to take a half day off.... It was just like a mourning. He stayed with us a week. Edwin wanted him to stay. He said, "No. The fact that I know where you are. I must go and get my sisters." At that time he was about 18. He just came, but I think somebody gave him a passport. We tried hard. You better stay. He was the only boy. He said, "No. I must go back for my sisters. They will suffer. You do not know what is going on at home. They will know that I have left. Nobody knows that I am here. But I must go and organise my sisters. We will all come." We tried hard to refuse, especially the father. He said, "No, we will find another way to bring the girls." He said, "Look all these years, you have not been able. I have found my own way to come. Now that I know where you are I am going to* find a way with them...." We allowed him to go. We sent him by air. Perhaps that was the mistake we made. They were still going to know that he came.

When he arrived [in Malawi]... he was detained, when they knew that he had come. Then... he was under restrictions. Unfortunately, the family was so shaken that they were making sure these children should not leave because if they [were to] leave ... [the family] will all be in trouble. And that was it.... They were just here [in the North] and he had no job. Nobody could give him a job. He finished his school certificate. He could not go anywhere. He was just staying. Missionaries could not give him a job, so they were just giving him something to help pass the time. All his cousins in our large family were all employed, but not him. He is the son of a rebel. Until much later on....

It was January 1968 when he came to Lusaka. April 1968, my husband died. Just two months after he had come. He tried to come. He was not allowed. And that just demoralised everybody. So then he stayed and then somebody was kind enough. They employed him in Malawi Airways... He worked about a year. Somebody told me that Roy is employed at Lilongwe, working in Malawi Airways. I was excited, so I said let me call him. I phoned him and he got excited too, "We are okay Mommy and this and that." That was it.

It was a Friday when I called him. Saturday, Sunday, Monday he came to work. They said, "There is no job for you." Why? "We don't know. We have just been told that he should not continue working." He went to the manager who said, "I have just received a word that you should not continue working with Malawi Airways." Poor soul. Mr Msonthi was then the Minister of Transport. He went and asked him, "Why have I been dismissed?" Msonthi said, "You better go and ask your uncle." [Qabaniso Chibambo was the brother of Edwin and an infamous and powerful Minister for the Northern Region.] And that was it. So he was just lingering around no job. After a year, in 1971 then he sneaked [out] and came and found me in Zambia. That's when we stayed together. I stayed with him. He got a job in Zambia. He was working very well. But unfortunately Zambia being what it is, people drink so much. He never drank in Malawi. He was then carried away with friends and so on... He finally felt free and he started drinking and it was so bad. It destroyed him.

He is back. He is here with me.

It became hard for her to talk at this point. So she broke the sad atmosphere by offering us a cup of tea.

Professionals like David Rubadiri fit very smoothly into academia once they decided to leave life under Dr Banda behind in Malawi. Gertrude told us how:

For him it was home. He had studied there at Bundo from Standard One up to Form Six and then to Makerere. So that was his home.

Ugandans were so accommodating. It's really Amin that disturbed our peace there. [The Idi Amin period] was a stressful time. Many friends had been affected, killed or disappearing. It was terrible. So when David's contract ended in 1976 May, in June we left to go to Kenya. I must say that people were very kind, especially in Uganda, they really welcomed us, the refugees. They didn't understand how you could be out of your country for a political situation, until they became refugees themselves and they found us in Kenya. The refugees were coming, then they knew what a refugee was. I worked with a small community that was attached to the church.... I remember one day one of the people was presenting to a certain person.... They said, "Mrs Rabadiri you should do the presentation. I said no that should be done by an Ugandan. So this person says, "Aren't you?" I said no. "And yet you are so vocal." It is just the experience I have had in Uganda that has sharpened my senses. I know what people are going through.

Thengo Maloya had always been an active, busy person and when he was resettled to Pangale Refugee Camp he found,

In exile, life was a bit frustrating.... In the first place none of us was allowed to do any work.... We were given food. But it was very frustrating. Like myself, I used to work and just to be put in a camp with nothing. We were active. I went to learn how to shoot guns. That was not my talent. We were doing that because we were in exile....

Families of activists lived in fear of the regime even in exile. Flora Mwakasungura tells of three incidents. She shows her awareness of the political situation of the time and her memory of the family detail is contextualised to those larger historical events. After a long period of frosty relations, Samora Machel, the President of Mozambique made a state visit to Malawi. Mozambique was bogged down in a never-ending war of sabotage instigated and funded by the racist regime of South Africa. Attati Mpakati had been the National Chairman of Lesoma and was assassinated in Harare by Banda's undercover agents. Mkwapatira Mhango and his family died when their house was fire-bombed in Lusaka. She had every reason to fear for her family's security which was complicated by the open-door house the family ran hosting Malawian refugees and Lesoma cadres.

Yes but, but some were enemies.... So it was one day 1994 [ed. probably 1984] *October. The first visit of President Samora Machel [to Malawi]... he was leaving at the airport going to Mozambique... he said..., "Dr Banda, don't worry we are going to work together, you and me we are two countries. Your enemies are our enemies."... It was the same day... we had a visitor from Malawi in the house.... I greeted him. I asked him, "Who are you?" He said something like... he was Mwambeni or something like that. I said, "Oh I'm*

Flora Mwakasungura

sorry. We are not Malawian. We are Tanzanians." He said, "No. You are Malawian." I asked why. He said "I saw the picture, the old picture of your father-in-law. Even now he is there [in Karonga]. He is your father-in-law. I know him and he knows me." I said myself, I don't know, but we are from Tanzania, Tukuyu Village.... I was worried about [Kapote] through Samora's speech. So I said, "Here at the estate, there are two Mwakasunguras. One is the owner of this house. This one comes from Tukuyu. The other one from Malawi. It is up the hill so let us go and escort you." So I was lying, because I knew that this visitor could do something with us.... So when we went outside of the house, he said, "Look here. I am not a refugee as you are." I said, "Who is a refugee?" He said, "You are." I said, "No" He said, "I can kill." I said, "I am ready to die. Kill me." So I [thought] this one is not a good visitor. So we went far from our house. There are two ways. A long one and a short way. So I rushed there until I met the Security Police from the office.... I said, look, you will see a man from Malawi. That man is not a good person. He is sent from the Malawi Government to kill Mwakasungura... When they arrived there.... they... handcuffed him. He was surprised.... Later on he started confessing. "I have been sent by the Malawi Government to assassinate Kapote Mwaksungura. He is wanted by the Malawi Government." So they picked him to Home Affairs in Dar es Salaam so they sent him away. Sent him back to Malawi. That was 1984. Attati Mpakati died 1983.

So we stayed, we stayed. 1986 they started again. Two boys rather than a man, to come again and kill my husband.... They said, 'We are countrymen from Malawi, Chilumba.... We want to go for further studies. We are told that he has channels to give boys to go outside for further studies. That's why we have come....' I said [to herself], "These people are not good people. They also want to kill my husband. They can kill us all," because I remember Mkwapatira Mhango all died at home.... My husband came... they were greeting each other.... "Who are you?"

[One replied,] "Oh I'm Stephen Mkandawire from Chilumba.... I am a teacher at Chilumba Secondary School.... It was last week we chased [away]... two students, so a Young Pioneer came and said why are chasing away these two students with no information nothing about what they have done here? We can kill you. So we said, 'Let us run away.' So we are coming here to have further studies. Where we can have a chance for a scholarship for further studies...."

So my husband said, "Here is your home. Feel free." But later on he sent [for] the security men to come here and ask them why they are here.

So the police came, two, with weapons because they were patrolling that week. They said, "You are from Malawi."

They said, "Yes," with a happy face....

"Have you got a passport?"

"Yes."

"Go and take your passports here." They saw the date of issue of the passports. "This passport was issued on 25 December. In your country, Malawi, you don't have Christmas holiday? Why are these issued this date?" …. "So these passports are issued on December 25 during the Christmas holiday. You people have been sent by your government to come and do something with him [Kapote]. And in your passport you are carrying all kinds of currency. The one who is running away can't have this currency. You said you are a teacher from secondary school. It is so difficult for a teacher from secondary school to have this currency." They had every kind of currency. Euros, Rand, pounds, dollars, Zambia kwacha, all kinds of currency they had. [The police] said, "Go take everything... you have carried here." They arrived with big luggage, new bags, new bedsheets, every clothes were brand new from the shop. [The police] said, "You have to tell the truth or we are going to shoot you." One of them said.... "Ah no. We are in exile." So the policeman said to them, "When you are coming here in exile did you carry all these things? All new bags. All new clothes.... We have no time for them here. Let's send them to arrest." So the police took them, sent them to Home Affairs, then back to Malawi.

We were very afraid. Everyone you can see [who] is a new face we were just afraid of them. We had a tough time....

Professionals

Since many of the people forced into exile were well educated, articulate and talented, they were able to integrate quickly into their new host societies. It is to the great credit of Tanzania and Zambia, in particular, that they recognised the contribution such people could make and allowed them to flourish in their professions. Ceciwa Nkhonje explains how her career path evolved once she was out of the country.

Contrary to the propaganda and lies Kamuzu was spreading in Malawi depicting the life of the exiles as miserable, starving and living under bridges, we were very comfortable and lived among our fellow Africans like we were at home. Many of us were in Zambia and Tanzania, two magnanimous African countries which welcomed us warmly, gave us jobs according to our qualifications and we had comfortable homes just like the nationals of those countries. These two countries accommodated exiles not only from Malawi but from all over Africa; Angola, Mozambique, South Africa, Southern Rhodesia, Namibia, Nigeria, Ghana, wherever Africans had to escape persecution.

I re-entered my broadcasting profession when we returned to Lusaka from Ndola where my husband had been deputy headmaster. One Saturday we had been invited to lunch at a VIP's residence and among the guests was Alick Nkhata, who, at the time was Director-General of the Zambia Broadcasting Corporation [ZBC.] When he heard that I was a BBC trained broadcaster, he told me to see him at his office the following Monday. I was employed on the spot and started working immediately.

A couple of years down the line, I received a scholarship to study at the Thomson Foundation Television College, at Newton Mearns outside Glasgow in Scotland, where I got a diploma as a television producer/director.

I left the ZBC when I was appointed Executive Director of Multimedia Zambia. Progress in my profession continued when I was appointed Head of Africa-English of the Netherlands World Service in Hilversum. From the Netherlands, I was recruited by the United Nations Headquarters in New York where I was appointed Producer in the Anti-Apartheid section. Later I was promoted to head the Africa Section of United Nations Radio.

While working in New York, I took advantage of the city's wonderful education facilities and first studied and obtained my diploma in French. I then registered at the State University of New York and got my Bachelor's Degree in Political Science and Media Communications.... Soon after I started my studies for my Master's Degree in International Relations, Secretary General Perez de Cuellar appointed me Head of a diplomatic mission to Nigeria, where I was Director of the United [Nations] Information Centre. My last posting as head of a UN diplomatic mission was in Zimbabwe, in 1994, from where I retired and settled in Pretoria, South Africa.

4.4 Divisions in the Exile Community

Frank Jiya had been a youth militant in Blantyre during the nationalist period. He had risen within the MCP structure and by the time Dr Banda carried out his putsch, Frank was part of the Southern Region loyalists of the younger leaders Dr Banda was expelling. He fled into exile and was a member of one of the groups sent for military training in Cuba. There are more details of his story in Chapter 7: Organised Opposition. He explains how disunity came among the Malawians in exile. He describes the scene in the Malawian refugee community after returning as a trained fighter. Unfortunately, the scenario that played out in the Malawian exile community is an all too common feature of exile life in general.

Unfortunately our leaders were doing nothing. They did not facilitate anything for us to do immediately while the fire was still burning for us to leave for Malawi... nothing happened." The [Tanzanian] *government there* said, "We don't keep people in cities. We settle them in rural areas. You Malawians, should go to Pangale" So we agreed. We were dropped there in the bush. We were given UN tents. For the first six months we were taught, given food rations... and we were asked to build houses....

This is now where problems started. In Pangale, there were two groups - one for the fight and the other one said, 'No!' This other group which was saying they were not ready to go and fight, one could say they were hiding behind Chipembere. They were saying they were for Chipembere. Automatically that was a division. There was a group headed by Chipembere saying they wanted to continue politicking, doing whatever they were doing. I don't know if they were doing it or not. Chipembere had left Malawi on the arrangement between him and the Malawi government, because he left peacefully from the airport, from Mangochi to America. I think Dr Banda knew everything. He just decided to clear his hands from Chipembere, so he left. He went to America. This time he was communicating with us, but unfortunately the divisions came into light. Those of us who were saying we should go and fight, we identified Yatuta Chisiza. He too was supporting the going.

Mary Mwale Mwahimba

One of the saddest stories is that of Mary Mwale who married Lutengano Mwahimba in September 1964 in the midst of the turmoil Banda unleashed upon the country. She was a young city-raised nurse who had finished her training in Salisbury [now Harare] and had begun her career at Zomba General Hospital. Together, Lutengano and Mundu Mwambetania fled from Kamuzu Banda on 24 hours notice. She followed her husband into exile on a path which was very similar to the story of subterfuge and fear that Mary Mwambetania recounts of how she and her mother left the country. Mary Mwale also lived in Pangale and recounts her disappointment with her fellow refugees and the bitter divisions that affected her very personally and deeply.

One of the things that disturbed me quite a lot was that when we got to Dar es Salaam, even though everybody had run away from the regime, there was still a strong element of Animal Farm[5]. When I came to Kyera... [I asked] What's happening... where is Mary Mwambetania? [She] was away to Nairobi. Where is Lutengano? He is in Pangale. So I jumped into a coach and arrived in Dar es Salaam. There I was stranded. I couldn't speak the language. Where I was going? I didn't know anybody. I ended up in a lodge or resthouse room. They were all men. I was scared. In the morning a kind person said, "Let's go to the police, they will help you." We went from one place to the other. The whole day. Trying to connect. Don't you know anybody at all....

---

5 George Orwell's novel about a farmyard animal revolt against human exploitation shows class relations that are later reproduced among the animals.

Clement in insurance. We went from insurance to insurance and finally we found Marama. He took me home.

We have come from posh government houses and we are looking for these people, I don't know where. Just the difference from what I remembered and what I was finding. Clement took me to his house and then Mwahimba came. From there we went to see Chisiza. I was thinking. We are suffering, How has the government given them these houses? [Tanzania treated the ex-ministers the same way they would their own ministers].

We were there a couple of weeks in Oyster Bay. It is not as bad as I thought [it was going to be].... When I stepped into the camp from the car and I am watching. We are having a meal, with boiled cassava and black tea. Is this what we are going to eat? He [Mwahimba] said, "Just eat....." Coming from a very spoiled background, I don't understand this. I asked what is going on?... I explained what I had observed [about the big houses and conditions in DSM and the camp conditions]. He wanted me to stay in Dar es Salaam because he didn't think I could cope with camp life. I said no I must see, so I went to Tabora. I see the place was very clean. Built nice houses, but to me the contrast... and I was told that it is better now we have nice houses and not the tents.... So right from there I felt there is something wrong. We have run away from Malawi and things are not good. We come to a foreign land, things are worse for other people, not for everybody.

So what do Malawians do? They fight. Those ones in Saigon, which is socialist, fighting those ones in Washington, and almost killing each other. And we who didn't have much experience, were wondering what is happening? And they couldn't mix at all. They were drinking together but fighting....

When the better animals came to visit the camp, people were bending backwards to make them comfortable. I was 22, I didn't know what was going on.

Mary is referring to the fact that the former ministers were living in ministerial-sized houses in the posh Oyster Bay district of Dar es Salaam, while all the ordinary refugees lived in the far away and sparse refugee camp. The rivalry between the ministers and their camp followers grew very antagonistic. It reached such a low point that the "Washington Camp" celebrated when they heard that Yatuta and her husband had died in the Shire Valley near Mwanza. She was particularly bitter about the reaction of her fellow refugees upon the news of the death of Yatuta Chisiza and Lutengano Mwahimba.

And then the day... they heard that Yatuta and Mwahimba had been killed there was drama. They were celebrating in Washington and Chipembere was there. So can you tell me about what people think of their leaders? That day is when I thought something is wrong here. Socialist. Maybe it was socialist. How come they didn't all go to fight? How come? They all divided the spoils.

They pocketed theirs. That's the experiences I had. They didn't change in the refugee camp, sadly to say. So I think we are people who are intrinsically selfish, because they danced. They had drama on the 10th of October 1967, when he was shot.

Back to why didn't they all go to fight....? There was one of those people, the big shots who was responsible for telling Banda that these other people have gone.

4.5 The Children of Exile

Today, children make up nearly half of the thirty four million people with whom the United Nations High Commission for Refugee Agency is concerned. Children are often the most neglected refugees. Political violence in the home country and stress in the family sphere in exile have a serious emotional and psychological impact on parents and this is passed down in an accumulated fashion to the children. Refugee children suffer from both the effects of escaping violence and terror and of adjusting to an unfamiliar culture.

In addition, host country citizens are poor themselves, and can be hostile and threatening towards newcomers competing for scarce resources. Being close to the homeland does not always diminish the culture shock. Adaptation to apparently similar settings is not necessarily easy, despite apparent similarities on the basis of religion and language. This is because the children have lost the familiar beacons of family and sense of community.

For younger children, who are with their families, which ever country they end up in perhaps matters less. But refugee children carry their memories of past events and live with the continuing consequences. Stress in the family sphere and exposure to acts of organized violence in the country of origin have been identified as major determinants of poor mental health. Children are very sensitive to the anxieties of their parents. Even traumatic family events that happened before a child was born can raise his or her risk of mental health problems.

Researchers have found that refugee children are often reserved and controlled, as a result of the fear, terror or harm they have experienced. They perceive that life is fragile and they are vulnerable. They see that the adults they trust have been victimised and persecuted. The parents who are supposed to protect them are rendered helpless. Often parents do not reveal the truth or the real reasons for their flight into exile and how long they will be away from their families. As a result, the children often feel alienated from the new environment and they also feel alienated from the adults in their own families who, more often than not, have had to struggle with their own problems and precarious emotional balance.

Frequently, these children struggle to be independent and self-sufficient. They must mature earlier than their local age-mates, and strive to prove themselves by high achievement in school and in jobs. Because of their forced migration, children lose valuable time and opportunities to develop their capacities and acquire new skills. In the host country, they have to make up for this lost time and put in extra effort to catch up with their local cohorts.

For the children, foreigners in the new country, a sense of family and community is often sought among fellow refugees who share similar losses. However, it is not always easy and the trauma and psychological loss often complicates the "victim's" quest to find help and solace. Others can feel very isolated from and distrustful of their compatriots.

Mary Mwale had two children with Lutengano. She stayed in Pangale for a short period before getting posted as a nurse into the Tanzanian health system. Eventually, she moved to the UK with her children and tragically lost one daughter. She felt abandoned and alone in her role as parent and that she was raising them alone without any support.

Yatuta Chisiza's death in the Shire Valley near Mwanza left his family fatherless. Vyande was 16 years old and Kwacha Chisiza was 11. They grew up in exile and were without a father for much of that time. Even in exile, the refugee community came together to support the family. Yatuta's wife was Mundu Mwambetania's sister and his house hosted his own five children and the three Chisizas.

Kapote Mwakasungura married a young woman from his home area and Flora joined him in Tanzania and raised her family of five with Swahili as their mother tongue. All the children of John Jando Nkhwazi were born in exile and grew up with Tanzania as their homeland. Frank Jiya married in Zambia and became a successful businessman and raised his family there. Kanyama Chiume and his four boys grew up as Tanzanians.

Two of our respondents told us their stories of becoming children in exile. Tujilane Chizumila was a lawyer, a former Malawi High Commissioner to Zimbabwe and a judge in Malawi's highest court. She was serving as Malawi's Ombudsman at the time we interviewed her in February 2013. Tujilane's father, Professor Michongwe, as a senior civil servant, had been assigned to the Malawi Delegation at the United Nations in New York in 1964 and suffered the same fate that Gertrude and David Rubadiri describe. She tells the story of becoming a refugee as a child.

My dad said that I have had to resign from our government and we are now refugees. We have to run away. At the age of twelve you don't understand what it means to be a refugee. What it was all about and what was in store for us.... So we left. We flew to London where we stayed in a hotel for a month.... He called another meeting and announced that I m following my colleagues to

Tujilane Chizumila

Zambia where the Chipemebere's, the Bwanausi's... he mentionned that group. I knew all of them because we grew up in Zomba and they were in Zomba and we used to know each other, especially the kids. That was our group. So in Zambia it was going to be fun [to see all these friends again]. It wasn't fun. We stayed for a very brief time in Zambia before my father called another meeting, he is good at calling meetings. "We are running away to Tanzania, for security purposes." Lusaka was too close to Malawi and there had been instances of Malawi Young Pioneers going to Lusaka and quietly abducting Malawians who had run away from home and bringing them back by force.

It was a big shock and the biggest shock of all was that we could no longer write letters to our friends and relatives in Malawi. We were banned. We were told, "Don't you dare for the sake of the people back home. Don't write letters to them." That was the biggest shock.

The other big shock was that overnight, we now realised what it meant to be refugees. We stayed in a hotel for about a week and then we moved into a refugee centre which was beautiful. It was flats that the Tanzanian government had built for all refugees from the southern region [of Africa]. I remember they were from the ANC from South Africa, from Zimbabwe, from Namibia. We were all there and us from Malawi.

But then the life was that for the first time, we had to sleep on the floor. Our dad had a camp bed at least. We were given metal plates and metal cups and to drink tea from those metal cups was something else. We had to queue up for our food every other week. That was a big shock to us now. Going from that kind of life to this one....

Then again culturally, overnight we were with fellow Africans like ourselves, but they did not speak our language. If you spoke English to them, they answered in Swahili, which we didn't understand. We went to a local school with all the refugee [children] where we had to learn the national anthem by heart. We had to understand that this was a completely different culture. We had to learn Swahili and we grew up speaking the language very fluently.

Culturally it was a big shock. Then I went to boarding school for my secondary education and that is where I felt it even more. "You are just being proud, because your father was at the UN. You can't speak the language. Why have you forgotten the language?" I tried to explain that this is not my language. I am not Tanzanian and we do not speak Swahili. "Why don't you speak Swahili in Malawi?" We grew up with that.

The stress of exile did not end as the children grow older. New problems and conflicts can arose. Tujilane's efforts to succeed in the Tanzanian context included her relationships as a young woman ready to start a family. She had no Malawian models around her.

The other cultural shock was that I grew up with Tanzanian boys throughout. The Malawian men that I knew were all cooks or drivers.... So when it came to marriage time, I told father I was going to marry my Tanzanian boyfriend. He hit the roof. For a whole year, I was there crying kneeling, you know our culture, I would kneel and say "Daddy, please give me permission to get married to this guy." And he said "No, you cannot. After all these years, you are getting married to a foreigner. One day we will go back home." And that was always the talk. "…. and then what do you do with a foreign husband?"

But Dad! I told him it was not my fault. Where are the Malawian men? None of them have come to propose to me. It is only this Tanzanian one. He just couldn't accept it… It took a long time. We had to call in accordance with our culture. We hadn't forgotten it. He called the elderly Malawians, to come to try to talk me out of it, but eventually we convinced him. We got married. I had my two sons with him. When I told my dad, I was in Germany, I wrote to tell him I was divorcing my husband, my step-mother told me that was the day she saw my father dancing. He was excited. "Finally sense has gone into her head."

Tujilane returned to Malawi while Dr Banda was still in power and that too brought on stress as a result of having been the child of a refugee. She relates the story of that difficult time in Chapter 8: Living with the pain.

Nettie Dzabara came from a well-known and prosperous Blantyre family. Her mother, Molly, was the sister of Augustine Bwanausi who was one of the Young Turks, the brains and energy behind the nationalist movement throughout the 1950s and early '60s. Nettie's uncle, Dr Henry Bwanausi, was one of the first African medical doctors licensed to practise in Malawi. Nettie later went on to become a pharmacist trained in Moscow through a Lesoma sponsorship. At the time of her interview, she was teaching Pharmacy at Kamuzu College of Medicine, was sitting on the Pharmacy, Medicines and Poisons Board and was head of the Young Women's Christian Association (YWCA) in Malawi, among other things. She recounts, through the eyes of a child, how she saw the family's flight out of Malawi.

Nettie Dzabara

I remember very little from the time before the actual time we had to leave.

I remember we were going to school with my sisters and suddenly although at the time I did not realise why, we had to stop going to school, and stay at home. My father had just bought a house or a farm area where we lived and we just stayed there all the time. Obviously I did not understand why.

Suddenly, I was told, we were leaving the country and we went to what was then called Villa Nova in Mozambique.... It was very hot.... lots of mosquitoes. My sister and I were both lying on Mom's lap and she was chasing away mosquitoes like anything.... I did not understand the goings on or where we were really going, but then suddenly we were coming back to Blantyre.

…. Before we came back, we were put in this area... in a sort of camp in Nsanje I think it was. I remember meeting somebody who was a driver to the late Chipembere, and a driver to the late Bwanausi. They were like prisoners there. We stayed there just a few nights. But I knew something was not right because of the silence between my mother, my grandparents, my dad and the others. That's when I was around seven. So we were transported back to the house in ....Chilomoni. We stayed in that house and we didn't go anywhere. We were just waiting. I did not understand what we were waiting for. I did not understand what was going on. Then suddenly, my sister and I were told, "We are going. Don't pack anything. Just carry a little bag as if we are going on a family outing."

My sister was so excited when we were leaving, we didn't know where to, that she even forgot to put on shoes. She was still in patapata. Finally, we're being taken to Chileka airport. We got on a plane, flew to Chipata, what is now Chipata, and at the border, they were asking, "Where are you going?" There was my father, my mother [Molly], their two children, my grandmother and my grandfather and a niece of the late Khonje.... "Where are you all going?" We are going to visit Dr Bwanausi. Later on Mom was narrating that we forgot to say we are refugees and they would just let us in. They were still hiding this fact that we were running away. Mom was arguing with her mother and father. You go [on]. We will go back. My grandmother was saying, "No! I cannot go on to Zambia and live in peace, not knowing what is going to happen to you in Malawi." Mom was saying that if we all go back, those people in Zambia will not know what is happening to us... In the end, mom remembered that she has got her [Post Office Savings Account] passbook and the money was just the same, because in the end they were saying, "You are so many. You have no money. What are you going to live on?" She showed him this passbook and they said, "Why didn't you show us this a long time ago. Go." So we flew to, I think it was Lusaka. I could be wrong, but I think it was Lusaka.

… From Lusaka we drove right through to Solwezi stopping on the way for breaks to where Mr Khonje and his family was. By then Dr Bwanausi, I think was in Balovalu. That is where he was practising. So we arrived in Solwezi and when we were passing through the Copperbelt, I remember as a child I was told that this is the Copperbelt. People are mining underground. I felt so uncomfortable. I thought I was going to collapse into the underground. I didn't want them mining under there. That was a horrible memory for me at that time. So we got to Solwezi and we lived there, I don't remember how long, but it was a lot of people in one house, one pot, one plate. It was cooking for this generation and then for that generation.

Like the majority of exiles, Nettie describes how in the early years they dreamed of returning quickly to pick up their lives in Malawi. She tells how slowly the reality of their situation became clearer and the family realised that the return to Malawi was not imminent.

Once we got to Solwezi it took some time for us to settle and start thinking, "What are we going to be doing?" because we all thought that we are going back home soon. We did not envisaged 30 years in exile.... It was "Ah, it's going to happen. We are going to go back." As time flew, then Mom and Dad started looking for jobs. My mother was the first to get a job in Chingola, so we moved to Chingola, she was given a house, but obviously we had nothing, so we had to put newspapers for curtains. It was quite an experience.

When queried about how much her parents told the youngsters about the reasons for their exile and what was happening, she replied:

Not quite. [We have moved] into a new place. Everything is... [left] behind. I think for me at that time, you know how kids are trusting that whatever Mom and Dad tells you is going to be true. "We are going back next month." We are looking forward to it and it doesn't happen. Then I realise that my sister is being sent to boarding school. She had just graduated from primary so they sent her away to boarding school and I was tagging along wherever mom went. I was in Chingola with them and then they started looking for schools for me. Language was a huge barrier, because I couldn't speak any of the local languages. So getting friends was a bit difficult. Then I started school as well. Lucky for me, I knew English, which most of my classmates at that time did not know. That was an advantage for me. So people wanted to get close to me.

I went through primary school. Little by little, as we started getting some income, the situation started changing... started to normalise.

Whatever the circumstances, the common sentiment of the first generation exiles was bitterness and victimisation. Most had contributed to the nationalist struggle and saw how the Banda takeover had highjacked the potential for liberating the people of Malawi. They also felt deprived of the chance to contribute their skills to developing a new society and benefiting from the fruits of independence. They were later frustrated by the less than warm welcome and suspicion they encountered upon returning home to a post-Banda Malawi. After years of suffering life as an unappreciated immigrant in a foreign country it was particularly galling to return home and be accused of having life easy in exile, while those who remained in Malawi suffered under the yoke of repressive dictatorship.

The disruption of life was another distress. The separation from family, the aborted end of promising careers, and the danger facing many who remained vocal opposition in exile contributed to perpetuating the stress and fear of life inside. Orton Ching'ole, Vera and their son, Fumbani Chirwa, were kidnapped from Zambia by the Banda regime in 1981 more than 17 years after they had been forced into exile and the dictatorship had been safely ensconced in power with very little threat to its existence from outside of the country. Tragically, Orton died in late 1992, after years of solitary confinement in the infamous Zomba Prison, and just months before the 1993 Multiparty Referendum and amnesty. No-one was safe even in exile.

The continuing oppression led many others to choose the path of exile over the daily grind of fear inside Malawi. Some, like the released detainees, left to get as far away as possible from the nastiness of life in Malawi. Often, younger Malawians chose exile as a path to further education or freedom of speech without having to constantly look over their shoulder for who was spying on them. These we call the second and third generation exiles.

Chapter Five: Exile – Second and Third Generation

Second Generation

5.1 Repression and Fear

5.2 Stigma and Discrimination

5.3 Safe Exit

Third Generation

5.4 Repression and Fear

5.5 Stigma and Discrimination

5.5 Political Opposition - New Political Culture

Why did many Malawians continue to flee the country long after the Cabinet Crisis? By the end of the 1960s, the internal opposition had been totally cowed and the culture of silence firmly implanted. Henry Chipembere had led a courageous resistance to the installation of the dictatorship following the Cabinet Crisis and after he left the country, his home district, Mangochi, was locked down and opponents either detained or exiled. In exile, the leaders were no longer united and with the death of Yatuta Chisiza in 1967, organised resistance literally dried up. In terms of security, there was no longer any need to continue the ferocious repression of the whole population.

Nonetheless, the multiple arms of security control were firmly in place to keep any form of internal opposition in check. Repression had become institutionalised along with brutal methods to enforce it. Tom Nyirenda was picked up and tortured in 1983 almost 20 years after Mordecai Gondwe and Carson had faced their beatings. If anything, his torture was more systematic and organised. Jehovah Witnesses were still being brutally persecuted because of their refusal to buy Malawi Congress Party cards. One detainee from 1967-68 talks of seeing their bodies hanging in the trees outside Maula Prison in Lilongwe. Professor Ted Pinney, an American and acting Principal of Bunda College of Agriculture, was deported from Malawi for protesting the similar treatment that the Jehovah Witnesses were receiving in Bunda Forest right beside the college.

A 1990, Human Rights Watch report, " The Suppression of Dissent," refers to the "Manipulation of the Machinery of Justice" to describe how what little vestige of fairness that might have been inherited from the British was entirely eliminated to prevent detained opponents from escaping the punishment the regime intended to hand out. The court system continued to be modified to serve the purposes of the regime. The traditional courts headed by loyal chiefs and their indunas (counsellors) were given expanded powers and jurisdiction including imposing the death sentence after trials that ignored minimum standards of evidence and basic justice. The concerns of Jay Jacobson about the introduction of the Preventive Detention Act and the Law and Order Maintenance Act came to be fully realised. Detention was one of the sticks in the arsenal of state terrorism and totally at the whim of the regime and its cohorts.

Educated people felt very vulnerable. Margaret Khonje points out how she and her husband watched as one by one their highly trained professional friends were being detained. She says, "They could smell it coming." Instead of waiting for the late night knock at the door, they fled into exile.

Regionalism became highly politicised and institutionalised. In the Southern Region, Mangochi people were particularly suspect and victimised. Many were detained and others were rusticated to internal exile in Mchinji for being Chipembere loyalists. People from the Northern Region featured largely among the senior staff and faculty of the University of Malawi and the National Statistics Office who had been detained.

In addition to detention without charge or trial as a punishment for whatever crime real or imagined they may have committed, the ex-detainees were shut out of work and even society after their release. In a small country with a limited economy and few job possibilities, post-detention ostracisation aborted promising careers. This prolonged injustice saw the likes of Mathew Kalambo waiting many years for "clearance," unable to work or even travel outside the country for work, while his wife was unable to teach for some years even after he got his clearance. Even on a social level, many ex-detainees found their friends and family reluctant to re-engage with them because they did not want to attract the attention of the authorities. They were effectively being punished twice for the same offense.

It is in this context that many Malawians felt fearful and unsafe at home and became the second and even third generation to flee into exile. Most left the country by making careful plans and clever subterfuge. For Makhumbira Munthali, there was no chance for a decent job and he felt unsafe and ostracised. His was a well planned flight into exile through a carefully mapped and executed escape route into Zambia. Margaret Khonje tells of the complicated charade they set up to make their departure look like a simple vacation.

Others, like most of the university staff and statisticians, were given carte blanche to stay in Malawi and work outside of government, or leave with the government's blessing. This uneven treatment simply added to the insecurity. People never knew how they might fare trying to restart their lives and careers.

6.1 Escaping Repression and Fear

Makhumbira Munthali's plight was worse than many others once he got out of prison, because Banda had publicly condemned him. Even before his release he was aware that his freedom would be very constrained. The Special Branch was not going to give him clearance when the word had come from the highest authority. After a futile search for work he decided to leave the country.

Somehow I had befriended a person named Kampunga Mwafulirwa from Karonga who had been detained in Karonga but was working in Zambia. He used to come into the country using paths and avoid police. He knew how to evade immigration. I befriended this chap Kampunga Mwafulirwa who later on became an MP. He told me how to get out of Malawi into Zambia without passing through immigration. You avoided being caught at Hewe immigration post. He told me how to avoid the Zambian immigration and a route which was safe. So after I was out and I failed to get a job in Malawi, I decided to leave the country. I had to make sure that my mother-in-law and sister-in-law had to leave the country before I left, because if I left them behind there might be trouble. I convinced them to leave the country and we dispatched them... So when we left the country in December 1977 they were already in Zambia....

I spent the better part of the year planning how to get out of the country. When we were ready to leave.... we left Blantyre saying that we are going home for Christmas holiday. When we were at home, we told them that we were going back to Blantyre for Christmas. They didn't know anything. The only people that knew we were leaving the country were a friend of mine in Blantyre that I trusted.... and he gave me addresses of his friends in the USA, "When you get out of the country contact them. I hope they will be able to respond to your communication." Then my mother and a cousin of mine. These were the only people that knew....

So we left the village and went to Hewe. At the [Hewe] border post we told them we were going to Chitipa, I had a cousin in Chitipa, who was an Education Officer. [At Hewe the road passes through Zambia] *You get out of Malawi and then you get back... when we had passed the Customs Post in Hewe we went to Chisimuka which is in Hewe itself. We stayed there until evening. This was because I had information that the Malawi army who was patrolling the area around Hewe on the Zambia - Malawi border around 8 o'clock they had finished patrolling and come back for dinner. At that time they are not paying attention to what is going on.... That was the time we should pass through this place and that was exactly the time we passed through... Once you get into Zambia there was a tsetse control station and they had police as well as tsetse control people which was between Muyombe and Isoka* [both are in Zambia] *and we were supposed to pass through this place after 10 p.m. because at 10 o'clock they would open the gate for the* tsetse control station... and they would abandon the post and go back to Isoka. At that place they had police as well as tsetse control people and if you pass through that place before 10 o'clock at night then you would be arrested if you didn't have papers. After 10 the place was wide open so that is exactly what we did.... so we drove straight to Lusaka without being stopped and went to see the UNHCR to declare myself as a refugee.

….They accepted me as a refugee. My wife wasn't accepted because they said you have a Zambian mother and you were born here, so you can't be accepted as a refugee. That was another issue.... I was in Zambia for about two years... For about a year I worked. I found a job with the United Nations Development Programme....

When I was settling down, the Zambia police called me. They told me that the Malawi Government was looking for me. They told me to be on the lookout for certain individuals. They showed me [pictures] of the people who were after me. I went to the offices of the Zambia special political police and they took me to the place where these people used to hang out. While there, they showed me the people and even showed me where these people were being accommodated. They were after me.... At that time there were other people in danger as well. Attati Mpakati, Stephen Mwaungulu, Mkwaptira Muhango. In fact they wiped out his whole family [of seven]. They told me I was in this group. They said if you are going out always go with somebody. Zambia cannot guarantee your security, but they have reported this matter to the UNHCR that your life is in danger. UNHCR approached the Canadian government, the American government, the Swedish government, the Danish government and the Australians to give me political asylum. It was the Canadian government that offered me political asylum first...I don't know if there were any other offers. As soon as the offer was made, arrangements were made to get me out of the country.... At first because of my age they thought I was too old to settle down in Canada, so at first I was rejected. It was after the second interview that I was accepted."

Even in exile, the danger was real. Dr Banda's Malawi Young Pioneer operatives that viciously killed the family of Mkwapatila Muhango in cold blood and later assassinated Attati Mpakati in Harare were looking for Makhumbira. In the same period, in Tanzania, Kapote Mwakasungura was summoned by the National Executive Committee of the ruling party to explain in writing why he was the most wanted man of the Malawian refugees by the Banda regime. The Central Committee advised him, "never to use my real name when I am travelling."

Margaret Khonje and her husband Tony could smell it coming. Even as they finished their degrees in the United States, they were reluctant to return home.

Margaret Khonje

We tried to get into Nigeria for job offers but lacked visas - we didn't want to come back.

She could not work right after her return because she had left in 1972 and quit a job in Community Development.

I guess they didn't like me abandoning a job in Community Development so when I came back in 1974, someone must have decided to give me a little bit of a punishment before they could take me on again... they needed people in community development, agriculture, but that's how it was... I was at home August 1974 when we saw that we had to leave. We came in April 74 and we left in August.

What happened was that Tony was given the position of pharmacist at Kamuzu Central Hospital, Lilongwe... You could see different characters there... they had habits that they became used to. Party people would be coming and demanding certain medicines and he said no, I'm sorry I can't. Especially someone who had just trained in the States, to give antibiotic drugs just like that. No, that doesn't work.

What frightened us the most was the never-ending stories of people being picked up and being thrown in Mikuyu or Mpyupyu. Almost every week we could hear Dr Munthali had been taken. Dr Mwanza had been taken. Doctor this one had been taken and we said, "Wait a minute. This is not going to be nice...." So we thought we should leave.... We did feel that the next stop these people would make would be at our house. We had no question about that because my husband was that type of a person who would stand up to someone. Rather than wait to stand up to someone, let us just leave.... had we been from the South or Centre, we would not have worried. The majority of the people arrested at that time were from the North, basically Northerners...

We discussed at length and spent sleepless nights planning the exit strategy until we got hold of Nigeria and asked that they send the tickets to Air Malawi. Fortunately the tickets landed in the hands of a person from home who knew us well and decided to keep quiet and to deal with us quietly. Not making too much noise about it until we collected the tickets. We managed to fly out of Lilongwe. Looking back now it becomes an interesting escape. Air Malawi was only in Blantyre in those days, so it meant me having to travel all the way to Blantyre to collect the tickets and having to come back to Lilongwe.

On the day of departure, we had this car. We had borrowed money from government so it had to be kept safely. So [Tony] took the family, we had two children, to the hotel where we would board the bus. He took us there first. Then he went back to the house and locked the car with the keys inside... then he joined as the hotel where we boarded the Air Malawi bus to the airport... being a pharmacist, he had drugged me a little bit, so that I don't get too excited. He gave me some Valium, enough to calm my nerves....

We took the plane to Blantyre just to find my sister waiting to see that we had departed alright. We didn't want to put our families in trouble, so it was just sign language. We met in the toilet, exchanged a few words quickly because we didn't want anyone to notice that these people are talking in the toilet....

The most nervous time was passing through the passport checkpoint. "You have just come and already you are leaving." You know I have a big family in Zambia, I just want to see them... Later we got on the plane and still I am not settled. There the air hostess comes who was a childhood mate from where I grew up. Oh we are going to visit friends in Zambia. She said to me. 'Mukuthawa.' [You are running away] Ah no. Anyway because she grew up with me she didn't say anything. We finally breathed free once we were in Zambia airspace. We didn't know where we were going to go in Zambia. All we wanted was to get out of Malawi. The rest, we are going to see what will happen.

6.2 Stigma and Discrimination

Sute Mwakasungura with Kapote

The regime's repression against its opponents ran deep. This included persecuting family members of those who had fled or been detained. Long after the incident that led to the fall from favour and regardless of age or gender, the family was stigmatised and discriminated against. Kapote had fled to Tanzania in the first exodus of opponents of Banda following the Cabinet Crisis in 1964. Many years later, his parents and his younger siblings were reaping the fallout of his actions. Charles Sute, a younger brother describes how the family had to live with a brother in exile.

Our family was seen to be anti-government, that is the new government of independent Malawi. We were labelled as such. I recall in Form 2, our father couldn't afford to pay school fees for all of us. So one time, I managed to get into Tanzania to try to get school fees from my brother. When I came back there was a police officer at our house. They had got wind that I sneaked out to Tanzania, so that was the beginning of my personal bad relations with the government. The government then was the Young Pioneers...The Police came and they interrogated our father and mother. They were asking my *whereabouts. They were told that I was in Blantyre. But they [police] said "No we have heard that he is in Tanzania." Lucky enough I came by another route via Hewe to Rumphi then down to Chiweta and went to school before I went home to pick my belongings. So that helped to confirm that I was really in Blantyre. That was 1972, I was in Form 2.*

Sute describes how his coach warned him to leave football camp to avoid being picked up after having objected to the national team having to play white minority ruled Rhodesia instead of a team from black independent Kenya. This was considered an attack on Kamuzu's warm relations with the racist regime of Ian Smith. It was not uncommon to be accused of being disloyal for such a simple act, but with his brother, a known rebel in exile, he was always suspected by the regime.

I finished school in 1974, I used to play football. I was in the Malawi Youth Team which was for schools. And while we were in Lilongwe at the Community Centre grounds, we were to play a team from Zimbabwe. As young people we were arguing about whether we should play a team from Zimbabwe - then it was still Rhodesia - or we should play a team from Kenya and in the course of discussing as young people, it appears, people say that I didn't want to play a team from Rhodesia. I preferred a team from Kenya. I don't remember. The coach then... Malola, he called me aside gave me K10 and he told me that I should leave the camp because he had been told that I was trying to instigate fellow players that we shouldn't play a team from Rhodesia.... By then I had already written my Form 4 so it was a game we were going to play after we had already sat for our exams. So I was told that I should leave immediately. I didn't even go to Karonga to say good-bye to my parents... So with the little money I had I travelled to Tanzania via Chitipa....

So because of the incident where they came to look for me in 1972 and also the record the family had with the government, so there was no way that I could stay. I just had to leave. Whether it was real or whatever, but you didn't have time to verify whether there was truth in it or not. [That was] July or August 1974.

6.3 Safe Exit

Despite having been released from detention and reassured by no less an authority than the Inspector General of Police that they could resume their lives and careers, none of the former detainees were re-hired by the public sector or para-public institutions. They faced considerable frustration at a number of levels with employers refusing to even interview them or relatives reluctant to associate with them. Those especially from the university and statistics office found the education and training they had worked so hard to acquire was going unused and unappreciated. The option of seeking employment in their field outside of the country was an obvious alternative to professional stagnation in Malawi, human rights violations, fear and repression. Despite the difficult situation, what marked their departure was the relative ease of it. The lower authorities appeared to want to quietly help rectify the injustice that they had been through.

Chifipa Gondwe's story is very indicative of wasted talent and the move to much greener pastures. He and James Chipasula had studied in France where he earned a PhD in Political Science. Dr Banda did not allow Political Science to be taught at the University of Malawi, so Chifipa was integrated into the Humanities Department where he taught Public Policy. He was detained in the purge of University of Malawi staff in 1975 and 1976 described by Kings Phiri. He was in the large group released after the demise of Albert Muwalo and Focus Gwede. After his release,

I didn't stay long at Nchenachena [His home in Rumphi District]. *My wife was the first to find a job. The person who sent a message was [Makhumbira] Munthali's wife.... I went with my wife to Blantyre. While there, I looked for a job as well. There was Professor Munthali working at a company called Hogg Robinson Insurance Brokers. He said, "Why don't you apply for a job as well...." So I applied for a job.... Mr King was the director then and he offered us both jobs. He said, "I am very sad that people like you have been detained....." Eventually Professor Chipasula joined.... He was very happy with us.... There were some people there who were not very happy, white people were not quite happy that... we had come....*

While there I was also looking for jobs. I applied for jobs in Mozambique... for a job in Maputo. I hadn't been there, but I just loved Maputo somehow. And then the University of Nairobi. Meanwhile the UNDP rep came to Hogg Robinson and interviewed me. "Would you be interested in working in the United Nations in New York?" I said, very much so. I accepted. But the offer from the University of Nairobi came a little bit earlier. I just wanted to move out of Malawi....

Many people had many problems getting clearance.... I had to go see the Commissioner of Police. Tell him about everything. He said as far as he is concerned there will be no problem. He was going to talk to the President that I had a job in Nairobi and that I would be an ambassador there, not an ambassador, but promoting Malawi....

Despite the reassurance, he remained concerned because everything requiring the President's attention went through his retainers. In the end everything worked out.

There was no problem. I had clearances here and there. Some people were having difficulties but we were able to fly and I went to the University [of Nairobi] and my colleagues there were very happy to see me. I told them

that I had been detained in Malawi. They said, "These are the kind of people we want to be teaching here...."

Chifipa Gondwe went on to teach for five years at the University of Nairobi and was about to made an Associate Professor when he was recruited by the UN Economic Commission on Africa to work in the subregional office in Lusaka in 1983. He was there for 17 years and in the main office in Addis Ababa for another five years before finally retiring to Malawi after he had had a stroke that made working difficult.

The story of the arrest of 18 members of the Department of Statistics is legendary and has become emblematic of the regionalism and irrationality of a regime with unchecked absolute power. As Kings Phiri pointed out, the Department was the institution outside of the university with a large concentration of highly educated Malawians. They, too, were released with reassurance from the Inspector General of Police that they could freely re-integrate into work and society. They also found the route out to be relatively painless.

Dickson Mzumara (DM) and Zifa Kazeze (ZK) agreed to be interviewed jointly. They explained the circumstances of their release and what happened after.

Dickson Mzumara and Zifa Kazeze

ZK *We were released. We were not told why we were detained. They were not sending us back to our jobs. We were sent out on our own and told we could find jobs wherever we wanted.. .. In my case I joined Commercial Bank. I was in Malindi for 13 months.... Thereafter, my brother [Dickson], who had joined the UN in Addis, helped me follow him to Addis....*

It was April 1978 [at the UNECA]. Even to go there you still had to go to police for clearance. It wasn't a problem. I went and saw Kamwana [Inspector-General of Police], so they cleared us without any difficulties, since they couldn't give us any jobs in government... But we thought they would stop us at the border, but... for me 26 years plus in the UN before I retired and settled home....

DM *I started making bricks for houses. After making bricks for some time, I reached a point of confusion, what to do next. I thought to establish my business in Dwangwa. And then, I thought of looking for employment and somehow I decided to apply for a job. I did apply and to my amazement*

I got offered jobs, first in Blantyre. I got offered a job.... As I was working... I found that being in employment was nice. So I applied for more jobs and then I got the offer at Addis Ababa. I also had the opportunity to work in several other offices outside the country but I chose Addis Ababa.

When asked if they considered exile to be a form of punishment the response was spontaneous.

ZK *Opportunity. We were outside.... We had a wider circle of international colleagues and we were coming home every two years, then every one-and-a-half years paid by the organisation.*

DM *Even in Addis... we were very careful. The Special Branch people, they had an office there. We felt we were being watched during the first year, early years.... Number one we felt we were being watched and number two we felt... that we were being ostracised by some of the Malawians who were not ex-detainees. And so you had that strange feeling. We were afraid of talking to some of them*

ZK *especially those working in the embassy*

DM *unless you knew them very well.*

DM *[the feeling of ostracisation] it was real. While we mixed extremely well with other nationalities, our links with fellow Malawians were kind of watched.... Otherwise we were very free with Zambians, Ghanaians... and that is where we had our best friends.*

ZK *The best of my time was out there.*

Augustine Msiska was a trained librarian and being groomed to replace an expatriate as head librarian when he got caught up in the purge of 1975-76. He faced a lot of stigma from family and employers in his quest to find a job in Malawi. Like other families, the problems started before his release, when his wife was dismissed from her government employment and according to custom returned to his family's village.

Unfortunately when she came home... I cannot hide... My uncle Mordecai said something which she didn't like. He said my wife had put me in trouble, which was not the case. So my wife went to her place at Usisya. She had to go there. It was very unfortunate....

When you are in detention you think everybody is sympathising with you. It's not the case. Now [that you are released] you have different trauma because not everybody likes you. Not everybody sympathises with you. Some people look at you as a spy, because you have been released, you should be spying for the government.... Getting jobs was a problem. I have a file like this [he shows with his hand how thick]. Regrets. Regrets. Regrets... Oh yes I was dismissed. I also have that letter here. My wife also. The ruling was that if you were detained and your wife was a civil servant than she has to go.....

I lost my premiums with Old Mutual. I remember when I got out I battled for that but I never got anything....

Not many people came to visit me at my home. They were afraid they might be implicated. You are visiting an ex-detainee. Later on you may be detained. They may get you. Others were just happy to say, "Aha. Here is a graduate. So what has he done with his degree? You know he is just rotting here." People were saying "Oh this Poka area. It's a beer place. In order to have your garden worked on you mobilise people with sweet beer." They would say, "Aha. This one is just drinking beer here. He is finished." Some would be very friendly to your face, but when they went somewhere they are not the same. "What is he? He thought he was educated, but now...."

I had friends at home, but not many people came to see me. One person did. He came all the way from Blantyre in a car older than myself. He had been working as an accounts clerk in the Finance Department of the university... Nedson Ng'oma.... When he heard that I was out, he came all the way from Blantyre to come and see me.... There were very few such people.

I decided after writing so many applications, I decided I should just be a farmer. After all, I hated going.... those people who were my juniors were now very big people. That pained me.... so I spent most of my time working in the gardens. I remember gardens which had been left in 1951, I reopened them. I was very settled. If I had had money I would not have gone back to town. Anger, yes. The idea that I should go and start again...

Here is a rejection letter.... My friend was Director of the National Library Service.... He knew that I was out. He met me somewhere... We had worked together at the University of Malawi, so a job for me was not a problem, because there were not very many qualified librarians. It was obvious, but the politics of it. You have been detained. He is the one who said, "Write a letter to the National Library Service." So I was very happy, I was getting a job. But then after some time he writes,

"Subject: Your application for employment. Dear Sir, We have just received notification from the Office of the President and Cabinet, through the Ministry of Education that it is regretted the authorities have not found it possible your being employed in the National Library Service. I am sorry that this is the reply we give after having waited for so long. Roderick Mbomba."

So going to Zambia was not by design, because I was frustrated here. I had a family. In fact what happened later on, I went to Blantyre and I was staying with Nedson Ng'oma. Some of my relatives did not want to keep me. Partly because they thought that I was spying on them, and not only that, in Africa, if you do not have a job, then you cannot serve someone. You are a nobody.... So I stayed with Ng'oma for 3 or 4 months. Taking that telephone directory with so many companies and writing. He even gave me his own key for his post office box, going in the morning, lunch, evening. So many regrets. Maybe there were about three interviews, for example at Air Malawi. The jobs I was applying for were like documentation officer, personnel officer, but then the issue was, "...but you have been detained. What about clearance. You need clearance."

One thing after detention, I became brave. I wrote to Malani Lungu [a MCP minister] and he wrote that you have to go to town and get a job first and then you will get clearance. So there was that game. They were wasting my time....

By that time the MDC [Malawi Development Corporation] had called back my wife. She was employed, so we were staying in a tiny house in Chilomoni. I remember we used to call it the microfilm reading room. It was just dark during the day... I spent so much of my early years in the University of Malawi library microfilm room. I had documented, in fact that is how I got this job in Zambia. - I compiled this thing, 59 pages, "A guide to Malawi papers in the Public Records Office in London. Correspondence between the colonial government here and the Foreign Office and Colonial Office." I documented that going through those microfilms. It was a big thing and I distributed it to many African Studies Centres [in] America, Canada, Australia, Africa, including Zambia. So when I wrote an application to the University of Zambia, the Deputy University Librarian said, "Oh yeah. This is the guy who produced this work," and then immediately sent me a telegram. "You are the sort of person we want here." That's how I ended up going to the University of Zambia. [I was there] eight years. Again I had to start from scratch, as assistant librarian. I arrived October 1979. Seventeenth October I started work.

After many months of frustration, things took a dramatic turn for the better.

There is this telegramme. You are wanted immediately. Now the issue is I have no passport. So I rushed to the Inspector General of Police. Instead of Kamwana, it is somebody else, I forget his name.... so I say. You know I have been detained. I have been looking for jobs here and I have got a family to look after and qualifications too. So I need a job. Here is the telegramme. They want me in Zambia, but I have no passport.... Within two days my passport and my wife's were ready.

Now going to Lusaka was a problem. My friends got excited. About 12 cars were there escorting me. From the microfilm reading room I was being escorted, when other friends and relatives were saying don't go. I am talking about a time when the Zimbabwe liberation wars were on. Bombing almost every other day. They said you should not go unless you want to die... "I am not afraid at all." ....There were shortages of essential commodities. I bought these with the money the Japanese were giving me [his pay]. I was buying *this and that, Surf* [laundry detergent], *Covo* [cooking oil], *this and that, toothpaste, everything.... Initially my wife didn't come. I was alone there, alone. I was afraid to get in the plane. I am going to be detained again with this convoy, so I got on the plane, I was waving to my wife and friends and kids, but still I was not very comfortable. I went inside the plane and I prayed. The plane took off.*

I arrived at Lusaka International Airport about 7:00 pm, 19:00 hours, and this man, a mzungu [a European], *the Deputy University Librarian asks for Mr Msiska. He has come to welcome me.... I am taken to Continental Hotel at that time the best hotel. So you can imagine the promotion from the microfilm reading room to Room 507 and I was told that you eat anything that you want.*

Augustine became Deputy Head Librarian in Zambia and eventually returned to Malawi because his wife couldn't work in Zambia and his son became quite ill and eventually died. In 1994, he rejoined the University of Malawi and finally did become the Head Librarian. After his retirement, he returned to his home area where Livingstonia had become a university. He took over the Head Librarian job there.

The Third Generation

By the late 70s and into the 80s, a new breed of exile emerged. Some carried the stigmatised name connected with exiled relatives who the regime continued to suspect, some 20 years after the installation of Dr Banda's regime. They could see that their educational and career possibilities were blocked in Malawi. Others inside the country became more and more aware that the Socialist League of Malawi (Lesoma), the largest and most credible of the exiled opposition parties, was active and recruiting strong students to send for studies in the Eastern Bloc. Still others were tired of the irrationality of the regime and of living in fear. With new technologies, it was increasingly difficult for the regime to block out news from outside, and they saw what a free and democratic society should look like. This prompted many to flee the county to join the opposition.

Ollen Mwalubunju and Undule Mwaksungura were also related to members of the exiled opposition. They had gone to their cousin's wedding in Tanzania and linked up with Lesoma. They became part of Lesoma's clandestine underground network after they returned to Malawi. Ollen later left the country in a a masterful demonstration of the ability of the underground to outwit the omnipresent security apparatus of the Banda regime.

5.3 Repression and Fear

Khwauli Msiska explained how he and his school mates fell foul of the system. He and his classmates knew their attitude at school was going to get them in trouble, they could smell it coming. They fled rather than risk detention for their disobedience. They got separated during their trek into exile and his two partners, Grant Sichale and Paul Munyenyembe, joined Lesoma in Tanzania and found their way to Moscow on scholarships. When we interviewed him he was a sitting Member of Parliament and recounts the events that led him to flee the country. Despite these being memories more than 30 years old, he could recall the circumstances in graphic detail.

Khwauli Msiska

It all started when we were at school, at Chaminade Secondary School... in Karonga. Myself with my two friends, Paul Munyenyembe and Grant Sichale, we were so close to each other and we used to pass our time talking about the situation in the country, to the extent that our activities, specifically it so happened at what we call Youth Week. Youth Week used to be the week where the young people would get involved in some development activities, like some construction, like clearing some paths into the form of a road or the construction of toilets at some places. The only problem we saw then was that it was being done forcibly and that did not amuse us. This was 1977. We used to have what they called the MYP instructor and these were posted at all government secondary schools, so we had one there, Mr Mzembe. So we started to talk about that, much as the idea behind it was not bad, [but] the way it was being done forcibly, we thought that was not proper.

Before I come to the outcome [of that incident], I used to receive magazines. These were magazines from China through the post. China Today, these were big, beautiful with beautiful pictures. I used to receive those and then one was intercepted. This was happening more or less at the same time as Youth Week and all that. Prior to this Youth Week which took place in Ngelenge, I was summoned to the police station Karonga to be interrogated. You can imagine that was my first time, young as I was to be interrogated by this policeman, so imposing in appearance.

[His possession of the magazine from China] Yes. That was a very serious matter, because... there was a query from Zomba. He told me that he was instructed to call me and hear my side of the story, how I managed to get such a magazine. Now with me, it was so innocently done, as far as I am concerned, because my father once worked in Tanzania at a diamond mine in Shiyanga and I did part of my primary education there. At Madui Primary School it was very normal to receive such magazines. There were many other pupils there who were receiving such magazines. Now when we came back

home, I still had that idea and it took time to operationalise it to write to them and tell them to send it. And that is how I was getting the magazine. I was just enjoying looking at the pictures, the kung fu and all that. They were beautiful pictures. But [in Malawi] it was taken very seriously. There, I was given a warning, and I was told that I would be invited anytime for further talk, for further interrogation. I was so scared. Mind you [he was] a big man, a police officer interviewing you. I was called - at least if I was in front of my parents - but I was all alone with this police officer. It scared the wits out of me. I was so scared, not even a teacher was around. It was just by myself. All that the teacher did, that was the headmaster, Mr Phiri, he drove me to the police station.... I thought he would be around. He wasn't around, he left. After that interview, the police drove me back, so you can imagine, I'm being driven in a police LandRover. I was so scared....

... After that, then there was this incident in Ngelenge where we actually protested. Our form of protest... was to vacate the place. We were supposed to be there for the whole week and we were only there for two days, so myself and my three friends, we just left that place. So my being interviewed was actually connected with what happened in Ngelenge. Then I was told that the headmaster wanted me in his office. Around the same time, I was told there was a police officer there waiting. I went, just to be told that, "We understand that you and your two colleagues who left Ngelenge are working together." Whatever they meant by working together. Since the schools were closing when I come back... before reporting to school, I was first going to meet the police, so that I give them more information. I must say they were sort of kind to me. They were not talking to me in a threatening manner, but it was just the presence of that same police face and this headmaster talking to me. Two days later, the school closed and we went back [home] and we had to go back in two weeks time.

That is the time I talked to my friends about what had happened to me. My friends were saying, "If you are in trouble, it follows that we will also be in trouble." So it was at that juncture we made a decision that we would actually go out of the country. So, basically, what we did was we used the money that was given to use for school fees. That time, it was 17 kwacha 50 tambala. My father gave me the 17 kwacha 50 tambala plus some pocket money, one kwacha... My father was very, very strict about it. My sister would be given two kwacha for Marymount Girls and I was given one kwacha and that one kwacha was actually in paper form. Even the 50 tambala was in a paper form. Those were the days. So instead of going to school to report, the three of us decided just to cross over the border to Tanzania. I was almost 19, in Form Three. I was so scared. I couldn't just contemplate going back there, because I didn't know, what was going to be the outcome....

This led to an epic tale of adventure and enterprise for the three young friends. They worked their way up through Tanzania and into Kenya to get as far away as possible from Malawi. All went onto further education and after 1994 returned to Malawi as successful professionals.

5.4 Stigma and Discrimination

Isyu Mwakasungura

Isyu is yet another member of the Mwakasungura family who found his path blocked because of his eldest brother's role in the external opposition. He was a very good scholar but it was clear that he was not going to be given a chance to study abroad, because of his last name. He also described the way the family had to live under a veil of suspicion.

I have some memories. I remember when my elder brother, Archibald.... was then being exiled. I remember the time he left Malawi, we were very young. I was still in primary school, just in Standard One. It affected us because we had to maintain secrecy about Archibald being in exile, together with Clement, it was a part of the family... they had left the country for Tanzania. So young as we were, we had to be strict about their whereabouts.

Dad was then based in Blantyre and Mom was staying in Karonga, and the aunties were still there. Mom was actually detained for that including a few other members who were suspected for [helping] Kapote escape from Malawi. So although briefly, still we were under investigations. We were being watched carefully. So you can imagine living under those conditions, it was very difficult. Whoever comes to our house in the village, especially those people who are not known, they have to be tracked. Who are these people coming to see our family? Those who are meeting your mom or your dad. You had to find out who these people were....

I had all the education I needed when trouble started. The government was refusing to give me a passport, and I knew that I wasn't going to get out of this country for further studies. Although I went to Chichiri High School for my Form 6, I knew there would be trouble, because after completion in 1977 I tried to apply for pilot and I had applied to study in Southampton in England and... I was the only student left out. The whole group of about 13 aspiring [pilots] went.... because I couldn't pass through the passport side, I couldn't leave the country. So I knew that there was trouble, so I never went....

I had to organise myself. I joined the National Bank. I worked there from 1977 to 80 then I resigned. I made an excuse that I was still young and I wanted to go to school in Zambia to take economics. The bank accepted okay. Of course I was questionned over this. I stayed from September up till December and left secretly by Mtendere steamer along the lake. I got off at Chilumba late afternoon. I left Chilumba by road in the night up to Karonga.

I slept at the bus depot. Early in the morning I took a bus, I didn't even stop at my home. I went right by. It was raining and somehow I reached the border where I was welcomed by somebody. We were together. We had planned in advance.... Early in the morning I travelled to Songwe to meet him and then.... Late in the afternoon we crossed the Songwe into Tanzania. There were some guides who led us across the river. They showed us the way. That was 6th December 1980.

On his trip up the road from Karonga to Songwe, he passed very close to his father's home. It would have jeopardised his escape had he stopped because his father, Kapote Sr., was under house-arrest as a result of the 1973 persecution of several chiefs following what became known as the Manoah Chirwa incident. Seventeen years later, the elder chief was still isolated in his home and Ishyu's passing by, for even a brief visit, would have aroused suspicion. The house was always under police and MYP surveillance.

Here is the nexus between the children of the first generation of exiles already grown up outside the country and this third generation leaving the country. Many people were very tired of the old repression. While still underground and clandestine, internal opposition was nonetheless growing. Isyu describes his participation in the Lesoma cells while still in Malawi. This part of his story can be found in the chapter on organised opposition. Even his escape resembles a well planned operation with subterfuge, secrecy, good timing and guides. No easy feat for a young man acting alone.

Ollen Mwalubunju also came from a family that had many connections with the regime's exiled opponents. He also faced considerable discrimination as he neared the end of his secondary education.

Ollen Mwalubunju

I graduated with good MSCE points. I had 21 points, but by that time [1987] there was a quota system that was introduced to limit that each of the districts should have a minimum of entrants to the university regardless of the points one would have attained... So people with points up to 30 would enter if they were coming from a district where it was not as highly competitive as most of the districts on the northern side of Malawi....

I was not selected despite marks. Therefore that experience was not conducive.... I decided to leave the country. We got passports under fake names. We had some friends within the immigration system who were also sympathetic to people who were struggling for change.

As a Mwalubunju, I had relatives, I had a step-grandfather who was in exile and he was a senior political activist when Banda was coming into the country.... The regime had that type of information. Secondly, I had uncles, the Mwakasunguras, who were also in exile, so the regime was fully aware of that and could even arrest me for wanting to leave the country.... Such type of families were not allowed to leave the country.

6.5 Political Culture and Differences

Khoti Kamanga grew up in Tanzania and lived there until he finished secondary school. By then his father had retired and moved back to settle in Malawi, his homeland, and Khoti followed the family in 1975. He reflects on the shock he faced when moving from the Tanzanian political culture of liberation and self-reliance to the Malawian culture of fear.

Khoti Kamanga

Dar was the mecca of liberation. We kept reading the paper and seeing Mugabe, Sithole, Haile Selassie was here, Kenyatta all these big names and events.... African-Americans were my tutors at Mazimbe Secondary school, so liberation theology, panAfricanism, I grew up in that atmosphere... So when I went to Malawi, the first thing that amazed me was the South African embassy. It really struck me.... There is no Frelimo here. There is no SWAPO. Those are details that never escaped me, bugged me. And this thing about Life President, these women going dancing, there were Young Pioneers all over the place, literally herding people to attend public meetings. It struck me very quickly that I have come to the wrong place. I am a fish out of water.

I got a job in a parastatal. I worked in Kasungu... 1975, 76, 77, 78 for four or five years. ... The Banda oligarchy was very known to me. We were always told that if you are doing business here, you must make sure you know who is who.... I was just a clerk in Chipiku. We were servicing other wholesalers, retailers and largely wholesale to the estates. I was familiar.... I was transferred... that is how I escaped Kasungu. Because sooner or later something was going to happen to me. Because sometimes, for example you would be required to remain behind, long after working hours. Why? Because a cousin or a niece or nephew of Dr Banda is coming to buy this or that. You would have to come to work sometimes on Sundays. Other traders will come and ask for something and you [would be told] you shouldn't sell this thing because Banda is coming.... I would not have survived for long. So I was more than happy when I was transferred to Lilongwe.

After leaving Tanzania, where debates on political issues were common and people held outspoken views, it was very difficult to adapt to the culture of silence.

There were people of a like mind. I was able to share in a vague way. "Cousin, do you think this is being done the right way? Do you think this could be done differently?"... Malawi was such... it was a police state so even the closest friend you were not too sure. So even with your closest you would speak in guarded terms. So we could even be talking about football and everyone was in denial about what they said.

If there were MCP meetings, the house where I was staying, we were several colleagues. We were known for not attending. So each day there was a meeting, what we would do was shut and lock the doors and windows were closed and draw the curtains. But still we would hear knocks on windows.... It was quite clear that it was closing in on me... It would have happened if I remained, certainly... because I was not carrying a card... so if you were observant enough, if I was a CID [Criminal Investigation Department of the police] person it would be very, very clear that if he is not with us then he is not with us....

Feeling the looming danger, Khoti hatched a plan to leave the country that would arouse no suspicion.

The biggest motivation [to leave Malawi] was self-preservation, yes self-preservation because quite truly my convictions were totally incompatible with what I found. Even some of the social aspects of life were totally incompatible. So there was no way. There were two things. Either, I had to abandon ship or conform. It was two options....

Because it was a police state, you would not want to leave a paper trail. What was characteristic of the Banda regime was that if you were discovered to be in opposition, real or even imagined for that matter, fundamental or even peripheral, it didn't matter. You would be convicted, arrested certainly, detention certainly and torture and all that but in addition to all that, as if that is not enough also the wider family, all of them would be victims. So if you have got a niece or a nephew, brother, either in school or a place of work, whether it is in a public office or private, they would make life very difficult for them.

So what I decided was rather than simply vanishing because that would raise issues and especially if you are working in a high profile office and earning a relatively good salary. Just to vanish would certainly leave a big stink. So what I opted to do was I went to the [Tanzanian] embassy. I found an opportunity to study in Tanzania and therefore I am resigning. So that was resolved.

So how do I leave the country? I decided to go by air.... I knew that I was leaving this country and probably might never return... so I had to carry as much documents and legal stuff, so I opted to travel by air and I bought a return ticket. What little money I had, I put into the air ticket, then when I got to immigration. "What purpose?" I am going to investigate opportunities to study. "When are you returning?" You can see for yourself. Here is my return ticket. I easily slipped past immigration and the CID and that was goodbye Malawi. That was 1981.

When asked how he felt upon returning to Tanzania he declared:

First of all an immense sense of relief - an immense sense of relief. I was in a country where I could be free... to have thoughts and convictions and also to practise those convictions I had about challenging colonialism, openly challenging apartheid, showing support to compatriots in the liberation struggle. Those things I was not able to do.

Although Margaret Khonje falls among the second generation exiles, she describes her political awareness and desire to see a different kind of politics. She credits her exile with shaping her political sensibility. She and Tony, her husband, had already fled Malawi and gone to work in Nigeria, but found something important was missing in their life in that country. They wanted to leave Nigeria for Tanzania but could not get their Malawian passports renewed.

We admired Mwalimu Nyerere and loved ujaama [Tanzanian socialism]....

This time the trouble was travel documents. We didn't have passports. It took only a few days to get documents to get to Dar es Salaam only. Okay we will try it and see what happens. We were just assuring ourselves that Nyerere's government was a people's government....

Indeed we come to Dar es Salaam airport, and what happens? "And what about you Madam? Where are you going to work?" Because Tony was showing them his contract paper for the University of Dar es Salaam. I said I haven't looked for a job yet. Right there at the airport they write a name for me. "Okay, when you have settled down, go to immigration and see Mr Mponzi." He was the perfect person to deal with refugees. He was so good. He was like a brother to everybody. It was so shocking. We couldn't believe that Tanzania just like that would be welcoming us. "When you go to see Mr Mponzi, he will give you travel documents." This is interesting. What's wrong with this Nyerere man? How could he be so good? So we didn't want to waste too much time, so the following Monday we were at Mr Mponzi's office. We filled in papers for UN passports - travel documents - and I gave the details of my qualifications and he tells me he will be in touch with me. It didn't take long before he got in touch with me to go see the managing director of Tanzania Food and Nutrition Centre.

.... Nyerere's government was very kind, very poor, very African. At the same time, they knew how to tap all the expertise of all those not wanted in their country. Why not make use of them?... Because of that reception in Tanzania. I have had a different perspective on how to take care of people who come into our country.

Exile was a blessing in disguise for me, because it made us see the other side of the world. What Nyerere's ujaama was about although he was disrupted in the process. Others didn't want him to succeed. I am a field person, I was out in the field a lot in Tanzania. What I could see in the villages was amazing you know. To see a village headman keeping statistics of his village. Statistics of the demographic breakdown. Availability of food. How many bags of maize, how many bags of... Nyerere was doing those things. I don't think it was wrong. I think it was proper. I feel our African leaders should re-examine the ujaama policy and improve on it.

Malawians continued through the seventies and eighties to choose exile over living in a state of terror. These second and third generation of exiles each had their own story but some common themes emerged. Repression under Dr Banda had not lessened in any measure as the years went on. The culture of silence and the politics of fear still held sway long after any form of internal dissent was effectively quashed.

Dr Banda with the full support of the western powers and their financial institutions proceeded to introduce a lopsided development favouring the primitive accumulation of the ruling cabal. This was the era of the West's Cold War and any ally that shared an antipathy to the communism received their unmitigated support, despite the regime's appalling human rights record. Meanwhile from Mozambique through, Rhodesia, South Africa, Namibia and Angola the national liberation struggles were being vigorously pursued. The Organisation of African Unity and particularly the frontline states were bubbling over with energy and enthusiasm to bring the movement of the sixties to its logical conclusion. Support for the liberation movements and debates about development strategies were open and energetic.

The exile respondents we spoke to were exposed to life in exile that allowed them to evolve personally, professionally and politically in ways that were impossible in the stultifying state of terror. Despite the trauma of their escape and the concomitant disruption of their lives, once in exile, they were able to live free of the oppression facing those who stayed behind and suffered in silence.

Chapter Six: State of Terror - Suffering in Bitter Silence

6.1 Victoria Sibanda
6.2 Kings Phiri
6.3 Lawrence Mwamalimu
6.4 Justin Malewezi
6.5 Traditional Leaders
6.6 Tujilane Chizumila

The full force of repression operated with the complicity of local elites and Western governments. The emphasis on stability, peace, discipline, order; the way the government was portrayed as efficient, moral, and clean; and, of course, Banda's fierce anti-communism and commitment to the World Bank's top-down development paradigm, meant that despite the excesses and despite what was known about the abuse of human rights, Western governments effectively turned a blind eye.

The people high and low who lived the experience could not afford that luxury. Fear permeated the landscape. Fear and silence were the operating principles for survival. In 1975, when Doug returned to Malawi after a three year absence, his old teacher friend, Justin Malewezi, had moved up into the Ministry of Education headquarters. On their first meeting, almost before Doug could broach any subjects as frankly as they had once talked, Justin told him that silence was the order of the day. The only way to stay safe was not to say anything. As part of our research, we interviewed Justin, the now retired ex-vice-president in order to gain insights into his years working directly under Banda. Despite his very senior position as Dr Banda's top civil servant, fear walked with him every day of his working life for that period.

Early precursors of this complicity and fear were apparent from the experience of Jay Jacobson and Colin Cameron, who both tried to defend democracy in the pre-independence period and warned of slipping into dictatorship should the *Preventive Detention Act* and the *Law and Order Maintenance Act* be passed into law. Jacobson writes about how Colin Cameron, the European Minister in the first Cabinet, resigned in protest.

In his view, the approval of the proposed constitutional amendment was too much of a wedge. "What," he said, "could the Ministers do if they walked into Parliament one morning and found the security bill on the Order Paper? The bill would be passed and the Ministers detained before they could get out of town."

The British complicity in the move to consolidate Banda as unchallenged power-holder was evident. Jay Jacobson had tried to build a critical mass of prominent jurists to write to Dr Banda and protest the idea of preventive detention. Jacobson was summoned by the most senior civil servant, at that time, Peter Youens, the Chief Secretary to Dr Banda, who informed him

Special Branch has determined," Youens said, "that you have been the instigator of correspondence from judges and lawyers in the United States and in the UK against the enactment by the Government of a preventive detention law. You have seventy-two hours to leave the country.

Already, any criticism was too much criticism. Dr Banda had specifically recruited an American lawyer to work in the Ministry of Justice to review and revise colonial laws. Now, he was being deported as *persona non grata* for doing his job.

On the streets, the Red Shirts, MYP, and the MCP Women's League ruled supreme. Ordinary villagers and townspeople could not get into the market or onto a bus without producing a paid up Malawi Congress Party card as a sign of loyalty. Failure to produce or buy a card was not simply met with refusal of service but harassment including severe beatings and even detention. Women whose skirts were deemed too short faced public humiliation and beating. Women of all walks of life had to leave their work and household chores to dance at party functions when they were called upon. They had to wear the official cloth wrap known as *chitenje,* which they were obliged to buy at their expense. Failure to perform was considered disloyalty. Every school had to have a MYP teacher whose role went far beyond school curriculum and was more enforcer, spy, and guarantor that obstreperous young people would not get out of line.

The truth was suppressed. Everything was based on concealment and, as Mapanje describes it, the "orality of dictatorship," with no written records. As a consequence, this also meant that rumours replaced informed news, which in turn reinforced fear. The November 2000 Article 19 report, *"Who Wants to Forget?" Truth and Access to Information about Past Human Rights Violations,* states the reality very clearly,

The exercise of these powers was whimsical and might even be considered amusing – had the human consequences not been so awful.... all Malawians knew the immediate danger that they faced – hence the culture of silence – no one knew the broader picture. Those who dared might refer to political opponents of the MCP being "meat for crocodiles" – a phrase used by Banda himself – but no one truly knew the extent of the regime's crimes.... (pg.13)

Chifipa Gondwe describes the fear he and the other lecturers experienced when they were called from their cells in Zomba Prison.

I was at Zomba Prison for about two months. And one day, the police came and said, "People from the University, lecturers from the University. Out!" We thought we were being released, but we were not sure if we were going to be released, because perhaps either we were going to be released

or we were going to be thrown into the Shire River.... because many, many, many people who were said to be opposing the government were from time to time taken from their houses by the police and then thrown into Shire River with stones, big rocks, so the bodies shouldn't come up. Many people died that way.

The fear was pervasive enough that most people followed the rule of silence to avoid drawing any attention to themselves. Malawians also spoke grimly about the dangers of being "accidentalised." The term came about because of the suspicion and rumours which followed the deaths in vehicle accidents of several prominent political figures, most notably that of Dunduzu Chisiza in 1962. The murder, in a clearly faked 1983 automobile accident, of Aaron Gadama,[1] Dick Matenje, Twaibu Sangala and David Chiwanga showed that even highly placed and powerful people would be 'dealt with' if they crossed the unknown line, and threatened the throne or the power behind it. The micro-management installed by Banda was perfected by the Kadzimira/Tembo cabal. In such a highly centralized and authoritarian structure, it would have been impossible for the police to murder cabinet ministers without the authority of Banda, or at least Tembo. No one dared question orders that came from on high.

Jack Mapanje describes his arrest in 1987, when the most senior police officer in the country interrogates him. What Inspector General Elliot Mbedza told him in a room of other senior police confirms Dr Banda's absolute unquestionned power.

...His Excellency [the H.E.] has directed me to arrest you and imprison you, Dr. Mapanje. He did not tell me why; I did not ask him why; and since it is a directive from above, I must tell you we are not going to investigate your case. It would be questionning the wisdom of the H.E., the highest authority in the land. I invited these commissioners from their posts all over the country, therefore, to find out if there is anything in our files about you. There is nothing, I repeat, Dr. Mapanje, these Commissioners say you are not in our books. (And Crocodiles are Hungry Tonight, pg.24)

A subtle but significant result of the state of terror and the culture of silence was a reluctance to take initiatives. Anything new and unusual, different and untested in this climate of fear was simply a matter of taking unnecessary risks and left a civil service stunted and incapable of acting without seeking authorisation from above.

One aspect of Banda's divide and rule was to foster suspicion within families themselves. In public speeches, Banda frequently exhorted his

---

1 In March 2014, we tried to interview Mrs Gadama, but a debilitating stroke had made it impossible for her to talk and remember the past.

mbumba,[2] in this case his women's league, to report their own husbands if they were involved in anything considered subversive. It got so bad that people would suspect someone of being an informer if he or she had been in a sensitive position for a long time and members of the family, counterparts or regional friends had been taken in.

It is well documented that the people who were detained suffered enormously. What is less well known is how the regime punished family members as well. Their treatment was also cruel and degrading.

6.1 Victoria Sibanda

In the case of Victoria Sibanda (a pseudonym), her husband's (W) detention followed the usual pattern. Within days of her husband's arrest, she was forced to vacate the housing she had been issued, and return to her husband's village. There she was much maligned by her mother-in-law who effectively held her responsible for her husband's arrest. Hers is not the only case of angry and upset mothers who suspected their daughters-in-law of reporting on their partners, especially if there were any sort of marital discord in the relationship. As a result, even 35 years later, Victoria Sibanda was our only interviewee who asked that her name not be used. She was more than willing to tell her story, but still feared the repercussions within the family.

Victoria Sibanda was talented at school and before she was 20 had graduated as a nurse midwife and begun working in Zomba. She met and married W from Karonga as he was studying at Chancellor College in Chichiri before it moved to Zomba. He became a lecturer upon graduation. In early 1974, they were in Zomba at Chancellor College's new campus. She was aware that:

...while in Zomba things started changing. Things started going sour at the university. There was a lot of speculation that some people were being taken for detention and things like that. There was a very big tension. People were afraid and it wasn't a happy situation.

As Professor Kings Phiri points out about that time, "people were being picked up left and right."

Victoria sensed something was wrong,

So one day, I think he knew that something was going to happen to him, but he didn't disclose it to me. So one day there was a wedding of my sister

---

[2] mbumba – In the Chewa matrilineal tradition this represents the lineage of child-bearers of the clan or family, effectively female relatives for whom a man is responsible. Dr. Banda applied the term to the women who danced and sang for him at political rallies. He symbolically took on the role of their maternal uncle or "nkhoswe," and because of his use of that term, it became part of the vocabulary of fear. Women were encouraged to inform on their male relatives if they were not obeying the four cornerstones of the MCP.

somewhere …. "You should go to that wedding and take all the grandchildren because your mom and dad are going to be there and the children should see their grandfather and grandmother." I said how shall I take all these children to a place that is just a wedding? He said, "Just take them all." I think he knew that he might be detained that time.

She took the children to the wedding and reality confronted her when she returned home late Monday evening.

As I arrived home, I found the house was so empty. There was no food in the fridge. There was absolutely nothing. I was tired. I was hungry. My parents had decided to stop over in Zomba to greet us, but when we came into the house, it was so unusual. I didn't understand. We didn't have food.... A certain woman, a neighbour came to me and said, "Things are not alright here. W has been taken." I had no idea. She said that things are not alright at the university and he too has been missing since Saturday.

Given the state of terror, distrust and fear people had of the authorities, Victoria found herself in shock and a state of helplessness. Even her parents articulated the hopelessness of the situation.

This was Monday evening. I didn't know what to do. Where to start. Three kids all under five. My mother and father were with me. They came in and they heard the story. There was nothing you could do. I just sat there puzzled. I could not do anything, I didn't know.... I just sat there.... The next day mom and dad left for Blantyre. They said, "We can't do anything. Just wait and see what will happen...." I just sat there along with my kids. I had no food.

Her employer was not surprised by the turn of events either. Victoria was advised to obey the rule of silence, since any emotional outbursts or angry reaction could worsen her situation. Since it had been happening so often in Zomba, her boss quietly offered her some more time off to sort things out and suggested a course of action.

The next morning Tuesday, I went to the hospital. I went to the matron's office. She asked, "Is it true?" I said yes, this is what is happening in Zomba here. She said, "Just keep quiet. It is the security. I will just give you some time to go to the police headquarters and find out...." So I went home. It wasn't nice. I could not sleep. I couldn't do anything.

It took a few days for her to overcome the fear.

Then on Wednesday, I picked up courage. I went to police station. EEEEH, the reception was very cool, very cruel. They asked me what I wanted there. I told them my husband is missing. They kept me there for almost half of the day without telling me anything. They were just looking at me. So I told them what do I do? They told me to go back home and come next week. I went back home after a week I went back there again. They said, "Yes, your husband is here. He is a bad man. He has not been nice to the president. Blah... blah... blah...." A lot of things. I said I don't know anything, but I have never heard him say such things. They said, "If you are not agreeing with what we are saying, you are also going to come in." Eventually they brought him out. There was nothing we could talk [about]. We just looked at each other. It was just a few minutes. He said to send a word to his mom to come and stay with me. That was all. The last time I saw him. That was all. I went back to the house and sent a word home.

The charges against Victoria's husband were clearly trumped up lies the police fabricated to detain him. They did not hold water. Given the climate of fear, even in bars and social events, no one dared broach anything remotely political, never knowing who was listening and how it might be taken. As if her husband's detention was not enough, the regime had another way of making people distrustful of each other.

When my mother-in-law came it was hell. It was hell because she was saying that I was the one who had reported him to police. She was crying every day. She was accusing me. It was hell. That's what the in-laws were doing those days - blaming the wife. They said that the women were reporting to the Special Branch people [because Kamuzu had said women should report their husbands]. She was very much angry at me. It was not a good relationship…. One day my mother-in-law sent the nephew to prison to tell him that I was removing all the katundu [baggage] from the house and hiding them. A thing I didn't do. I didn't even touch a teaspoon.

Without her husband, and sharing a house with a resentful and angry mother-in-law, the regime ratcheted up her punishment for being married to a detainee.

The University office told us to vacate the house. They sent us transport, we packed the luggage and we left for Karonga. At that time the Ministry [of Health] didn't fire me. They just gave me a sort of holiday to sort out these things…. When we arrived at Karonga, it was hell…. She was crying like as if her son had died. She couldn't face me. I couldn't face her. The relationship was so bad and I was staying in her house. There was no one to run to.

Once Victoria was far away in the North and W was transferred to Mikuyu, the police and Special Branch found another way to rub salt in her wounds to increase her misery. Visiting her husband became a marathon of obstruction and indifference.

So after I stayed there for one month, I went to visit him again this time now at Mikuyu. It was not two days [of travel from Karonga to Zomba] because you had to go to the police to beg permission. That would take two weeks. When you had that okay, so then you move down to Zomba and you went to the Special Branch office to beg for permission and then you wait two weeks again to have an okay. Then you started travelling, walking down. In those days there was no transport on those roads. I had to walk from a place called ndege [airplane] near the airport, all the way to Mikuyu [approximately five kilometres].

In the patrilineal tradition, she was expected to take the children to her husband's home and stay with his people. However, the distrust engendered by the regime made such situations very unhappy. She had to ask W's permission to rejoin her own parents.

I didn't want to tell him about our relationship [with her mother-in-law], but I was forced to do so. He said, "You can move. Go to your parents." I was broken-hearted. I returned to Karonga and said I am going home to my father's. And the people in Karonga said, "You are going with all these children? You are not going to arrive with them because they will die along the way." The Karonga people were so bitter with me. "You are not going to arrive with these children home." I was so much afraid. I didn't know what to do. But I picked up courage and said whatever happens will happen, but I left [my first born boy] there as young as he was. I sacrificed for him to remain there. I picked two and came back home.

Her ordeal was far from over.

...and then the Ministry decided to remove me from Zomba to Ntchisi. They allowed me to continue working for a while. But I didn't last a year. I found myself with a letter saying that you have been dismissed. It was 1975....

Ironically, she finally felt safe and somewhat free of pressure.

I went to my daddy's place. He said, "Just come. You are most welcome. You can't just sit there. You should be doing farming to support your kids." I was growing maize and selling it. I had a little peace of mind. I was at my daddy's place 1975, 1976.

Her reaction to W's release was a combination of astonishment and joy.

Periodically, I would go visit him. It was the same process to have an okay and I used to go visit him.... The day he came out I had visited him that same day. When I came back [from Mikuyu] I was arranging to come back home then we heard that they had been released, so I waited for him in Zomba. We met there. It was like you don't know what is happening. Is this man really out? Is it true what we are seeing? I can't believe it.

When they were finally re-united as a family, they were both unemployed, living without income, and still facing stigma and ostracisation. Some good friends nonetheless came to their aid.

The friends, when they heard he was out said that he couldn't travel by bus, he was very weak ... they contributed some money and put him on the flight and flew him to Karonga. He said that I should go to [home] and pick up the kids and join him in Karonga. So we were there in Karonga. We created a small garden so that we could have some income. We created a vegetable garden at the village and we were selling the vegetables to people for the income, buying soap. Later on we decided we should be going and buying cattle and slaughtering them at the market. I was selling meat at the market. But still the relationship with my in-law was very sour.

The strain on the family relations forced her to seek employment elsewhere, but then she faced the problem of getting clearance to work. Most employers steered clear of former detainees and their families to avoid attracting the unwanted attention of pervasive spy networks that would monitor the movements of all such people.

I said enough is enough.... I should look for work in these CHAM [Christian Health Association of Malawi] hospitals, I couldn't work in the Ministry hospital. Even in CHAM it was difficult. I applied in several places, but nobody could accept me. Luckily enough I applied to the Anglican hospital in Nkhotakota, St Anne's. "Come. Come. We don't have registered nurses, we need you here." I left him in the village and took the kids with me and went to Nkhotakota. And after I left him, life was not very kind to him. He, too, decided to leave and go to Lilongwe and get a job.

They were finally able to regain some semblance of family life when W got a job at the Dwangwa Sugar factory owned by Lonrho at the time. They lived there almost three years. She became the staff nurse at the factory clinic, but the regionalism fostered by Dr Banda reared its ugly head once again.

It wasn't enough for us. The politics still went on. We are foreigners wherever we are.... The story was that he [W] was only employing people from the North, not from the Centre and South.... and it was so bad again.... the Minister Gadama came down there to address the meeting. After the meeting, the Minister told him that, "Today, you are not spending the night here. You should get out. People are so bitter with you." It was the Minister who tipped him to get out of Dwangwa.... He came home and he said. "I am driving to Blantyre. You are remaining here. You will pack the katundu [baggage] then follow me. Just do what I am telling you." He didn't even stop. He just went to Blantyre. I was stranded there again with three children. It was bad, really bad....

The family was not out of danger even with W safely away from Dwangwa. Victoria still felt threatened and feared for her and her children's safety. This time, she was rescued by a brave couple who come to her aid.

He and his wife used to come to Dwangwa every weekend to come to the lake. So that weekend they happened to be coming to visit and they met him on the way. "Where are you going?" "Ah I am going to Blantyre. The situation here is not very good for me. I have been told to get out of Dwangwa. I have left Victoria with the kids. You are going to sort her out...." So he came and found us there. These politicians were ready to ambush us.

Yeah. So they saw [him] and he came out with a gun. Then they were afraid to come to the house. They wanted to attack us. If it wasn't for [him], I don't think we would be here now... [He] stayed with me over the weekend. He waited for me to leave that house in proper manner. We packed our katundu and his wife helped me. Then on Monday they [the company] sent us a car and a lorry to get our luggage out.... He was still working with Lonrho.... Lonrho did not chase him, it was the politicians.

W had been detained in 1975. Victoria was dismissed as supplementary punishment in 1976. W was released in 1977, but it still took until late in 1980 for Victoria to get clearance to work in the public sector again. W would never be allowed to work for a government or parapublic organisation as long as the Banda government remained in power.

We moved to Blantyre.... He worked with Lonrho. When we settled down there, [that] is when I applied to the government, to the Ministry of Health. When I took my application to Queen Elizabeth Hospital, the matrons were very happy to see me. They welcomed me. They processed my letter and the Minister said, "You can start working." [That was] in 1980.... After all that we settled nicely in Blantyre. The politicians there didn't follow us.... So life went on smooth after that.

We asked Victoria how she must feel after undergoing so much misery, pain and suffering. Despite her story of ostracisation, intimidation and fear, she emerged from the ordeal with pride:

I think I was very strong. Psychologically, I was very strong. I didn't break down after all these hassles. I felt very strong. I didn't really go down. I didn't break down. Let God sort these things.

6.2 Kings Phiri

Professor Kings Phiri tells of his terrible first two years at the University, watching some of the most talented and experienced senior people being picked up by the Special Branch Police. He is a terrific story teller and he describes the terror of waiting for his turn and his understanding of the politics of geography. He describes watching as his colleagues were taken away one by one.

So I decided to come back at the end of 1971 and was engaged immediately.... My immediate reaction was one of regret having not taken up the offer from America, because from the first day of starting to teach at the University of Malawi, colleagues were being arrested left and right. And believe you me, especially those, because on the African side those who were well established as part of academia were mostly from... the northern part of the country. They were the ones being picked up almost on a daily basis. You would wake up and, "Did you hear? So and so. The police came and searched the house of so and so and they asked them to go [with them]" At that time

I remember seeing colleagues like Chifipa Gondwe, Dr Chifipa Gondwe. They came to arrest him. He was in the same department as I was. He had studied political science in France, but we did not have political science. Dr Banda did not allow political science to be taught in the University of Malawi at that time, so they said, "If you want a job in this university then you must opt to teach in a related discipline...." They came and arrested him. His colleague Frank [ed. Note, James] Chipasula, he was from Likoma. They came and arrested him. Dr Bernard Harawa, who was an educationalist from Rumphi, they came and arrested him. It went on and on. Dr Felix Munthali, Dr Peter Chiona. All these were arrested within my first two years of being a young lecturer at Chancellor College.

It was a terrifying moment. The reason why I and Boston Soko... were spared was because we had just returned from universities abroad and so we were too junior for them to worry about. They were initially targetting all these academics from the North who were well established and were making an impact. It went on and on. It was so many people. Professor Peter Mwanza was arrested. John Banda all these academics, because it was Northerners on the African side who were running the University of Malawi at that time. Augustine Msiska who was a key librarian. It went on.....

And Mr Shumba, you know, the greatest shock I had was... when they engaged me the Principal said, "You know, Kingsley, you are still very young and we do not have any housing for you. But we can give you accommodation on campus if you agree to serve as a warden for the male students." I said I don't mind, so they gave me a flat with four rooms in it, attached to one of the dormitory hostels for male students and who did I have as mentors in that job of being a warden? What to expect of it. How to prepare myself for it. One was Mr Mumpha Shumba and the other was Dr Dominic Milazi from Mulanje. These were the ones who taught me the ABCs of how to be a warden.

And believe you me, within three months of working with them, both of them were arrested and I watched terrified as security people, members of the Special Branch...., as wardens, all of us had flats on the campus, they came, "We are looking for Mr Shumba's house." I went there to see what it was they were doing. They searched the house, the entire flat, from the sitting room to the bedroom. They turned everything upside down and telling the owner, "You will accompany us," while the wife and children wailed hysterically because.... At that time, when they came for someone, there were two possibilities. Either they were going to release them and they would come back after two or three days of inquisition or they went for good. But for the family it was trauma. So I watched this relative to Mr Shumba's family, then I watched this happen to Dr Milanzi, his wife, we were neighbours with whom I was working. It went on for a whole year....

It was not only lecturers who were being arrested and detained. Some of our students also underwent the ordeal. As a warden I ended up in my flat keeping the suitcases and possessions of the students who had been arrested, once it was clear they were not going to return. We had a very bright student who had a position on the Student Representative Council, by the name of Lance Nguluwe from Mzimba. There was Akim Kaunda also from Mzimba....There was a certain Thindwa from the Chiweta area. I forget his name, but I kept their possessions for almost a year until their parents or relatives came to claim them. Then there was Leonard Hamuza, I think he was from Thyolo. This one, I remember vividly the circumstances under which he was arrested. He had gone to visit his parents who were in Zambia at that time. Then at the beginning of the term, soon after he returned, they came and picked him. The impression they gave us was that while in Zambia he had got in touch with some of the groups that were anti-President Banda. This was 1975, early 76. There was Gerald Chaponda. I think he is a relative of George Chaponda who is a politician in the DPP - Democratic Progressive Party. They came and arrested him. It was mainly students from the North and from the South. They were the ones suffering this. It was that period when Dr Alifeyo Chilivumbo was arrested. The first generation of very talented and able lecturers. They were put in one after the other.

You see it was a nightmare, because you would go to bed. They usually came to arrest the colleagues at night. I do not know why they operated like that. It was only the students they came for during the day time. For the lecturers they would come at night. I remember going to bed and every time you heard the sound of a vehicle outside you would say "Aha Aha. My time has come." On going out, it would be a friend or colleague who was maybe passing by. "I just wanted to say hi." What a relief. It was just for one year.

I remember, it was October of 1976, when we heard that the Chief of Special Branch, Martin Focus Gwede, who had been behind all these arrests, had been arrested along with the late Albert Muwalo, the powerful Secretary General of the mighty Malawi Congress Party. That was the jinx that brought the arrests to an end, but we had lived through it for a whole year. By that time, believe you me, the lecturers from the North, they had arrested almost everyone who had a name and who had been making an impact on the community either because they were good teachers or they were good at organising.... and I think if it had not been for that break which came with the arrest of Muwalo and Gwede, they had now reached a point where they were eyeing us who were very small and had just returned from university. But we were going to go too. There is no doubt about it, because I remember colleagues from other parts of the country coming to Boston Soko and me, and saying,"Aren't you lucky. There has been a turnaround in the way events are developing politically because you were now next in line. You see because they have arrested all the lecturers from your part of the country who were established. Now they have no choice but to go down and pick the tubers that are not yet ripe."

I remember one meeting we had as wardens. Our meetings had to be with Alex Kalindawalo. He was the Registrar. We were trying to make provisions for those students who were needy, arranging relief, cash packages... Mr Shumba had been in administration prior to crossing over to the teaching side. He was conversant with administrative procedures. I remember Mr Shumba at that meeting was explaining to the rest of us that the best way of going about this... going into the technicalities of it. Kalindawalo tried to say something that did not quite hold water. Then Mr Shumba corrected him. "It can't be that way. Technically we have to go about it this way..." Mr Kalindawalo blew up into a rage and started banging on the table. "You cannot tell me how we are going to run this college." I was new and quite intrigued by what was happening. Kalindawalo obviously directing his remarks at Mr Shumba..... What happened was that within that week members of the Special Branch came to arrest Mr Shumba... [The link was very evident] Yes. Yes.

Mr Kalindawalo was a close friend of Martin Focus Gwede, the head of the Special Branch. They were very close. People used to joke about it. It was a "brotherhood of two very ugly people." Both of them were not just dark in complexion... they had gruesome features....

6.3 Lawrence Mwamlima

Fear permeated all sectors of society including high up the ranks of the civil service. Lawrence Mwamlima was a successful civil servant who rose to the senior position of District Commissioner soon after independence. He escaped detention by virtue of a spokesperson in the President's Office defending his interests. His former boss knew his character and integrity so instead of detention he was rusticated to his home in Karonga as a form of internal exile. Lawrence Mwamlima started his story at the point where trouble was about to begin.

1976, I was called by the Office of the President and Cabinet [to be accused] that I was telling people not to go to Sanjika where there had been tree planting. It was a lie. At the same time I was supposed to be telling people, I was the other side of Lake Chirwa. Possibly someone wanted me to be dismissed, I don't know.

He speculated that it might have been a former classmate at Zomba Secondary school who was then Regional Minister.

In 1976 April, I was called again by the Office of the President and Cabinet for a meeting. When I arrived there I was told by the Secretary to the President and Cabinet that the President had received reports that some people were speaking against the government, but I did not stop them. I told him that it was very difficult for me to say that somebody did that because I never went to pubs where people drink and I didn't drink. So I felt that that was a lie. He said that I was sympathetic to those who were detained. At that particular time, a number of lecturers from Chancellor College were detained. The person who reported said I was sympathetic to those who were detained. I told the Secretary to the President and Cabinet, that it would be very difficult for me to say I was not sympathetic to those who were detained, because anyone who was detained, I feel sorry. Someone may say I am not displeased with that but we should have sympathy.... We don't even know why they were detained. He said, "Because of that the President has ordered that you be dismissed effective immediately..." from that particular day, 14 April 1976. And I was advised by the Secretary to the President and Cabinet that the best thing for me was to come to Karonga and stay for about two years before I look for employment again.

Fortunately he assured me, you know he was our Permanent Secretary in the Ministry of External Affairs, so he knew very well my character and so forth.... He said he tried to defend me, but the President was not very happy. "How can you defend Mwamlima in Zomba and you are working in Lilongwe?..." "No, I worked with him in the Ministry of External Affairs for two years so I know him..." He was trying to defend me. So from that time I came home. I stayed here for two years. In 1978, in December, I went back to Blantyre and I was employed by the Christian Service Committee.

I can say that from the time I was dismissed it was not until after 12 years when I received information that the government had decided to give back our terminal benefits.... I was dismissed without anything. I understand from the Secretary to the President and Cabinet at that time the President wanted me to be detained. After he had defended me, he was allowed to tell that I was dismissed and should stay at home. So I came here.

Now when I looked at the whole story, the reason was that I think ... the chief security officer at that time was Mr Focus Gwede. Focus Gwede worked with me at Karonga here in 1957.... So we argued on issues. I didn't know that he was on the security side. When I was posted to Mzimba he was also posted to Mzimba. When it came to the State of Emergency [he was picked up] he was also there. What surprised me was that when I was dismissed he was now head of the Special Branch. The same Gwede, when I went to Britain for studies, I visited the Malawi High Commission and the person who welcomed me was Gwede. He opened the door for me and before I saw the High Commissioner, he took me to his office. The first question he asked me was, "Mr Mwamlima, are you still interested in politics?" I was shocked. I said look Mr Gwede, I would not have come back to you if that was the case. I knew that he was the one who actually recommended that I should be detained, because we had quarrelled on political issues. We disagreed, only *disagreed, but he kept that. When I was posted to Mzimba, it seems he was the person who influenced that.*

And even this dismissal, I believe he was the one who actually did that one. Why I am saying this because, I was dismissed on Friday, and Saturday I went to the bank in Zomba. I met him. He said, "Mr Mwamlima, are you still here?" ....So he was very surprised that I was found there. He thought I was already whisked away... That is the suspicion I have that he might have been the one....

When I came to Karonga that was in April. In August, the President came here. I was cycling and I met one of the chaps, a police officer who was a Special Branch chap. We had worked together, so I knew him. The time they suspected that I was stopping people, I was with him on the other side of the lake. So when he saw me he said, "Sir. Can you come? Please don't leave this country. We were all surprised to see you have been dismissed. And the people who actually did that are in trouble. You will be hearing shortly they are in trouble." That was in August, I was dismissed in April. Just a week after I was told that Gwede and Muwalo were detained. The chap who told me was informing me what was going to happen to those fellows. He said all the policemen there, even Mr Kamwana, the Commissioner was very surprised to see that I was dismissed.

Mwamlima's career had been cut short by a malicious, vengeful police officer, who coincidentally he also believed betrayed him to the British during the State of Emergency in 1959. The continuity of that officer's service as an undercover political informer from British colonial times to independent Malawi was exactly the kind of complicity the former rulers used to bring a man like Dr Banda into power.

6.4 Justin Malewezi

Justin Malewezi with Kapote

Justin Malewezi rose through the ranks of the civil service, and eventually was appointed the Secretary to the President and Cabinet, the most senior civil servant in the country. As such, he had regular, close contact with Dr Banda when he was in his nineties. Despite his position, he tells how he lived in fear thorough the years he held the position. Just performing his job in a conscientious fashion forced him to do unpleasant things, put him in a very compromising position and left him terribly upset. He starts his story when he was still in the Ministry of Education.

I made a deliberate move to never participate actively in politics. I was a good athlete, track and football. That kept me very busy. Being a professional at Ministry, we didn't really [have] much problems until the Muwalo problems 1977... I was now head of Basic Education, that would be primary, secondary, special education for the blind and deaf and teacher education. It was quite senior. You will remember that Mr Muwalo after his detention, another lady was also detained who was the Deputy Minister in Social Welfare, Mrs Fern Sadyalunda. Mr Sadyalunda was our chief accountant in the Ministry of Education and we were classmates at Kongwe. So when his wife was out of favour, I was instructed to dismiss all their children in school. All of them. It was written instruction from the Minister to PS [Permanent Secretary] to me... It was either Bakili Muluzi or Munyenyembe. But the orders came from MCP headquarters of course. I was called, "Look here. Find out where these children are and dismiss them." That was one of the most difficult and heart rending things to do. Particularly the youngest, who was only in Standard One - a six year old... so that happened, and of course Mr Sadyulunda lost his job....

Then a few weeks later I had another problem.... Mr Muwalo had an accomplice called Focus Gwede, who was head of intelligence in the police Special Branch. It was Gwede who had come to my PS. [He] had come to tell me to dismiss the Sadyulunda children. I was called by the PS because the PS was also quite afraid that he himself should not pass this on to me. "You come to my office" and that was the first time I saw Focus Gwede. He was in a turtle neck and if you knew him his face was not symmetrical. One side was very funny... you couldn't focus on him even if his name was Focus. It made you afraid, although I didn't know him, I was really afraid.

That was the irony, then a few weeks later Gwede was taken in. So one of the literature books in ChiChewa being used either in secondary schools or I think it was primary schools had a character called Gwede. Predictably, I was summoned. "There is a book with someone named Gwede. Find out which one it is and bring the page." So I looked and I found it and of course it was a literature book so the character was mentionned in several places. So [they said] "...you black out [all the references to Gwede]...." I said, I don't think this makes sense. I went back to my PS and said let's just withdraw it. Not blacking out all these.... So I issued instructions, "This book is withdrawn." You know those are the things that you experience and you can't do anything about it. You feel it is wrong, that it's bad....

Justin rose to a very senior rank as the Permanent Secretary.

Dr Banda was giving a speech in Ntcheu where he castigated some principal secretaries for thinking that they are very powerful, that they were this and that. It was a very hot speech obviously targetted at somebody but we didn't know who it was. It happened to be targetted to the Secretary to the Treasury who was a young man called Mphande.... who later on was fired. So John Ngwiri called me to his office and says, "I want you to go to the Treasury...." So Mphande and Mbisa were the two who were moved out.... then I was promoted to Permanent Secretary. In those days we were called Permanent Secretary. I stayed in Health for three and a half years....

I had just been appointed, this is a young professional who had just been appointed and now I was in a semi-political post and we were required to go to Parliament, of course as principal secretaries, and he gave this speech about some Secretary for Health... thinking that he was 'Permanent.' I can fire all of you, whatever.... I was so shaken because I was the Secretary for Health. But of course it wasn't referring to me it was my predecessor, Mr Salima, who, I think wasn't fired but moved.... So that is why... I built this house here. I got quite nervous and started building houses in case I got fired. Particularly that we had children and they were in school etc... [I had been living in government housing] since that time, it was like a benefit that you expected. You were given a house and a house of your grade. If you were promoted you were expected to move to a bigger house.... "

Later Justin became the Secretary to the President and Cabinet (SPC). Normally John Tembo, as the senior party man, should have introduced the new SPC to the President at their first meeting. Tembo refused to escort Justin, because he was not Tembo's choice for the job. Dr Banda had chosen Justin over other candidates favoured by Tembo because he recognised Justin's American Ivy League education. Justin described how the audience went.

I presented myself alone to the President without a party heavyweight.... I arrived at Sanjika. I was briefed [on] what happens in audience with the Life President. You know there were three levels of security people at Sanjika. There was the Malawi Young Pioneer guards, who wore white and those were the ones who ushered you in. Then there was the ADC [aide de camp] from the Malawi Army who was more ceremonial and his deputy, and then there were the police people, presidential guard. Manning the gate was the police. Then you go and report to the ADC who was in charge of the formal appointments. Then you are ushered in by the MYP guards. They tell you what to do, how he is announced and how you are received, etc.... They would take you and show you your seat. Usually I sat on the eastern chair next to the President. The lion, the famous stuffed lion was facing you and you face the lion. It was a big table. Us, the officials, sat on his left and the politicians sat on the right... then the lion was over at the end of the table. You could see it. I learned later on that the eye of the lion was actually a camera... it surveyed and photographed everybody.

Justin describes an incident which illustrates the extent of Banda's control and the fear he instilled. During the period of the World Bank/IMF structural readjustment programme, Justin was the Permanent Secretary in Finance when they were supposed to tell Dr Banda that they had to break up his commercial empire, Press Holdings, which had a stranglehold on large parts of the economy.

This was the time of the SAP [Structural Adjustment Programme]. I was responsible for implementing them. A real challenge. I first came into contact with Dr Banda. Matenje was my Minister.... [for] Malawi the economic crisis came with the first oil shock in 1975, and again 1977 and then the Mozambique war when Nacala was closed, the import and export routes. We had to come up with alternative routes. I negotiated the northern route to Tanzania, the fuel tanks at Chilumba, the Canadian - Malawi rail route to Zambia to connect through to Kabwe. We began the privatisation progamme because of the costs of the parastatals. Fertiliser prices started rising. Highly subsidised fertiliser ... and ADMARC taxed the farmers and highly. ADMARC diversified and bought hotels and other non-agricultural [holdings]. Press Holdings Company had over 20 companies in all sectors and controlled over 6% of the GDP.

When the crisis came, this became very political. It too was nearly bankrupt. I had the unenviable job of reporting to Dr Banda that we were in trouble. He did not like to hear that. We decided as technicians to do whatever we could at our level before reporting some sort of good news to him. We rescued several progammes. The institutions who we owed money to decided to call in their loans. The creditors assembled at the Capital Hotel. I told them to call in their debs. We have no money so we cannot repay. They accepted and we renegotiated.

The big one was Press, because this was Dr Banda's private company. Press was too big to fail. I led that negotiation. It meant changing the ownership. We had to take the company away from Dr Banda. Sadar Sacranie was our lawyer and he [found] a really clever solution. He created Press Trust for the people of Malawi. The chairperson and sole owner was Dr Banda. We gave him one million Kwacha per year to disburse as he wished. He was still in charge and he had his money to build houses for his women.

He was old but still sharp.

When asked if he felt he was receiving special treatment, Justin replied,

I can say that all the three-and-a-half years were very nervous years, because you never knew what will come out of any audience. Any audience. You never knew. You just had a sigh of relief at about 12 o'clock or one o'clock when the audience ended. It was like walking a tightrope. And that position was very difficult, because you had access to the President at least once a week, sometimes many more because you would escort him to meetings. You are not allowed to be in the forefront. If you look at all the pictures where Dr Banda was addressing a meeting you never see my face. You must always be in the background. But you must take notes, be attentive and follow up. You must do that. After every meeting I would go to Sanjika. If he had promised anything or someone else had promised anything, I would have it in written form at his desk. If it didn't come you were in trouble. He would remember.

Justin's fall from grace was just as predictable as that of his predecessors. A protocol situation at a Commonwealth Summit in Zimbabwe left Dr Banda unassisted as he walked up some stairs, tripped and fell. The politicians around Dr Banda framed the incident as a major embarrassment for the President and a protocol failure on Justin's part. They resented his easy access to and relationship with the President and concocted a scheme to oust him. Justin was sacked just as the 1992 Lenten letter from the Catholic bishops came out and deflected attention away from him. He became active in the politics of change and was a very positive force in the transition from dictatorship to democracy.

6.5 Traditional Leaders

Traditional leaders were equally vulnerable to the wrath of Dr Banda. William Sinkara is a retired school teacher and was a confidant of the late Kyungu, or paramount chief, father of Kapote and the current Kyungu. They explained how an incident at an MCP convention in 1973 led to Kapote Sr. being punished, dethroned and he was placed under house arrest, along with his wife.

When Archibald Mwakasungura fled away from Malawi in October 1964. The big man here Kapote Mwakasungura [senior] was in problems.... Then in 1968 he became the Kyungu [Paramount Chief of the Nkhondes]... everything seemed to be going on well. But then 1973, when Manoah Chirwa had written a letter to ask Dr Banda to allow him to come back to Malawi. That was the time Dr Banda had called a Malawi Congress Party Convention. It was held in Mzuzu. So Dr Banda opened that meeting... saying there was a letter from Manoah Chirwa [who] was asking forgiveness, that he be allowed to come back to Malawi.

And so Dr Banda asked the audience to discuss and come to the conclusion whether Manoah Chirwa should be forgiven or not. So all the chiefs that accepted that Manoah Chirwa should be forgiven were removed out of their chieftainships. The first one was Chief Mwase who was removed from chieftainship and the government sent a bulldozer to pull down his house. The second chief was Chief Katumbi from Rumphi. He was removed from his chieftainship. The next was Chief Mwasambo by then he was Chief Mwafulirwa. He was removed from his chieftainship and his young brother took over. The fourth was Chief Kyungu, by then Chief Kyungu was Raphael Kapote Mwakasungura. He too was removed from his chieftainship and then was given house arrest. Nobody was allowed to pay a visit to him and he was not allowed to move to any home. I was the only person who used to pay him a visit from Malungo where I was teaching, to cheer him up and then back to Malungo.

It is this same incident that led to the detention of G.K. Mpango, after Chief Mwase was dethroned and forced into internal exile in Mlanje. Such treatment of even senior traditional leaders reinforced the fear in people that no one was safe from Kamuzu's anger.

6.6 Tujilane Chizumila

Tujilane Chizumila tells the story of studying for her Masters degree in law when she got a surprising invitation to return and work for the Malawi government.

When I was in Germany, I got a letter from the Malawian government, I don't know how, because that was the Kamuzu Banda era.

Her father had fled the Banda regime at the time the Cabinet Coup and settled in Tanzania where she had grown up and gained her first degree. She returned home following her mother after her parent's divorced. Even after being invited home, she could not work in government for more than one-and-a-half years as she waited for security clearance, so she took a job with an international NGO and was happily settled into her new work.

That is when I got a phone call from the Office of the President and Cabinet.... "I have been directed by His Excellency, Ngwazi, the Lion of Malawi..." and he went on and on "...Kamuzu Banda. You have been cleared. You should report with immediate effect at the Minister of Justice as a State Advocate." Now, not having grown up here, my first reaction, my instant reaction was - oh no. I don't need that job. I am comfortable. I have got a job, which I love. I am okay. Thank you very much. And he said very calmly, "I repeat..." and he started all over again. I said thank you and put down the phone.

My Afro American boss told me to stay with [the NGO] to continue as a social worker and go for the internship and become the deputy representative. I was so excited....

But then I went to my colleague, a fellow Malawian, and when I told him he was white in complexion. He shut me up. "Please shhh... shhh..." We were only the two of us in his office and he tiptoed and locked the door with the key, knelt and held my legs. He literally begged me. He said, "My sister. Here is the phone. Call the OPC and inform them that you are reporting for duty with effect from tomorrow morning." I argued with him... My rights.... He said, "This is Malawi. You know what will happen. Jacques [her boss at the NGO]. He is going to be deported if the worst comes to the worst, but you and I by the latest tonight we will be meat for crocodiles. This is not a joke. Our relatives, our families will know what has happened to us, but they dare not follow up on our case." I was just crying and he picked the phone and phoned that gentleman. And when I told that gentleman that I would be reporting for work tomorrow, that gentleman, laughed and said, I knew that common sense would come into your mind. So by 3:00 p.m., [the NGO] were throwing a farewell party for me, and I was just crying and crying. The next day, I used to live in Kawale, I walked on foot to Capital Hill to report for duties.

Even after two years or more back in Malawi, Tujilane had not clearly understood her situation when the call came from the top. She had not fully absorbed the lesson of fear that Malawians who stayed in the country had built into their everyday lives. Her colleague's pleading saved her from facing serious repercussions for ignoring an order from the President's Office.

Chapter 7: Organised Opposition

7.1 The Crisis – Chipembere in the Bush
7.2 Early exile – 1964-66
7.3 Yatuta Incursion
7.4 Post 1967 - The Political Vacuum
7.5 The Lesoma contribution
7.6 Internal opposition
7.7 Lesoma's role in the democratic transition

Mary Mwale lost her husband, Lutengano Mwahimba, in the battle between Yatuta Chisiza's UUMA - Ufulu Umodzi Malawi Party brigade and Dr Banda's armed forces in Mwanza in 1967. She remains bitter about the fact that this important piece of history has been so little recognised. As she says about their deaths:

It is a very long story... they died in vain.. Even the daughter thinks he must have been 'chigawenga'[1], because nobody speaks about him.... They remember Chilembwe and the events of 1915, but not 1967. How did President Muluzi remember somebody from 1915 but not 1967.... What is it about?

Malawians of all political stripes proudly refer to their radical tradition of opposition and resistance with the proud example of John Chilembwe and his short-lived revolt against colonial rule in 1915. They may also mention the activism of Clements Kadalie in South Africa, Oscar Kambona in Tanzania, and Dunduzu Chisiza in Zimbabwe. The Young Turks and their role in the nationalist struggle during the 1950s and 60s carried on this tradition until it was driven underground or into exile after the Cabinet Crisis of 1964. The Banda era of rule by terror and stifling repression effectively silenced or obliterated from the official memory the brave freedom fighters who had led these struggles. Their fall from grace and subsequent tarring as *chigawenga* remains more a part of the current national discourse than the evidence of principled struggle and sacrifice their stories carry.

Inside the country the repression was so brutal and effective that all opposition ceased. From an initial willingness and capacity to work together, exile politics soon led to fractured opposition, jealousy and ineffectiveness. The unity of the former ministers had started to splinter even by 1966, almost as an inevitable consequence of a protracted exile. The solidarity of purpose immediately after fleeing the country in late 1964 slowly decomposed, as different tendencies, personalities and politics came into play. The PanAfrican

---

[1] *Chigawenga* is ChiChewa for traitor or rebel, used to describe anyone identified as an opponent of Banda.

Democratic Party (PDP) had been set up by the ministers with Chipembere as the President and Chiume as Secretary-General. By 1967, it too had splintered with the disagreements between the two leaders becoming open and vicious.

Kapote Mwakasungura was a young student during this period and witnessed the turn of events. He describes how,

Chipembere had been employed by Tanzania's governing party, the Chama Cha Mapunduzi [CCM] as a lecturer at the party's ideological college in Dar es Salaam. That provided him with a privileged access to the CCM Party structures and even to President Nyerere himself. This rankled with Kanyama Chiume who had grown up with and went to school with many of Tanzania's key nationalist leaders. Prior to exile, he was always the person with the Tanzania keys in his pocket. He had been at secondary school and at Makerere with many of them, so he had always had easy access to senior Tanzanian government officials. In many ways he was the Malawian that the Tanzanians looked to as an authoritative voice on what was happening in Malawi.

However, with Chipembere at the ideological college, Chiume feared that he was losing that influence and so he began to slowly undermine his previously close colleague. He accused Chipembere of having CIA connections and questionned his status as a Malawian. Chipembere fought back about his nationality and wrote a pamphlet affirming his Malawian roots, "My Malawian Ancestors."

In the context of the 1960s Cold War, the Tanzanians took the CIA allegations very seriously. CCM Party officials removed Chipembere from his post at the ideological college, which was considered too sensitive for a person under suspicion. He had already faced personal and political attacks when he wrote a letter from the United States in 1966 to "His Friends in the Camp" which appears in this chapter. Upon his return to Tanzania, the treatment he received made Chipembere even more bitter and he finally left for good for the United States in 1968. The ultimate humiliation for a man who had dedicated his life to African liberation and panAfricanism was the excessively thorough search the Tanzanian officials subjected him to as he left from the Dar es Salaam airport.

As the dictatorship continued long into the 1980s the internal opposition to the regime's autocratic tendencies slowly began to surface. The murders of the four senior MCP ministers and MP in the Mwanza incident of 1985 marked a major turning point in the regime's ability to enforce the rule of silence. The majority of churches had maintained a submissive silence in the face of the regime's terror throughout the 30 years. That made the courageous release of the Lenten Letter of the Catholic Bishops in 1992 such a remarkable event. It marked an end to the rule of silence and opened the door to active opposition.

Once the floodgates were opened, opposition was vigorous and irresistible. The once mighty Malawi Congress Party and its omnipotent control of the country wilted in a relatively quick and peaceful movement from dictatorship to democracy.

Nonetheless, one of the points that rankled many of our interview subjects was the way people who remained in the country and suffered under the Banda regime accused those returning from exile of having had it easy, or enjoying a life of luxury and freedom. In this chapter many of the actors reveal how they forsake careers and family life to carry on the struggle to restore democracy. People in exile were committed to fighting the dictatorship, took risks and suffered in many ways as a result of their militant opposition.

7.1 The Crisis – Chipembere in the Bush

The anger and disappointment at the move to dictatorship was met with armed resistance from the beginning. Henry Masauko Chipembere had been widely regarded as the most articulate and capable leaders of the Young Turks in the pre-indepedence period. Immediately after Dr Banda unleashed his reign of terror following the Cabinet Crisis in 1964, Chipembere went into the bush of his home turf around Malindi and frustrated attempts to corner him. British security prevented his return to Zomba to confront Dr Banda in armed battle. Eventually his weakened physical condition placed him in an extremely difficult situation. The British got the Anglican clergy to convince Chipembere to abandon the struggle and flee the country. They are even purported to have facilitated his departure in secret from Chileka airport despite heavy security and surveillance where the MYP and informer network was on the vigilant lookout for him.

Henry Masauko Blasius Chipembere participating in a demonstration in Dar es Salaam after his exile in 1964

We were extremely fortunate when we met John Jando Nkhwazi to stumble on his treasure trove of documents, including this correspondence from Masauko Chipembere written from Harvard on 16 August 1966, and addressed to Dear Brother Chikwakwa and all the Malawi Friends in the Camp. It is a telling tribute to the greatness of the man and his determination to continue the struggle even though many frustrations had set in.

23/8/66 From: H.B.M Chipembere
Harvard, USA.
16th August, 1966

Dear Brother Chikwakwa and all
Malawi friends in the Camp;

I write in reply to the letters I have received from some of you since your arrival in that camp.

First of all I wish to say how deeply I sympathise with you in all the difficulties to which you refer in your letters. It gives me a lot of pain to think that I am unable to do anything to relieve your suffering at the present moment because I am so far away. However, as a result of your letters which have touched me very greatly I have decided to return to Africa earlier than I had planned. I do not think that I can do much to change a state of affairs which is the result and culmination of mistakes which have been made in our own movement since last year. But I wish to come and be with you, my friends and loving brothers of many years, so that I can share in your suffering and so that we can sit together and discuss what should be done next. I dislike the habit of each man moving in his own direction and each man acting as a separate entity, not as a member of a group or a movement. We are men of one group and men who left Malawi for one common reason, to pursue one common purpose or goal. Difficulties have arisen, but they must not make us break up into isolated individuals. Indeed, if we act one by one and not together we shall ruin one another.

There is one thing I know and which strengthens me all the time. It is that the Government and people of Tanzania are our friends and desire to help us. We ourselves sometimes abuse this kindness, but the Tanzanian intention is to help us.

In a camp such as the one to which you have been moved there are bound to be difficulties of the pioneer type. Every beginning comes with problems. But as you settle in, you will find changes coming, however slowly.

As you know, I never agreed with the idea of leaving Malawi to go and fight tyrant Banda from outside. Through every possible means I tried to point out that leaving Malawi for Tanzania was not the right way to fight the monster, and this is why I tried to remain in Malawi, and to fight from the forests to the best of my ability. It was not until illness made me too weak to fight or wait that I left the country. Any nonsense that weapons could not have been found in Malawi is disproved by the fact that I managed to collect 72 guns and rifles in my constituency alone (from the people) in two months. When we stormed one police station and made it surrender we captured 82 more guns and rifles, as well as thousands of rounds of ammunition. If my health had not broken down we were going to seize more and more weapons from the enemy, and there were men in the army and police willing to obtain such weapons for us from their places of work. I believe that through this process we were eventually going to wear down Banda's resistance and win vic; however long it was going to ta But this idea was laughed at and mocked!!!

If I were a man of pettiness and spite, I would stay outside Africa for 5 or so more years, so that you could prove to me that Tanzania was the best place from which to fight Banda, and not Malawi itself. I would have given you a chance to prove your theory to me, the theory of basing a struggle outside the country, not within.

But I have decided to forget all the past mockery and all the past mistakes and come to join you my brothers in your moment of sadness and hardship. I bear no grudge against any man. When I come I will come as everybody's friend and will want to meet each man. In the meantime please co-operate fully with the authorities, especially the Commandant and his staff. Yrs. Chip

It was clear that the freedom fighters felt that they were on a winning path. At this phase of the struggle, Dr Banda was still dealing with widespread unrest and had not yet been able to cow a population still filled with nationalist fervour aroused over the previous few years of struggle and organising for independence. Chipembere had a lot of credibility with the people of Malawi and a widespread following. His choice of rooting his struggle in his home base in the Malindi area ensured solid local support. His untimely illness robbed the resistance of their leader at a critical moment.

He addressed the letter to his 'Friends in the Camp' in sympathy with their plight. Regrettably, by 1966, when he decided to return from the United States and join them in Tanzania the splits and differences among the exiled leaders had grown very apparent and become hurtful. Despite the bitter differences, he demonstrates in his letter a magnanimity of spirit, which was unable to survive the internecine politicking that had taken over the Malawian refugee community.

Thengo Maloya was an MP at the time of Banda's Cabinet coup. After trying to appease Dr Banda and find a middle path, he joined 'Chip' and his forces in the bush.

Thengo Maloya

I was arrested in Zomba. I was there for almost one week..... Then after about a week I saw two policemen, they were in civilian clothes.... "We have been asked to arrest you. After arresting [you], we think it is possible you may [go] missing, so we don't want that. We don't want to make you missing. So we are asking you to move away." Imagine! Police officers who were sympathetic to us.... I had never run away in my life. That's when I knew the matter was serious. I went in to my mother.... and said good bye to my mother....

So I left and that is when I now started joining Chipembere. I went to Mangochi and found Mr Chipembere in hiding....This should have been in October... He was already in hiding. There was a young man who was feeding us. He would prepare us food at his sister Mary's home and then go the other direction and it was carried from Chipembere's home to a certain point.... We didn't trust anybody with our lives. From there we would make zigzags.... We would come very close. Meanwhile, many people thought we were very far away in the mountains, but we were close to the lake at Kamoto village. This is where the guerrilla warfare was planned.... As I said, people would prepare food and take it to the mountain, but we would take that food and bring it to the village right near the lake....

It was only when one of our agents was arrested.... He used to get in some bullets, so he was arrested and we were unable to get any bullets....

The sinking of the ferry is what precipitated some of us to go away. ...... The army was divided. Most of the army was pro-Chipembere and the message they sent was that they would help in the coup d'etat.... Two weeks after I had left... they broke into the Fort Johnston boma[2] to get the guns, to get the vehicles, anything they could use.... That was also a wise move with a popular uprising. Then on the way they met a person, a white man who was innocently going to Monkey Bay.... People wanted to get his car and kill him... and Chipembere said, "No! No! No! ...." [and they let him go]. That was a big mistake, because this man came to Mangochi and saw the trouble at Mangochi and he is the one that reported the incident from Monkey Bay. So the message was transmitted to Zomba and the soldiers came in at Liwonde crossing. There was a ferry there. So they were on the other side. This team with Chipembere came in on the ... western side. The soldiers were on the eastern side and the ferry was pulled by chance, by providence ... to stop it from crossing.... When the people came to the crossing they wanted to call the ferry to keep the appointment to go meet the people at Mulunguzi and arrest Dr Banda. Then some people were going to move from Blantyre and answer the call.

Silombera took his role, he was the leader, a soldier..., but by then he was tame. Chipembere had tamed him... Later after this failed at the ferry and they discovered it was the army on the other side, it was a matter of running away. This is where everybody ran his own direction except a few. Now they were moving away from the house along the lakeshore. Now it was real war, being hunted by the soldiers... after Chipembere had gone to the United States, Silombera became the leader, but he was not a good person. This Silombera put me in more troubles as an individual. He was hunting for chiefs who were pro-Dr Banda...One of the chiefs was my chief and the home was just very close to mine... he killed chief Nyambe, killed the other chiefs, killed the village headmen,... Silombera put petrol on the house and lit it.....

Thengo Maloya had been sent on an external mission by the guerrilla resistance to garner international support before the fateful ferry incident and so he missed the events he relates here but they are very similar to other accounts of this incident. He describes his escape from the country.

I was out. I had put on a police uniform and looked like a police officer and another person.... carried me to Monkey Bay in a police uniform. People thinking I was a police officer. Then from there I went on Ilala ship. We were four people travelling to Mbamba Bay [Tanzania].... Kanyama drove all the way from Dar es Salaam to greet us. He was very good. He was fluent in

---

2 A small fort or district government offices.

Swahili...."*Ali Sikelo came and Siliya and John Chipembere, they were the people who escaped mysteriously.*"

7.2 Early exile - 1964-66

John Jando Nkhwazi (JJN) and Kapote Mwakasungura (AKM) both left Malawi after the Cabinet Crisis of September 1964 with the Banda regime hot on their heels. We interviewed them together and despite not having seen each other for many years and recalling long distant 40-year-old memories, they picked up the threads of their story seamlessly passing the narrative back and forth like a well-rehearsed dance team.

(JJN) Life was not bad then. We shared stories [of how we escaped]. The ex-ministers were coming to visit us. They came as a team the first time. They visited us together. The frequency would begin to disappear. We thought it was for security reasons. Then later we began seeing them come one by one. This one comes. He selects a few people. People could see this. Maybe they are relatives and they are discussing [family] things. Maybe tomorrow this one comes and discusses with a few. Later it began to be rumoured that these people are disagreeing. What is the problem? We couldn't know, but then we said okay.... It doesn't matter. We shall remain one, until they come and split us....

Later on there was a sense of insecurity. How can we defend ourselves? If now these people [Banda's thugs] start coming, hunting for us, we don't have anything, so how can we defend ourselves? We began to pressurise these people [the ex-ministers]. "Are we going to stay like this forever? Banda's thugs are going to come armed and we are left without any knowledge of how to defend ourselves. Can't you discuss with all these people around [the senior Tanzanians that the Ministers knew]. Why can't they teach us?" Later, somehow they agreed with some few officials from this way and that way, so we began to get some small training somewhere, just for defense purposes....

When the [Tanzanian] government began to see that there was a misunderstanding between these people [ex-Ministers]. They feared that we were going to split and it would happen as it did with the Congolese, who started killing each other. So they decided to shift us from Dar es Salaam to Pangale; that was 1966.

Carson Kayuni, Machipisa Munthali and Frank Jiya all tell of how they were sent to China or Cuba for military training. It was a busy, exciting time and they were strongly committed to returning to the country to overthrow the dictatorship. For the first two years, the exiled ministers maintained unity and carried out a programme of training and military sorties. There was a strong sense of unity and purpose amongst leaders and the larger refugee community. Many people refused to integrate into the host country workforce in order to reserve their total commitment for the struggle to return to their homeland.

AKM The problem began at the Bulani camp in Dar es Salaam because every minister wanted his team of loyalists. Yatuta had his own. Chipembere had his own. Kanyama had his own. Ching'oli Chirwa, the same. Except for Bwanausi. He had gone to Zambia. During the 1965 period, that was when the tactic was to send sorties of 10 or 5 people but all of them with loyalty to a minister. Yatuta sent his people to Karonga. Kanyama sent his people to Rumphi. Ching'oli sent his to Nkhata Bay.

JJN Chipembere sent his to Blantyre. Machipisa led the team that was going to Rumphi under Kanyama. Kayuni was at the head of people sent by Yatuta to Karonga and Chitipa...to Nkhata Bay, it was Ching'oli's young brother [who led that team]. Munthali was the biggest victim of those sorties, but the others managed to come back.... He was captured, because he refused to listen to the advice of his comrades. When they were returning, he said, "You go ahead. I will just stay..." He said he was not sent to fight, they all did, but they were armed.

The sorties ended as the Malawi Congress Party apparatus firmly imposed its iron rule and security network over the whole country. In addition, there was less and less unity amongst the leadership in exile, as Kapote explains:

...the fighters realised they were being sacrificed, because all of them [the ex-ministers] were afraid to accompany them on these sorties.

7.3 Yatuta Incursion

Accounts of the Yatuta incursion are still written with the bias of the Banda regime. It has yet to receive the attention and recognition it deserves. The operation was clearly an extension of the nationalist independence struggle through the 1950s and early 1960s. The participants and their many supporters saw the need to fight against the subversion of the independence struggle by the Banda dictatorship. Theirs was a very principled and dedicated commitment to freedom and even today, many years after the incident, those involved in and around the action remember it in vivid detail. That it was viewed differently by the Banda regime is understandable. That other refugees could celebrate its failure was reprehensible. But that it should be relegated to less than a footnote in history and its heroes, in unmarked graves, lost to memory without mention is a travesty.

There had been bickering amongst the leadership of the armed resistance, over who would lead the fighters. As early as 1966, the united front initially presented by the exiled ministers had begun to crumble. During his early career in Tanganyika, Yatuta Chisiza had risen to a very senior position in the colonial police force. After Banda's return in 1958, Yatuta was responsible for his security, and became the Minister of Home Affairs in the first independence cabinet. While Yatuta was committed to leading a force of trained fighters into Malawi, the other ministers refused to personally go into battle. However, those who were reluctant to accompany the fighters, feared that if Yatuta led the guerrilla force and succeeded in overthrowing Banda, he might very well leave them out in the cold when it came time to form a government. As a result, the other ministers called back all the trained men who were loyal to them, thus dividing the fighting force. Loyalties to the individual ministers really manifested themselves after this, largely along a Chipembere – Yatuta divide. Chipembere and the rest of the ministers remained under the PanAfrican Democratic Party (PDP), with Chipembere as the leader and Kanyama as deputy. Yatuta stood alone with his Ufulu Umodzi Malawi Party (UUMA) and carried through with his vow to return and fight inside the country.

The pundits of guerrilla warfare at the time Mao Tse Tung, Fidel Castro and Che Guevara espoused the idea that a small spark can cause a prairie fire. In their view, a small, highly motivated group of well trained, ideologically minded and well armed cadre could begin a guerrilla war that would lead to a successful outcome, as in China and Cuba. Yatuta and his group saw their effort as the spark and expected it to fan the flame of internal support for their effort. Regrettably, the support did not materialise.

His group was very small, 17 in all, but well armed, highly trained and highly motivated. On the day of the battle in October 1967, oral accounts from participants recount that Yatatu's forces fought almost the entire day and that the Malawi Army was backed by Rhodesian forces. In a sad twist of fate, the leader was the first to die on the first encounter leaving a demoralised cadre behind. Yatuta Chisiza, Lutengano Mwahimba and Felix Mwayambwile lay dead on the battlefield, while seven were captured alive and five managed to escape back to Zambia. Of the entire group, only Frank Jiya was still alive to contribute to this project.[3]

Carson Kayuni was one of the trained guerrillas loyal to Yatuta and would have been on the incursion to Mwanza but for a stroke of bad luck. Through his narrative one can sense his commitment to struggle and determination to fight on. He had fled Malawi after being seriously wounded from a savage beating at the hands of the MYP.

When I got better, I started getting involved in guerrilla warfare, I trained in guerrilla warfare. I refused to take any job in exile pending one day to go home. I went to Cuba where I met Sam Nujoma [leader of the Namibian liberation struggle] and these friends of ours from South Africa, Oliver Tambo [leader of the South African liberation struggle]. We were with Nyirenda, I

---

3 We were only able to identify 15 of the 17 fighters.

was with Lutengano Mwahimba, Jomo Chikwakwa ... Michael Mwambande. We had Chisausau Msowoya.[4]

Coming back we started [mid-1967]. I was put to the section of reconnaissance, through Kyera, through Sumba Wanga. So the trip of this fighting of Mwanza, I paved the way for these fighters [who] moved from Dar to Pangale to Mwanza [Malawi]. It was me. The way I moved. I left Tabora. I was staying at Pangale Camp. I went from Pangale for Mpanda, Sumba Wanga to Chesa on the border of Tanzania and Zambia. I had no passport, so to go through there I had to drop [from the bus] and move this side of Tanzania along the hills making marks where these guerrilla fighters would be moving to the other side of Zambia....

Then I went to near Lake Tanganyika where I found Amnon Phiri. We need you Amnon. We left from Lake Tanganyika for Abercorn [now Mbala in Zambia]. From Abercorn, we proceeded to a certain place where I had made a mark so the car to take these guerrilla fighters should stop there. We removed tires, pretending to be repairing in case they haven't arrived. I showed him [how to pick up the fighters]. I came back to Tabora and I reported to Dar es Salaam. [They said], "You went alone. You may be dead or missing, so you have to walk it with a second man." So I had to take the same route with George Akogogo [Kanyanya]. After coming back is when we sent a telegram indicating that a baby boy is born....This is how Chisiza had to leave....

We had an oath, of course. We had a dove. We had ground peas black and you put it in your mouth. Then you had a cigarette of opium. .... We had the dove and made a small cut and took a drop of that blood in our mouths. We swore never to disclose anything if we were arrested. "I will die on my oath, no matter how much torture. I am not going to disclose [anything] even under torture...."

Yatuta stood up and said a word to my mother. "Pray for us." Mother prayed, prayed, prayed. "Go in peace. That is your home. Souls of all who died should protect you." Yatuta took hold of the hands of my mother and he said, "We are going home. In case of good luck we will meet at home. In case of bad luck, heaven will tell..."

.... After Chisiza arrived in Tabora, for security reasons the whole shoot [18 guerrillas] had to hide. They gave me money to buy tickets from Tabora to Mpanda by train. While I was at the window, I think one of the police had to wonder about all the tickets I was buying. When I came out from there, immediately, I handed over those tickets [to my comrades]. That policeman

---

4 There may be a memory issue here because, according to other sources, Jomo Chikwakwa was sent to China for training and Ian Kasambo Munthali and others were in Cuba with him.

was looking for me and I was arrested. Searching me they found me with one ticket only. "Where are the rest of the tickets? There is only one ticket...." They took me to the police [station] and detained me. My friends left. They left the word that if Carson is released, he should not follow us, he should take Kyera route and start from Karonga because I knew who to contact. One of them was this Mordecai Gondwe and another Dan Mphotwa.

I stayed in custody for 42 days, until someone came to bail me... We were refugees. We were not allowed to leave the camp without permission of the camp commander. When I was released, it is when the news came that Chisiza had been shot. I was called to Dar es Salaam and then sent to Kyera. There I sent for Dan Mphotwa who brought me a newspaper which was bearing the picture of Yatuta after he had been shot. I took this newspaper to Dar es Salaam and then we knew that it was true that he was dead. We conducted a very limited funeral [for Yatuta] together with Lutengano Mwahimba.

Frank Jiya was a member of the incursion force. In response to a question about what they hoped to accomplish he explained:

Frank Jiya

To start with, we were saying that we were not going to fight with the army as such. Our target was Dr Banda. As we were discussing, we agreed that it is Banda behind almost all the atrocities in the country. Once that one is not there everything else will change. Why? Because we believed Malawians were being dictated by Dr Banda himself and the Malawi Congress Party. The way we analysed it, the way Dr Banda was running the government administration and the party, we concluded that it was a one-man party, a one-man government. Dr Banda appointed almost everybody to positions. He appointed people to the National Executive. He appointed people to become officials in the regular positions of the party. He even appointed chairmen of the district committees. He went on appointing people of his liking in various positions. So we were saying that the government is Dr Banda.... We concluded it is just Dr Banda. "Once this man disappears, then Malawians will be able to sit down and talk to each other and find solutions to the problems created by this monster."

So we targetted Dr Banda. Wrongly or rightly... we underrated... somehow, somewhere, we must admit to say we underrated this... because before you get to Dr Banda, you meet many who will try to defend him. So in the process you meet the police, the intelligence, the army, whatever.... So somehow, somewhere we underrated this one... Our aim was to do away with the man.

The strategy was to get into Malawi and not to start fighting far away from Blantyre or the cities. Why? Because we thought we could convince our brothers in uniform just as Chipembere had talked and convinced them that time.

That failure made Dr Banda get organised. So we knew it was going to be difficult.... Our job was to get there, get in touch with our contacts. We wanted to organise ourselves [clandestinely]. We wanted to beef up our weaponry. The army took over from the colonials and whatever they took over from there were not the arms to talk about. ... We had superior arms. Malawians as a people are fighters, but a fighter cannot fight without weapons, real materials to use. We wanted to renew our contacts, hit and run here and there until they recognised our being around....

Jiya describes the trip through Tanzania, Zambia and Portuguese controlled Mozambique until they arrived in the lower Shire River valley near Mwanza.

Unfortunately we did not cross the Shire to the other side. We were cornered [at the Shire] not because they were clever enough to trace us. Unfortunately, it was the baboons who started making noise. We managed. We travelled. We fought several battles. We split this group there and this group somewhere [else]. But the group of seven which was the command unit. My group, the Yatuta unit. We never fought anybody. While in Mwanza, we were forced to talk to chiefs, because people were coming. "You have come at the right time here. Dr Banda's government is oppressive. Agriculture products, we are forced to go and sell in Mozambique. Here we have no markets.... Please. Please help us." So we talked to them... my comrades were Tumbuka speaking, so I was spokesperson communicating with those people..... They wanted to join us. "No. We will call on you when we are ready. Meanwhile, we just want to do it ourselves...."

Unfortunately, the police got the information and came. They found us somewhere. We were trying to cross.... So they came in a LandRover. We were hiding... and we saw them. They entered the area. They didn't know some [of us] were this side and some that side. Some were behind. They entered our trap where we could just finish them. We said [to them] our weapons are not for people like you, but you can only become a target should you resist or try to defend something you do not know, you do not understand. You will become a target and we will show you. But as of now, I am giving you five minutes to clear [out] or I ask you to drop your guns. They are not guns. To us, they are just sticks.... Their leader tried to resist. I started counting. Five. Four. Three. They started trembling. They jumped into the LandRover and called everyone else, I think they were seven of them.... We said we are not interested in that small vehicle - not even your guns. We have more than enough. Please go back and tell him that "Yes they are around. They haven't killed us. They are not after us." They left.... We walked quickly and disappeared.

When we got to the Shire River.... we found some small canoes to cross. Let's [hide out] somewhere so we get here during the night when it's dark. We used to see military planes, the small Beavers flying along the Shire. When it was just around three, the baboons started to make noise because we were in the thicket of the forest just along the Shire.... In Malawi we were some 7 or 10 days or so....

This [other] group met and fought.... They said Felix Mwayambwile committed suicide.... We don't know. So the baboons started making noise. I was somewhere. I was the most used person for reconnaissance.... Then I saw someone in uniform, from afar. Who is that one? Baboons were making noise.... Enemy, in Malawi military uniform. He [the Banda soldiers] started shouting. I informed my comrades, Yatuta my immediate boss. I said, "Prepare yourselves, we are about to enter into battle. The enemy has appeared. We have been seen." And with this noise [of the baboons], we went somewhere down, down. So I said, "We cannot fight from here because here they will finish us by using hand grenades or whatever bomb thrown into here. We will not be able to climb [out].... Let's climb slowly. When we are at a level where we are able to see far that's when we will engage them." We agreed and started coming up. We reached a summit where it was clear now. We saw them from afar. Far away there. They were shouting "Ipha, sim'bale wako. Sim'bale wako." Kill. Kill. Kill. It's an enemy. They are not your friend… They were many. They were coming. We agreed we should target those we saw to be leaders.... We were aiming. They were shooting aimlessly, but we agreed we should aim at certain individuals we believed were their leaders "Ipha sim'bale wake."

In the process, some discovered where we had come from and they used that same [route] behind us from where we had climbed out. From there, that is where the bullet that killed Yatuta Chisiza came from. They hit Lutengano Mwahimba. I saw him lying down just like this. I knew he is hit and then Yatuta who was close to me. First of all, just before that Yatuta exploded a bomb, a bazooka.... There was confusion in the enemy camp because they could not see. That was number one .When the dust was settling...Yatuta wanted to shift moving from this place to check on these people not knowing that someone has now come from behind... That's the one who shot Yatuta. I saw him going up. Down.... He was not shot from behind... He was moving trying to get around and [he exposed himself.] He was hit in the tummy. He went up. The air inside you takes you up. I saw him going up and I knew he was hit. They pumped in several bullets then or else they pumped into him when they collected the body. I guessed we were still five left.... I got hit by the same person. I never said anything. I remained quiet... I signalled Kanyanya and told him Yatuta was no more. The enemy shooting stopped.

We exchanged fire for about one hour.... Once it was quiet, I decided to spray whatever I had to clear the way. I stood up and checked and decided to take my five comrades from here. We stood up and the five of us left and disappeared. We were walking in the dark.... We agreed to withdraw. We went some distance before I told them I had been hit. Blood all over my uniform. I had to use a knife because it was a Soviet type of uniform.... I had no medicine, so I used urine. My comrades wanted me to surrender to avoid dying. I said "No. Surrendering is as good as committing suicide. " I will die along the way rather than committing suicide by surrendering to Dr Banda. They agreed to walk me back to where I could enter a safe hospital.... We were walking back. We walked and walked... we were fighting battles with the Portuguese, but we were trying to avoid that.... It healed on the way, before we arrived in Zambia and when I entered the hospital it had dried up.....

I was reminded by Rose Chibambo that the day Yatuta was killed was the same day her husband died, 22 September 1967. The other group was fighting battles. The rest were captured before our battle. They told us that only for us to hear but wait for the next day and we would hear that they fought another battle....[5]

The other group lost one to suicide [Felix Mwayambwile]. All the others were apprehended, captured. They would not have given themselves up. They too fought a battle. They were captured maybe when they tried to withdraw, they went into the army's trap.

They were captured in 1967. Dr Banda hastily constituted a kangaroo court, I say kangaroo court because traditional chiefs cannot try treason cases.... Banda confused the legal fraternity by saying that the best people to try a treason are the chiefs. He would call them, brief them and meeting them every afternoon after the court sits until these people and ourselves the surviving five were all sentenced to death. We were sentenced to death, the five of us in absentia. The rest went to Zomba Prison. February 1968, they were executed. Mwambande survived as a state witness.... He only saved his life and not his freedom. He led a miserable life until his death.

The Yatuta incursion was an important moment in Malawian history, one that reveals the courageous determination to overthrow Banda. It is a sadly overlooked chapter with a devastating conclusion. Yatuta Chisiza died on the field of battle, as did Luthengano Mwahimba. Felix Mwayambwile committed suicide rather than be taken alive. Seven were captured, Simon Chidawathe, Harry Phombeya, Simon Moyo, Jhimo Mwambetania, Raphael Kamanga, his nephew and Micheal Mwambande. The first six were hanged. Michael Mwambande turned State witness to save his life and died in Zomba Prison.

---

[5] They were listening in to the government station which was broadcasting disinformation.

The five survivors of the incursion were George Akogo Kanyanya, Frank Jiya, Ian Munthali, Stain Msiska and Manson Chiumia, who all managed to escape to Zambia.

Mary Mwale lost her husband, Lutengano Mwahimba, in the battle. She is bitter that this important piece of history has been so little recognised.

It is a very long story... they died in vain.. Even the daughter thinks he must have been 'chigawenga', because nobody speaks about him.... They remember Chilembwe and the events of 1915, but not 1967. How did President Muluzi remember somebody from 1915 but not 1967.... What is it about?

7.4 Post 1967 - The Political Vacuum

Up to early 1966, there was a united front and Yatuta fought under that banner. All the ex-ministers had cooperated in sending militants to Algeria, China and Cuba for military training. After their training, the fighters were waiting for deployment when the ministers started to in-fight. Thereafter the parties that evolved were formed around specific leaders who promoted their cults of personalities. Meanwhile the PDP tried to fill the vacuum that was left by the departure of Yatuta as a united political force.

The refugees had already broken into the Washington and Saigon camps in the debate over armed struggle. As relations deteriorated between the former ministerial allies, Kanyama left the PDP and established the Congress for a Second Republic (CSR) with himself as President and tried to undermine the large base of support that Chipembere still commanded within the exile community. Everyone claimed to be acting in the name of freedom and democracy but nothing was really happening which played nicely into Dr Banda's hands. The dark veil of repression at home and disunity abroad is what we call the political vacuum which continued from 1967 till 1974.

Yatuta's death marked the end of military resistance to Dr Banda's dictatorship and almost smothered all anti-Banda political activity amongst the Malawians in exile. With the death of the Yatuta heroes, the refugee community was left demoralised. Banda had won the day. Even Dr Banda feared Yatuta the most for his bravery, strength and capacity to lead an effective military opposition. Once he was eliminated, Banda felt little or no threat from the other exiled ministers. Even more telling was how the incursion reflected the tensions in the refugee community. Some people mourned the loss of their comrades, but others apparently were happy that they had failed. Mary Mwale tells of hearing celebrating from the Washington side of Pangale camp when news came back of Yatuta's death.

For the next six or seven years there was a political vacuum. The National Chairman of the Socialist League of Malawi (Lesoma), Attati Mpakati summed up the situation of the exiles in a speech he made at a meeting of the Malawi Support Committee in London in 1980:

.... The opposition, however, suffered many setbacks; lack of unity, political immaturity, and the underestimation of Banda's ruthlessness. These factors combined to weaken any organized opposition to Malawi's dictator. Indeed, the opponents of Banda's rule remained fragmented, lacking the co-ordination and direction of an organized grouping. During this period of confusion, Banda consolidated his power and entrenched his personal control throughout Malawi. (In Review of African Political Economy, Vol. 7 No. 19 (Winter 1980), pp96-99.)

Lesoma's entry onto the scene contributed to further splintering. Orton Chirwa was very unhappy that the Lesoma initiative had bypassed him and that he had not automatically been invited to take the leadership as the senior of the ousted ministers. He could not accept a secondary role, so he and his wife, Vera, set up the Malawi Freedom Movement (Mafremo) in 1974 in Dar es Salaam as a counterweight to the Lesoma initiative. In any case, times had changed from the 1950s and inspired by their hosts and the wars of Southern African liberation, Lesoma had adopted a socialist programme which neither Kanyama Chiume nor Orton Chirwa could have accepted. Ideologically they were probably just as distrustful of socialism as Dr Banda was.

7.5 The Lesoma contribution
Origins

In the same speech, Dr Mpakati explained the logic underpinning the creation of Lesoma.

....Thus in 1974 after a number of abortive attempts to overthrow President Banda, The Socialist League of Malawi was formed to achieve the reorganization of Malawi's exiles and to build an internal party network within the country itself. In this way, we are working to create the conditions necessary for the successful overthrow of the Banda regime and the creation of a democratic and socialist society.

By 1974, the message was clear amongst exiles young and old. They were tired. They did not want to die in exile. Lesoma, the Socialist League of Malawi, was established as a new kind of party representing people from all walks of life and cutting across the various divisions. The call for action came from the younger generation as well as from older unhappy militants. It appealed to a membership that cut across the linguistic, geographic and ethnic divisions exploited by tribalists like Dr Banda. The founders acted on the recognition that the 1964 crisis was not a personal power struggle between Banda and the ex-ministers but between democracy and dictatorship, between progress and reaction. The exiles had learned from the progressive examples of Tanzania, Mozambique and Zambia and were inspired by the revolutionary spirit of the Southern African liberation movements.

Lesoma brought a new level of organisation. It was membership based and followed the principles of democratic centralism. It established regional and national representation among the exiles throughout Tanzania and Zambia then later to Zimbabwe after it gained independence in 1980. Lesoma was well structured and active. It had a dynamic youth wing, military training, education and scholarships, foreign affairs, as well as committees in national and regional localities.

Different allegiances that had arisen amongst the followers of the exiled ministers were overcome to rally around the new formation. Professor Michongwe came from the Chipembere camp as did Attati Mpakati and Jomo Chikwakwa. From the Kanyama side came John Jando Nkhwazi and Chisausau Msowoya. George Aghogho Kanyanya, Carson Kayuni and Mundu Mwambetania, Yatuta loyalists, threw their hats in with Lesoma to all together make a very strong and formidable grouping.

John Jando Nkhwazi (JJN) and Kapote Mwakasungura (AKM) were two of Lesoma's founding members. They were re-united in Mzuzu after many years to tell the story of founding Lesoma in a joint interview.

JJN Chirwa came to see us in Dar and asked why they had been left out. "We have been here for ten years and nothing is happening...." After we had seen that nothing was happening, we began discussing. What about the people inside? People are suffering. And we just keep quiet and look at them there. We may not go there to fight as our friends did... but we can still rescue people. Let's try and work out so we try to look for scholarships. Let's collect people from inside and send them for education. And send them for sensitisation and..... make them feel we are still with them....

AKM - Another major motivation was the forthcoming independence of Mozambique. So we got equally motivated. If Mozambicans can be free, we will get more space to argue for our case... and then Chipembere also died.... so that set free many people who would have opposed joining or even the formation of Lesoma.

AKM - In fact, we first called it the Progressive League of Malawi...

JJN - When we were forming it. So when we were telling our friends in Zambia

AKM - I had gone to Lusaka for research on my Masters. There I met people like Akogo Kanyanya, Suzgo Kabuzi Munthali, Frank Jiya and many others. So they went through the programme document and one of them says, "Ah you Kapote. Why are you being shy or timid? This is a socialist programme. Why don't you just call it the Socialist League of Malawi?"

JJN - "The name and the content are not together. You are talking about socialism but you are calling it Progressive Party."

AKM - So when I came back, I told my comrades, that our friends are happy with calling it the Socialist League of Malawi....

…. to add more spice we had to get Jomo Chikwakwa from Pangale to come and be with us at Mwenge. He was very important for many reasons. One, he is a very steadfast person. He was very loyal to Chipembere and at the same time he is a man who has no tribalism in him. His thinking is always along military lines. So it was good for the party. He was from Chiradzulu. [In] 1976 we continued making branches in Tanzania, Zambia, Eastern Europe and even Zimbabwe.

JJN - Reginald [Mhango] was posted there just after Zimbabwe independence.

AKM - He had been seconded to start the newspaper, so he too went and started a branch of Lesoma there. The headquarters was literally his [JJN] house. He was the secretariat and he did a wonderful job really.

JJN - ...and we also got Mpakati to Lusaka at the United Nations Institute for Nambia…. Then later we discussed with the Mozambican government. We have our leader here... "Oh he can come here."

AKM - … then he got a job at the Central Bank of Mozambique.

….We kept on organising right until the [1993 multiparty] referendum. We could count the number of Malawians who were not with Lesoma [in Dar es Salaam]. They knew about us. They supported our cause.

JJN - Each time I went to Europe for a conference, we would find students who were supporting us…. Just imagine. We were able to ferry young men from inside the country to come to Tanzania, I was responsible for making passports for them [UN Travel Documents]. The executive knew just how many we are ferrying from Malawi, Zambia. When they come back most of them used to be trained. They are still here [in Malawi]. They are working in government and so on. We just keep quiet. I have a list of those people. They would infiltrate to do political work and just mix with the crowd.

AKM - We had one fellow at the Central Region Water Board, but he spotted me one time I was in town in Lilongwe, "Mdala you here." Then when I was High Commissioner in Zimbabwe, one young lady came and said, "You know I am one of your students you sent to Cuba." She was a medical doctor.

The Lisbon Conference hosted by the World Peace Council was called on the first anniversary to commemorate the beginning of the Soweto uprising in South Africa June 16, 1976. All the leaders of the exiled liberation movements were present as well as solidarity groups and activists from around the world. Lisbon was the first international conference Lesoma was invited to, just three years after its birth. It was a matter of great interest and enthusiasm that a delegation was to be sent to this conference. Money had to be found even though no one was rich. Rank and file members in Zambia and Tanzania all pitched in and this mobilisation towards a common goal contributed to unifying the new party. The money collected by the Zambian members was needed in Dar es Salaam to buy the air ticket, but transferring money was difficult because of strict currency exchange controls in both Tanzania and Zambia. Doug and Nellie Miller were running the CUSO Zambia office in Lusaka and were very sympathetic to the Lesoma cause. The Zambia Lesoma members gave their office the Zambian kwacha they had raised and CUSO in Dar es Salaam released an equivalent amount in Tanzanian shillings from their bank account to pay for the ticket for Kapote.

AKM - 1977 was that conference that took ... [Doug] and me to Lisbon..... That was a big, big breakthrough for us. Because after that, scholarships started coming. The World Peace Council was always on our side. If there was a conference anywhere, "Lesoma. There is a conference in Burundi, in Algeria, many places." Mundu went to Cairo....

JJN - When he had just returned that is when I left for Ghana....

In Lisbon, the Lesoma delegation interacted with many international delegations and was warmly received as was their message of solidarity and explanation of their struggle. The delegation consisted of Kapote and Mahoma Mwaungulu, who was Lesoma's Eastern European representative. There were many meetings with a number of delegations including the Afro-Asian Solidarity Committee of the Soviet Union, which included several highly placed Politburo apparatchiks. This led to an official recognition of Lesoma and much greater international visibility and credibility as well as substantial support in the form of scholarships.

Lesoma took up the military struggle after the mid-seventies. Cadres were sent for training with the Palestine Liberation Organisation (PLO), China, Libya and several Eastern European countries. The training followed the model of the African National Congress (ANC) of South Africa. The military training was obviously important but political education was the main goal to ready the population for the fight back. Trained cadres skilled at cell formation, information dissemination, political education and gathering intelligence infiltrated the country.

Isyu Mwakasungura described his experience with some of these cadres inside Malawi.

[In] 1980, for Lesoma, we had leaflets. We had circles which were meeting. Some of them came through Zambia and introduced it to us. [From] the Zambia side it was easier to infiltrate Malawi. Internally, we were very secret, although the regular people were not suspected. Some people had family in Zambia. They had no connection with any political problems. So they were free to travel up and down. Those are the people we used as

our connections, knowing that there were certain materials for us inside we were happy with.... So we were encouraged by that. Internally there were certain members of Lesoma who would meet us maybe once in a while at night. Those guys would disappear. We wouldn't even know where they have gone. Such people were frequently young people... especially those along the border like in Karonga and Mchinji side.

Ollen Mwalubunju was a trained cadre who infiltrated Malawi to undertake this clandestine work. He and another militant were leaving the country to rejoin Lesoma in Tanzania when they were intercepted by an MYP patroller. His description of the encounter reveals the sophistication of the training they had received and their courage.

We also had some small passport size photos of people who had been recruited as Lesoma members, young students. Fortunately, they didn't open our bag. Lesoma used to recruit young people inside and send them to the Eastern Bloc, Soviet Union, Bulgaria. They would go for short courses, and when they are back, live in the country and continue their contacts. Even at high school. We even had literature and we knew how to keep it [discretely] because you were in danger. You could get killed and involve other family members. So I was looking for further education and also to participate in the struggle fighting against the regime and perhaps utilise my contacts within the student movement to strengthen the party structures. Young people as you know are always active and adventurous and easy to recruit, and also a source of information and a source of propaganda.... It was much more cell building 5 to 10 people. I could communicate with one or two people and those two people could also communicate in their own way, because we were trying to avoid that information should go into the wrong hands. [We educated ourselves] mostly through literature and those colleagues who had gone out to the communist or socialist countries. They could share their information and some brave ones would conduct a session of two or three people. And those two or three people, each one of them would conduct or orient sessions.

We were carrying pictures and also information on what was happening inside the country. The person I was with had already been recruited and had already gone for short course training and come back to the country. That's also why the issue of the [false] passports and caution. We were going in and out of the country.

I left with a friend through Chitipa side to Tanzania. As we were leaving, we passed through the immigration. Then we walked on foot a distance of approximately 20 kilometres to the Tanzanian border. On our way, it was the night, we missed the path to cross the river to the other side and we were intercepted by a Malawi Young Pioneer. "Where are you going?" We were asking for the path to Tanzania, we want to cross. "No you are running away. You are the young people that have been recruited. We know it and I have to *take you to the police." It was at night and the police station was distance of about 15 kilometres. He decided to take us to the chief's home. He explained to the chief that these are young people running away. "Can you keep them so that tomorrow morning they should be taken to the police station?" The chief was kind enough, he gave us a place.*

[The MYP] was asking so many silly questions. "Do you know Nelson Mandela? Do you know Winnie Mandela?" Obviously these are political figures. They are fighting for justice in South Africa. Their names are all over the radio. So the chief after he left was complaining to us, "You know that person is an informer. I don't know why he is making life very difficult for you people. You're young people. You've explained to him that you are going to a wedding of your sister who is being married on the other side," because that was our story... We had some champagne and all sorts of things....

[The next morning] Went by bicycle to the police station. It was four hours away.... We wrote our statements. Our passports showed that we had passed through immigration. We had stamps. The police said there was no case. So we slept at the police station. Sichale took us home for a bath and food and we slept with the police. [In the morning] ...we hired bicycles, we picked up our documents and entered Tanzania.... We finally met [the] leaders of Lesoma at Morogoro and met Lesoma cadres. [By] 1990, access to scholarships became a challenge as the USSR was collapsing so support to liberation movements began to waver.

We were part of the student movement of Lesoma. We attended the World Congress of Students sponsored by the socialist wings. I went to Ethiopia and Uganda. I was on the executive of the Tanzania Chapter. We went to Makerere and we used those forums to tell the world what was happening in Malawi to combat the Western pro-Banda propaganda.

Lesoma grew into the largest and most organised of the exile movements. It remained true to its democratic roots and escaped the personality cults that dominated the other groupings. It remained politically principled and disciplined right up until the first democratic elections when it effectively dissolved itself into the United Front for Multiparty Democracy (UFMD) in the interests of opposition unity.

7.6 Internal opposition

The 1983 Mwanza incident proved to be a pivotal event for the iron triumvirate at the top of the Banda regime. Since the 'orality' of dictatorship meant that such internal debates were never recorded, much of the background information to the incident was passed from person to person and gravitated between rumour and fact. Nonetheless, the split in the MCP that opened up over the succession issue at that time destabilised the throne and those immediately behind it.

The story has it that Dr Banda wanted to go to England on sabbatical and appoint John Tembo as acting president in his absence. At the time, Tembo was Treasurer-General of the MCP and Governor of the Reserve Bank. The constitution stipulated that the Secretary-General of the MCP and two senior Cabinet Ministers would fill the role of President in the case of the incumbent being unable to do so. When some senior ministers pointed out that Tembo did not fulfill those conditions, Banda felt that his authority was being challenged and saw disloyalty in their pointing out his mistake. They paid very dearly for their temerity.

In 1995, after the democratic dispensation, Justice Michael Mtegha was appointed to chair a Commission of Inquiry to establish the circumstances around the deaths of the Mwanza Four.

….The Mwanza Commission, as it came to be called, found that on the night of May 18-19, 1983, Ministers Aaron Gadama, Dick Matenje and John Twaibu Sangala and David Chiwanga, member of parliament for Chikwawa, were taken to a remote spot on the Mwanza Road, beaten with sharp instruments, including hammers, thrown into Matenje's blue Peugeot, and pushed over a steep incline into a ravine. This was done to make the murders look like a car accident. Police officers admitted to having carried out the murders, and it was widely believed that they were acting on instructions issuing from the highest level of government. In the subsequent criminal trial, the prosecution tried to argue that such an act could not have been perpetrated without the knowledge of the president and his close associates, given the assumed monopoly of political power by a small number of people. (Powers, p171)

While they got away with this travesty of justice, it was the beginning of the end of people's patience with the repression and fear. It took another decade to remove the dictatorship, but the story of how the ministers had died and for what reason as well as the injustice of the treatment meted out to the families thereafter was so widespread that it could not be wiped from the collective memory. Ollen Mwalubunju was in secondary school at the time and experienced the event with one of his classmates first-hand.

…. Three senior cabinet ministers … were assassinated on the assumption that they were trying to run away. They were assassinated around Mwanza

district *[along with]* a Member of Parliament called Chiwanga. Chiwanga had two sons. One of them was our classmate at Blantyre Secondary School.

When the news broke students were quite concerned about the situation. Of course, the state radio was giving the other side of the story. We had the inside story because the son of one of the victims was our classmate. The real story was that they were killed and then dragged, pushed into a vehicle disguised as [if] they were involved in an accident. Of course the family members knew exactly what had happened, even within the Banda regime there were also networks. Some were sympathetic to the three senior cabinet ministers. We understand they were assassinated because of the transition arrangement. They... opposed Dr Banda [who] wanted John Tembo who happened to be an uncle to the Official Hostess and these senior ministers resisted. More especially Dick Matenje who was more senior as the Secretary General of the Malawi Congress Party, so that was the scenario.

[After] there was a lot of intimidation and also the hostel where we used to sleep there was a lot of security officers in plain clothes to see what was happening around. They knew that the truth of the matter would have been known by the family members.

Dr Banda abandoned his intention to take a sabbatical leave. In that sense, it was a defeat for Dr Banda and a tribute to the courage of those ministers and MPs who stood by the constitution even at the risk of their lives.

By 1990, change was in the air all around the world. Solidarnosc (Solidarity), the independent Polish trade union movement slowly whittled away against its totalitarian regime until the communists stepped down. Perestroika was introduced into the Union of Soviet Socialist Republics (USSR) and within months the fall of the Berlin Wall led to the implosion of the Soviet Empire. The most important event in Southern Africa was the release of the mighty Nelson Mandela in February 1990. The change forced upon the intractable white racist regime of South Africa made it possible to dream of change elsewhere.

In Malawi, resentment was present, but could not be publicly registered under the regime of silence and state of terror. Nonetheless, resentment simmered under the surface and by early March 1992, Malawi was ripe for change.

The Turning Point

Pope John Paul II had worked behind the scenes in his homeland, Poland, to bring about the end of communist rule. In May of 1989, he ended a nine day tour of Africa in Malawi and privately urged the local bishops to take a public position on the abusive aspects of the Banda dictatorship and the lack of free speech. After the 1964 Cabinet Crisis, the majority of churches in Malawi had remained submissive and silent in face of the widespread and heavy-handed repression.

The Pastoral Letter or Lenten Letter of March 1992 represented a key turning point. Eight Catholic bishops signed their names publicly to a document that gave a critique, in polite but clear terms, of the system which had been in place for 28 years. Much as it is famous for the change it triggered, we found it was a hard document to acquire in Malawi. In the course of our research we visited the Mzuzu University of the North (Mzuni) Library to offer a transcript Machipisa Munthali had given us for their archives. While there, we explored their Malawiana collection and could not find the 1992 Lenten Letter. Nor could we find Dunduzu Chisiza's *Africa What Lies Ahead,* or even a copy of Justice Mtegha's inquiry report written as recently as 1995 on the Mwanza incident. As a result, we are including a copy of the *Pastoral Letter of the Catholic Bishops of Malawi* in the appendix so that readers can refer to this historic document in full.

The cumulative frustration of the Malawian people and the work of a variety of activists became an explosive combination. Not unexpectedly, the regime's reaction was to arrest and interrogate the bishops. University students in Zomba demonstrated in protest and spontaneous demonstrations occurred in other major centres. The regime responded with heavy-handed police intervention, but the demonstrators did not back down and army officers came out and protected the students from the police, even encouraging them to exercise their right to free speech. The position of the army was critical to how the change process unfolded.

The Lenten Letter coincided with the meeting of the United Front for Multiparty Democracy in Lusaka, March 20 to 23. Following the conference, Chikufwa Chihana returned and called for multiparty democracy and was summarily arrested. This led to more demonstrations. Meanwhile, rumours circulated that tapes had been recovered in which MCP leaders discussed assassinating the bishops. This triggered more demonstrations.

The final evidence that popular resistance was unstoppable came in the form of a strike by 3000 workers from the David Whitehead textile factory. While their demands were rooted in working conditions and labour relations, they went far beyond to clearly expressed political demands. Once again, the regime responded with typical repression, but this time the Malawi Young Pioneers (MYP) thugs met active resistance which quickly turned to urban warfare. Unemployed youth, students, and other workers joined the battle. Through their militant resistance the people of Malawi declared an end to their submission to autocratic abuse.

Joey Powers, in her book *Political Culture and Nationalism in Malawi: Building Kwacha,* points out how in fact the "riots" that took place were not driven purely by passion nor as mindless as they might have appeared. In fact, the anger of the people was clearly focussed on who and what they identified as their oppressor. They attacked possessions of the Life President, the Malawi Congress Party, the Malawi Young Pioneers and when need be the police who were defending all of the preceding.

The riots began in early May 1992. They started at the David Whitehead textile factory in Ndirande, a densely populated township in Blantyre, the commercial capital of Malawi. When their demands for higher wages and better terms of service were ignored workers resolved to occupy the plant until management would speak to them. This began on the night of May 5, when the night shift remained in the factory as the graveyard shift arrived. In the morning, the managing director, an expatriate, refused to meet with workers. Instead he called the Malawi Young Pioneers (MYP) a kind of paramilitary arm of the ruling party the Malawi Congress Party. Vehicles carrying armed MYP members soon arrived and entered the plant where violence was met with violence. Over the next few hours and days, hostilities spilled out of the factory and into neighboring Ndirande (a large periurban village between Blantyre and Limbe towns). Rioting and looting spread to Blantyre and Limbe proper, and its character demonstrated that this was not simply mob action based on bread and butter issues. Middle- and working-class "pillagers" targeted specific businesses, in particular, The People's Trading Company, Bergers, and Chipiku Stores all establishments associated with Life President Doctor Hasting Kamuzu Banda's consortium, Press Industries. And in some places like Ndirande, crowds not only looted but burned the very buildings that housed these enterprises. One Ndirande resident whose grocery shared the same premises as the Press-controlled Chipiku Stores was politely asked to vacate his shop. "Looters" even assisted him in clearing his stock before setting the building alight. In other words, this mob action was not random. Crowds of ordinary men and women removed windows and door frames from shops and destroyed MYP and MCP buildings. There were reports that some women wearing the MCP 'chipani' cloth (with Dr Banda's face emblazoned on it) were accosted and even assaulted as the cloths were torn from their bodies. Similar events occurred in Lilongwe, Mzuzu, Zomba and elsewhere over the next few days....[6]

Slowly but surely, other churches gained courage and by August individual churches had joined in broad ecumenical campaigns and declarations in support of multipartyism. The Muslim community joined with the Christian churches. By this time international pressure had also been mounting and Dr Banda finally agreed to hold a referendum on whether Malawians wanted their country to become a multiparty democracy. The referendum occurred in

---

6 Powers, Joey. Political Culture and Nationalism in Malawi: Building Kwacha, University of Rochester Press, 2010, pg 1

June 1993 and the Malawian people decisively declared the end of the Banda dictatorship by voting 63.5% for multiparty politics.

Once again, the army intervened in its "Operation Bwezani" to disarm and demobilise the Malawi Young Pioneers. In one clean, rapid intervention they collected weapons and shutdown bases of this paramilitary wing of the Malawi Congress Party which answered directly to Banda and his senior cohorts. This occurred after the referendum and in the run up to the first multiparty elections in 1994. It helped to ensure that one party to the elections was not able to mobilise a private army to intimidate the electorate in its favour.

7.7 Lesoma's role in the democratic transition

Even before the Pastoral Letter of the Catholic Bishops in March 1992, Lesoma had sensed that change was in the air. Early that year, a call went out for a conference of the opposition in exile and change agents from inside Malawi to meet in Lusaka March 20 to 23. In order to make it possible for as broad a range of political opinion to participate as possible, a new umbrella organisation was set up and called the United Front for Multiparty Democracy (UFMD). Lesoma enrolled as a member to help build a broader movement to overthrow the dictatorship. Events snowballed very quickly and the opposition found a new energy. Exiles, who had previously feared to speak out because of repercussions on their families at home, started to form groups and act for change.

Lesoma sent their revised manifesto to the United Democratic Front (UDF) with a view to encouraging them to use it as a model, particularly with respect to agricultural and economic policy. Fear still ruled and in order to be discrete, Kapote tells how, "*We sent everything to the Muslim Association of Malawi, P.O. Box Blantyre, c/o The Chairman so they [the Special Branch police] would think it was Muslim documents.*" It was then passed on to Bakili Muluzi, the United Democratic Front, (UDF) leader.

The Lusaka Conference, while a high point of external organising, nonetheless, showed that the path was fraught with difficulties. There was a clear effort by foreign actors to railroad the conference into accepting the leadership they were trying to impose. The democratic spirit of the participants prevented such a turn of events. After having failed to achieve their objective at the Lusaka Conference, these same foreign actors then tried to achieve their goal by flying Chakufwa Chihana, the exiled union leader, from Johannesburg to Lilongwe airport. Chihana's controversial return to Malawi, the growing public resistance in the country, as well as the international outcry over Malawi's abysmal human rights record, and the pressure of the international financial institutions led to the referendum on multiparty democracy in June 1993 and the dam had burst.

Not everyone could return from exile right away and expect to be safe. The regime's long history of violence was a disincentive for many people to return to the country. Kapote Mwakasungura, Mundu Mwambetania, John Jando Nkhwazi and others were high on the regime's hit list and their lives had been threatened publicly by Banda and his people. Frank Jiya tells how he and George Akogo Kanyanya faced more serious problems as a result of their participation in the Yatuta Chisiza incursion into Mwanza in 1967.

For the first returnees, myself and Kanyanya could not come back because of the death sentence against us. We were pushing for a general amnesty and we came back after the referendum. He [Banda] was forced to do it.

Once amnesty was declared, then the many people in the diaspora returned to take their seat at the table to build the new democracy. The Lesoma leadership was present throughout the process and at all levels. Their collective knowledge of law and public policy contributed greatly to the framing of the new constitution and the many legal instruments and institutions needed to implement a functionning democracy after the dictatorship and single party was displaced. Kapote Mwakasungura picks up the story from his position as Secretary General of the UFMD in 1993.

Once the referendum was held, and it became clear that Dr Banda had lost in the referendum, we waited until a general amnesty had been proclaimed by the government of Dr Banda so that we would be able to return.... There was a wait and see, but for us, the leadership of Lesoma, of the UFMD in Dar es Salaam, five of us, myself, Reginald Muhango, Mundu Mwambetania, Clement Marama, and Jomo Chikwakwa, we all decided to come back on the 28th or 29th of June, immediately after the referendum, although while we were still in Dar es Salaam we went to seek assistance for travel from the office of the United Nations [High Commission for Refugees]. They refused any assistance to us from the UN Office, because they said that you are actually coming back to your death, because Dr Banda could not be trusted.... Nonetheless, we did come.

To the question of whether people were truly free to campaign and get down to the business of converting a dictatorship to democracy, Kapote replied:

Yes we did. We went flat out. The Public Affairs Committee [PAC][7] had been fighting with the government to establish a transitional organisation which would be able to interface the government with the opposition.... The result of that was the National Consultative Council [NCC] and the constitutional

---

7 The PAC was a grouping of civil society actors which became an informal watchdog of the democratisation process.

making body which we named the National Executive Committee [NEC]. They operated almost side by side, because the National Consultative Council was the transitional parliament in which about 7 political parties were grouped.... [They] were meeting to thrash out issues that were burning at the time. That would have been about 35 people, representatives from each political party, whereas in the National Executive Council, it was principally seven people [one from each political party] who were thrashing out the draft new constitution of Malawi.

All the parties cooperated by providing one constitutional expert each to serve on the technical team mandated to give the principles worked out by the National Executive Committee the legal language required by a formal constitution. The Lesoma contribution was the Soviet trained lawyer, Dr Khoti Kamanga, who was brought in under the UFMD umbrella. Kapote explains the process.

Mostly the seven members were lawyers, although I happened to be the only non-lawyer. The other political parties had people in and people out. The MCP would have Louis Chimango, UDF was represented by Mr Chizumila, the husband of the Ombudsman and many others...

... They were very heated debates, some were constitutional, some were political issues generally, but overall it was shaping the new Malawi that we all wanted to create. The one [constitutional issues] that I can remember offhand was the recall provision, Section 65 in the new constitution, because we felt, particularly those of us coming from outside the country, who were refugees and knowing how power was being abused, that if people could not live up to the expectations, doing something else instead of representing the people, the constituents, the voters should be able to recall these people based on non-performance. And that has remained a very burning issue to this day. Crossing the floor, we advised against anybody crossing the floor. Those were new issues in the constitution, brought by people who had been in exile which people inside the country were not used to.

The election date was set for 15 May 1994 and the new draft constitution was passed a day or two before the actual election. We agreed to extend the life of the old parliament [composed solely of MCP MPs].

One downfall of the process of democratisation in other countries was a fractured opposition. Kapote explained how this was overcome in Malawi.

We didn't escape that malaise, because the Alliance for Democracy, Aford, refused to enter into alliance with other opposition parties like the UDF, the UFMD and other smaller parties. So they went into the elections on their own which was very sad. But because the UMFD had teamed up with the UDF and other smaller parties, we managed to tilt the scales and the UDF and the opposition won the election. But otherwise it was a very closely contested vote because Aford refused to enter into an alliance with the other political parties.

The Common Electoral Group [CEG] was set up to provide a united front against the Malawi Congress Party. It was proposed by the UFMD and the UDF bought into the idea as did several smaller parties. Regrettably Aford refused to participate in the CEG. They mistakenly believed that their party was so popular that they would win the election and form a majority government with nationwide support. Once Aford realised it had not won the popular vote, it joined forces with the UDF and a coalition of the two parties gave them an absolute majority in Parliament against the MCP. For his cooperation, the post of second vice-president was created to accommodate Chikufwa Chihana.

Kapote ended by paying tribute to Dr Banda for acknowledging the end of his Life Presidency and stepping down after losing the election.

To the credit of Dr Banda, once the National Electoral Commission announced the result that Dr Banda had actually failed on the elections, Dr Banda graciously enough called a national press conference to announce that he had failed in the elections and he congratulated Bakili Mluzi as the new president.... He stepped down.

Despite their intelligent and constructive contributions, most of the UFMD leadership were viewed with suspicion as too radical. The MCP old guard had spent so long absorbing Kamuzu's ideological prejudices that the exiles with their panAfricanism and connections to the Eastern Europe were anathema. The returnees were useful, informed and connected but too pushy for the old guard who feared for the possibility they might upset the old guard's applecart. While one or two were given ministerial posts within the new government, many of the others in the UFMD leadership were given diplomatic postings and sent into golden exile outside the country which effectively removed them from the political scene and neutralised them.

The downfall of the Banda regime while it was long overdue, nonetheless came dramatically, relatively quickly in political terms and very peacefully. All sides seemed to show goodwill to bring about the long dreamed of democracy. The "new" Malawi started on a very hopeful footing even if there were a number of birth pains associated with the transition. However, within the next decade, troubling signs of the residue of Dr Banda's long, iron-handed, autocratic rule became more and more apparent. The rest of this book examines how our respondents lived this part of their life-experience.

Chapter Eight: Living With the Pain

"Bay kou bliye, pote mak sonje"
"He who gives the blow forgets; he who carries the scar remembers."
(Haitian Creole proverb)

8.1   The Exiles Return
8.2   Physical Scars
8.3   Psychological Scars
8.4   No Compensation and Rehabilitation
8.5   Dispossession
8.6   Cultural Alienation
8.7   Contribution of the Returnees

Detainees and exiles shared much in common as a result of their treatment by the regime. Prison conditions were so bad that even prisoners who were never tortured still came out with permanent physical and psychological damage. Exiles often came back in poor health, having suffered many of the social and psychological consequences of forced dislocation. Detainees and those who had been beaten or abused by the regime's enforcers before escaping into exile often carried serious and permanent physical and psychological scars. On their return to their homes in Malawi, they found themselves stigmatised and even ostracised by workmates and friends and sometimes even by their family and community.

Almost without exception, they were bitter about the treatment they had received at the hands of the regime. Many were even more upset at being forsaken and forgotten after the change of government in 1964 that removed Dr Banda from power. The truth about what had happened under the dictatorship was inconvenient for many people in high positions after the democratic dispensation, and they short-changed the compensation process in order to keep their role under the dictatorship from coming to light. The lack of compensation and rehabilitation was an additional source of bitterness. Furthermore, they had been dispossessed by their detention or exile while MCP stalwarts expropriated their opponents' possessions like spoils of war.

Former exiles, in particular, often found themselves shut out of society. They had absorbed cultural and political values that ran against the values instilled in those who had remained in Malawi and been acculturated to the underlying values Banda imposed on the society. One noticeable example is the strong anti-communism promoted by Banda that had permeated Malawian society Even today, many years after the fall of communism in Eastern Europe and the demise of Dr Banda's regime, there is still deep suspicion among Malawians raised under Banda of anyone coming from Russia and the education they may have acquired there. Moreover, the deeply conservative elements of traditional society did not accept the non-Malawian habits and cultural values brought by formerly exiled family members. Calling a returnee a Tanzanian became an insult, despite those who grew up in that country being proud of what they had gained from their experience. Still others found their families dispersed around the world and reluctant to re-engage with a new Malawi.

Our respondents reflect this wide range of challenges and issues in their testimony.

8.1 The Exiles Return

People were initially very excited to return home after 30 years of exile. Many came home soon after the referendum of June 1993 led to a political amnesty. However, hopeful expectations for the return soon turned to serious disappointment and, almost without exception, there was a sense of shock at the difficult reception they often received on their homecoming. Some, like Ceciwa Bwanausi Khonje, had had successful careers and gained international recognition. She was disgusted at the way the role of the heroes of the national liberation of Malawi was erased from public memory and how those who had been in power under Banda still exercised so much power after his regime was brought to an end. She and many others were scandalised that the likes of JZU Tembo still enjoyed wealth and power rather than being called to account for their abuse of power and the people. Ceciwa retired into a second exile rather than live with such hypocrisy. Mary Mwale stayed in the UK until her "second retirement," almost 15 years after the democratic dispensation, before she finally returned to settle in Mzuzu.

Frequently, their stories were about aborted professional careers or how exile blocked them from advancing in their careers because they were foreigners. Instead of being welcomed on their return to their homeland, they often faced still more problems. These uncomfortable landings, and hostile homecomings affected people like Carson Kayuni who found himself the focus of much animosity from local people. He had to struggle to re-integrate into life at home and now finds himself in his 80s having to farm potatoes to make ends meet.

John Phiri, Paul Munyenyembe, Nettie Dzabara, Sute and Isyu Mwakasungura all trained in the onetime Soviet Union. With their education and training they could have brought a fresh outlook to government institutions in Malawi. However, they found themselves locked out by the deeply ingrained anti-communism in the civil service which had been instilled by Dr Banda. Dr

Banda's rabid anti-communism had become so firmly implanted that even after the fall of the Soviet Union, anyone associated with the Eastern Bloc remained suspect and their education treated as inferior. After 1994, many were disappointed because they were denied employment opportunities, despite being highly qualified, simply because they possessed Soviet degrees. Even when they took charge of their situations and created NGOs, they were accused of being a clique of Northerners monopolising the local NGO scene.

John Phiri trained in international law in Moscow to the Masters level. He was one of many that Lesoma sent to the former Soviet Bloc countries. He describes what it felt like being frozen out by the people who had remained inside the country.

Why were they afraid to accommodate us? Because if you were a minister, I have gone to school, I would talk to you as an equal. Tell you where you have gone wrong. Discuss it with you. I'll not take that word

John Phiri and Kapote

"Yes Sir" [with emphasis]. *I would take that word, "Yes Sir. I have agreed with you," out of your reasoning. This is how we can resolve the issues... What are the pro and cons and move forward not as enemies, but our friends would take us as enemies."*

I remember the time I was supposed to work for the Ministry of Justice. I had to talk to the late Chizumila. He was the Minister of Justice. He came to me when we were drinking and told me, 'You are too idealistic.'

He never got the job. In order to contribute to the democratisation process and still make a living he and other Lesoma militants applied the skills they had developed in exile.

.... we had to come together, whether it was by design, it is unfortunate that we were from the Northern Region, but we were sharing the same common purpose for so many years, so forming the organisation for us to be together was not a problem. It was quite easy. We used to share everything. We used to share our food, accommodation - we were staying in the same house. Me, Ollen Mwalubunju, Undule Mwakasungura, unfortunately we have lost one colleague, Grant Sichale and the fifth one who came to join us was Grifford Msiska. We remained together in four houses....

Sute Mwakasungura, with a technical degree as a veterinarian, found getting a job was not a big problem. Nonetheless, he had problems with his work colleagues who had trained together inside the country and resented his presence. Eventually he left the milieu to set up an NGO where he could use his skills outside the confines of a government workplace.

We were so much longing to come home.... I came in 1994 and threw around applications for jobs and I went back to Tanzania. Finally 1995, I came back alone. I left the family behind and found a job... I got a job with National Parks and Wildlife and was posted to Kasungu as an extension officer. I didn't stay long. After six months, they transferred me to Nyika National Park in the same position.... I didn't have a problem [finding a job] maybe because I came earlier and threw around applications. Also I was in the agriculture sector which was not as sensitive as the law or something like that. Agriculture didn't pose any threat...

[But] ... the resentment was there in the field. Not at headquarters where they were interviewing, but in the field. Malawi being a very small country, so all those that go into National Parks as employees, they know one another. I was the only one out. They didn't know where I was coming from. The National Parks is like a military institution where a bwana is a bwana and I didn't behave that way.... I didn't go through that training. I was a pure civilian and my fellow bosses were not very happy with me, the way I was conducting myself. That created a problem, because the juniors started coming more to me... because they saw that I was someone who was approachable. So my problems were with the [hierarchy]..."

Isyu Mwaksungura had a softer landing although getting back to Malawi had been a problem.

[By 1992]... My refugee status was a problem. I first of all had to find myself, "What am I in Australia?" My refugee status was denied because by the time I was hoping to apply, there was change in Malawi. So I couldn't proceed. After facing a few problems, I said I am a doctor. Why should I mess myself up? So I wrote back to Malawi. I wrote the Office of the President and Cabinet introducing myself, who I was and that I had all my basic education [in Malawi]. I pursued my medical degree in Moscow, that now I was in Australia and now I was ready to return home. Then I got mail by DHL [courier service] from the Ministry of Health that they wanted me. Of course [I got the letter] with suspicion because I didn't know what this was. I had to plan how to open the letter, because the Attati Mpakati experience was still alive and Mkwapatila Mhango. So you can imagine that the fear is still very much there. I opened it and ... then what do I do now? I was in Australia and not working. Still getting financial support from the Red Cross. Then I had to apply to come here. To tell them that I wanted to go back home.... I was given an air ticket and a letter attesting that I am a genuine refugee returning home....

[Upon arrival] There was suspicion, because I used documents from Tanzania. It was a travel document that was acting like an Alien Passport. When I got at the airport they took it away together with the letter as a returnee. I said you can't take that one back. That one [the letter] is for me. I need to have it with me all the time I am here in Malawi.... They kept the passport, but after an hour or so I was given back the letter.... The folks

from home came to see me. They were happy to see me. From the airport, I went straight to the Ministry to tell them I am here. I didn't go anywhere else. I went straight to the Office of the President and Cabinet on Capital Hill. Then I was given a letter to take to the Ministry of Health. Then I was told to go home. They said that I will be hearing from them. It didn't take even a month. Just about a week or so, I was told to come back. I had just left for Karonga and then I was called back to Kamuzu Central Hospital. Dr Kazembe was the pediatrician and the director then. So I did internship there from 1995 because it was like orientation. They were taking other students, a new intake from the College of Medicine. "Why don't you just go along with them? Do as though it was an internship with them." So I agreed. I was excited to be home. I did internship with them for one year and completed successfully. Then I was at Mpemba for Hospital Management. After that I was posted to Karonga.

….I think what helped was that I was born here. I have been to many places. I knew Lilongwe very well. I knew Blantyre. All my secondary education, my A levels, my O levels, I have done here. So language was not a problem for me. I know the languages... so I didn't have much of a problem.

In contrast, Professor Michongwe from Zomba had had a successful career in Tanzania in many post-secondary institutions. In Malawi, he was refused good jobs commensurate with his experience. The jobs he was given seemed intended to humiliate and belittle his extensive experience.

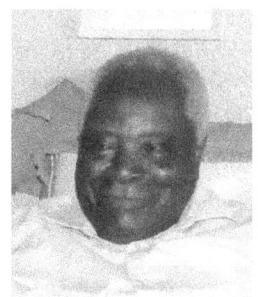

George Michongwe

In the end I decided to come back here. Now I regret. I wish I had gone to India. I would have been much richer?...

Everybody was asking me to come back... My uncle, my sisters, everybody. You come back. Life is okay here....

When asked if former President Bakili Mluzi had invited him back, the professor responded,

One of the people he sent was the late Chizumila. All the way to Tanzania to invite me to come back. But when I came here the job they gave me teaching at Domasi. Acch! Rubbish. I really hated that work.... A person who has been doing a lot of research work, a lot of consultancy work now to go sit in classes... I really hated it.

Khwauli Msiska by force of personality and determination found his way into the system, but recognised the hurdles he and others like him faced on returning from exile.

…. What I went through, at a personal level. I think it taught me a lot. One it humbled me. I think I have emerged out of that possibly a better person than if I was just here and possibly look at things differently than my colleagues who have spent their entire lives in Malawi. Having said that

I know there are those of us who were out there who have not been able to make it and those years have weighed on them mightily and have come out of this possibly weaker, not able to stand on their own feet as a result of being denied the right to be home.... Also another challenge was getting accepted back. It was not easy for us to get accepted back. You were nice and welcome when you are out there. People talk about we miss you so much. We want you home. When you come home, it is a different story. We were more or less treated like an intruder. You really have to fight for your space. And this is what I have seen. I have had to fight for my space. It is not like, "It is here. You are welcome." Even to get jobs, "Oh he is from Russia." We had to create our own institutions, set up the Centre for Human Rights and Rehabilitation. And that is how our friend Grant got a job out of creating our own institutions because we felt we were not being accepted. My good friend, Sute, created his own NGO, Small Scale Livestock and Livelihoods Programme [SSLLP], all this because we have not been accepted. You just have to do something about [it] yourself.

There are obvious cases of more comfortable landings, often professionals whose careers in Malawi were aborted by detention without trial or charge who were forced to seek employment outside the country. They found their talents well recognised and they prospered in their foreign careers. Chifipa Gondwe, Dickson Mzumara, Zifa Kasese flourished in exile and returned home to retire as soon as the situation after Banda's demise allowed their safe return. These cases are held up to support the myth of golden exile.

Exile was a long struggle for Ali Sikelo who was nonetheless able to come home and be accorded the honour he deserved as a former freedom fighter with Chipembere in the bush around Malindi. He was elected as an MP with widespread support to represent the people of the area where he had fought so bravely. He died shortly after his return to Malawi.

8.2 Physical Scars

While our sample was limited, it is clear that the physical damage inflicted upon Malawians by their fellow citizens beggars belief. We met and interviewed an elderly man in Chitimba, Mr Mzembe. In the mid-1960s he had settled in Kitwe, Zambia as a driver and, at some point in the early 1970s, Kanyama Chiume, the ex-minister, visited him as a home boy. In 1974, he came to Malawi on vacation to visit family. He travelled via Chitipa (Kamwala) where immigration handed him over to the Special Branch police because he was on their list as a rebel sympathiser. He was beaten mercilessly and sustained a serious spine injury. In his old age, he is permanently hunched over and severely crippled. He has lost touch with his children in Zambia and Tanzania. He wants to live his final years in Malawi and die with his ancestors, but sadly, no one remains from his birth family at his home to look after him. He is destitute and dependent on the charity of the community around him.

Mordecai Gondwe still carries his scars and blindness as a reminder of the treatment he received. In a dramatic gesture during his interview, he reached up into his thick grey hair and parted it to reveal a dramatic scar, a reminder of the serious wound inflicted on him in a beating meted out by British inspector John Savage.

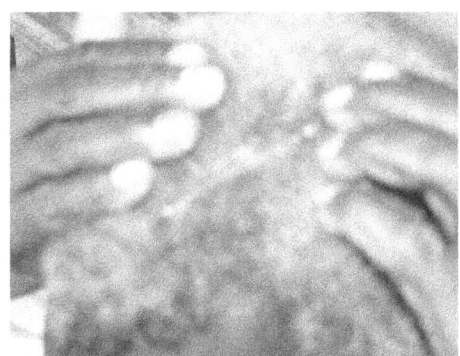

Mordecai Gondwe shows the scar he still bears from his beating by Inspector John Savage.

.... I was beaten and the beating was very heavy and I was crying as a small kid. Anyhow, anywhere, mostly the head. I tell you I am [lucky] to be alive. I have this scar. This scar was very alive then. [He parts his hair and shows a wide scar extending from front to back]. *It was very wide then. It was over one inch wide. I lost the sight of this eye which I only got to know later on....*

Tom Chabwino Nyirenda still carries scars, is lame in one leg, and has reduced eyesight. He demonstrated how he and other prisoners had been chained to the floor. His wrists were cuffed and then a short chain attached the cuffs to a ring on the floor in such a manner that he could not free his legs. He had to feed himself from this position and it was in this position that they beat him.[1]

Even today I don't eat easily, because of the broken ribs. The beatings lasted for just a matter of a month. They were through with me within a month. The beating it was only a month - each and every day. Naked, not even a pant, no underwear. [He crouches to demonstrate how they were shackled in the sitting position with the arms through the legs]. *For seven months like this, but it was only one month we were beaten.... they took me to the hospital after the seventh month when I fainted. The leg got infected. Five months in Nkhata Bay to heal. Worms had formed in the wound and were coming out...*

They used pepper in his eyes and the burning has left him with considerable vision loss. Thomas showed us the scars on his broken leg. Because of the mistreatment, it took six months to heal and he now walks with a permanent limp.

---

1 * He demonstrates this position in the picture on page 82.

I am not in fashion. I am mentally derailed and physically derailed and so financially out of it.

In the case of Kirby Mwambetania, conditions were so bad that even though he was not physically beaten, he suffered permanent damage to his health equivalent to torture. From among his father's papers, Lwitiko Mwambetania scanned and forwarded two medical notes attesting to Kirby having acquired diabetes mellitus and hypertension as a result of his incarceration. Signed in September of 1996, by Dr C.M. Nyirenda, Chief Consultant Physician, one of them reads as follows:

<u>MEDICAL REPORT: MR K.K. MWAMBETANIA – HYPERTENSION, DIABETES MELLITUS AND VERTEBRAL DISC LESION</u>

Mr. K.K. Mwambetania is a known case of diabetes mellitus and high blood pressure which developed while he was in detention.

He also developed lumbar vertebral disc problem as a result of trauma he was subjected to while in prison. This gives him severe pain, numbness, and pins and needles type of sensation in his legs and feet.

He is being referred to Garden City Clinic Johannesburg for further management with computer scanning non-available here in Malawi.

Kirby died the following year, his death no doubt hastened by his treatment in prison and the terrible conditions he experienced.

8.3 Psychological Scars - Bitterness

The long-term impact of the organised violence and torture visited upon the citizens of Malawi by the Banda dictatorship manifests itself in many different ways. Bitterness is a common thread through most of the narratives we collected. Bitterness may not be labelled a clinical condition, but most of the respondents felt bitter about being arrested without cause, denied career possibilities, dispossessed of their property and having to flee into exile, and bitterness at the treatment they continue to receive lies at the root of many of the testimonies that we collected. They were bitter that those who were in power in Banda's time are still enjoying the fruits of power, despite their complicity in perpetrating the crimes of the regime.

Mary Mwale Mwahimba expressed her frustration and bitterness at the current crop of political leaders and how they have subverted the second liberation, just as they did the first. The greed and venality of the political classes in Malawi stands in stark contrast to the selflessness of the nationalist leaders that Banda ousted in his Cabinet Coup and the brave men and women who fled into exile and struggled and died trying to restore some form of democracy.

But I think what the problem is that when we got multiparty. It didn't achieve much. What was missing was instead of those people being dedicated to the multiparty and bringing everybody to enjoy the ufulu. That didn't happen. They left people behind and they enjoyed by themselves, which is the reason why they didn't mention anybody else. [They talk as if] it is them who brought multiparty, basi! Nobody else. So they failed. I think the people who did all this, they shouldn't have been singing, "We have achieved it without having to fight." Our friends tried to fight for this [liberation]. They [inside politicians] were scared of the dead ones.

Mary is equally bitter about what we call the forsaken ones. The feeling of being forgotten and forsaken comes up frequently.

That's really the sentiments I have... either the country is ashamed of them... Banda is long gone... Now there is multiparty and now there is democracy and people still can't talk about it at all.... I've been here six years now and at least this name Chisiza appears because of the brother, but if it was Yatuta on his own he doesn't exist in the history of Malawi. As for Mwahimba, he was just an incident which just happened to be there at the time. Basi...

[Lutengano] To me that name doesn't exist. Only because of Malawi, He never existed.... It is a very long story... they died in vain... Even the daughter thinks he must have been chigawenga, because nobody speaks about him....

They remember Chilembwe and the events of 1915, but not 1967.

I am not angry. I am just disappointed about Malawi. If it was a struggle and everybody was into it, then we would go forward together. We failed to do that. They failed even those people who died and they are forgotten... the people like Mwahimba, it's a dead memory....

....So many people feel bitter, forsaken and forgotten. Completely! .... People are being ignored... which is the reason why they [the current crop of politicians] didn't mention anybody else except themselves.... nobody else counted.

Her bitterness runs deep and she has lived with it for a long time. In order to get on with her life she suppressed as much of the past as possible.

So that is why I say my experiences, I put them there [behind her], because they leave me puzzled very, very puzzled.... Suteni [one of her daughters] died. Nobody educated my children and yet their father died for them [the Malawian people]. They never went anywhere. They never saw a penny. What I have done, I have done it myself. I helped myself. Nobody said Mary you are one of those widows we should help, even though they said you are young and they can go to school and do whatever you want... Not a penny. Not a single penny to say Mary go to such and such a place...

My parents educated my daughter. Not a penny. So this memory of Malawi is very... selective for me. Other people benefited... others didn't.

We tried to reassure her that it was important to get her story out but it was hard for her to deal with what she had tried so hard to put behind her. Her tragedy is doubly sad because of the very few months she and Mwahimba were able to spend together as a married couple over three years.

Let me get used to it [talking about my husband]. These are some repressed memories that I guard.... I didn't live long with him. Maybe 8 months in totality.

Mary was quite young when she married Lutengano Mwahimba and claims to be unaware of much that he was involved in. Nonetheless, she recounts in vivid detail the important role he played in saving Chipembere by helping him leave the country.

What I know was in Zomba. And yet Chipembere wouldn't have left this country alive if it wasn't for Mwahimba.... He is the one who went to Mangochi to give him a warning, three times... I read in Malawi Journal [The Society of Malawi Journal] that talks about a black man but they didn't know who it was who carried the warning that you are in danger. But I know it was him because he left me alone in the house and said, "I am going to Mangochi, I might not be back." It started here playing with his life to protect the ministers... Later on when I met him [Chipembere] in [Tanzania], he could mention to me that I am alive because of him [Mwahimba]... it is unwritten history.

In her later, unrecorded interview she detailed the purpose of each trip:

Mwahimba went 3 times to see him. First to warn him. Second to provide details of how he should leave. Third to take him the tickets.

Her bitterness resurfaced when she finished this story and said,

How often is it I tell the history which is coming from my mouth... people will just laugh... look at her, she is just daydreaming....

The bitterness is tinged with despair sometimes and cynicism other times. We are not the first to have asked for her story and she has put materials together, but again despairs at what she sees as the futility of the exercise.

I have got my story written, it is that size [she holds up her hands to show the thickness]. *I think to myself, that they will think this woman is eccentric... Does she really think that happened?*

S.K. Mpango's bitterness at Banda's betrayal still sits badly with him 20 years after Banda is gone. He has been left penniless and forsaken. From a position as a senior *induna* to Chief Mwase, the most influential Chewa chief of the time, he has been reduced to an old age mired in poverty.

> Only God knows why Banda was so angry. We had welcomed him warmly as our son.... But because of his advanced age he was listening to the Gadamas for everything. Dr Banda came many years later to apologise but only after we had suffered terrible torture under detention.... Despite his apology, he never gave us anything, despite having lost everything, during our many years of detention.
>
> Bakili Muluzi became ruler.... He asked to meet all those ex-detainees. I went to meet with Bakili Muluzi. I told him my story and Bakili Muluzi apologised. They gave us K20,000 relief money to each one of us. At least Muluzi gave us a token, but not from Banda. He only said words but nothing else. When I went to see Muluzi, all my colleagues had already passed on.

Rose Chibambo told a truly sad story of how she had been forced to send her children home to Mzimba as conditions deteriorated after September 1964 and it was no longer safe for them to go to school in the Blantyre area. They had to be left behind when she fled into exile. She was doubly punished when the Banda authorities refused to allow her son and daughters to rejoin them in exile. Her son faced discrimination in school and employment because of his parentage and had been punished after visiting his parents in Zambia. Eventually, he too fled into exile but it did not go well for him. Rose picks up the story:

> That's when we stayed together. I stayed with him. He got a job in Zambia. He was working very well. But unfortunately Zambia being what it is, people drink so much. He never drank in Malawi. He was then carried away with friends and so on... He finally felt free and he started drinking and it was so bad. It destroyed him.... He is back. He is here with me.

It became hard for her to talk at this point and she proposed a tea break. His psychological problems had clearly been a major burden for her.

Many respondents, exiles and detainees alike, turned to religion to find meaning and solace. The late Lawrence Mwamlima told us that he had accepted Christ only a few weeks before he was summarily and unjustly dismissed. He found strength in religion when facing his difficulties after being ousted from his post and sent into internal exile.

> I had accepted Jesus Christ six months before I was dismissed. I asked the Lord why I should be dismissed. You know I am innocent in this affair. I think the Lord has something that he would like me to do at home. But should it be?... For any Christian, I said there must be a purpose. The Lord has a purpose. Remember the story of Joseph.... Two months after I had come here I was told I should be a church elder and two months later the Synod asked me to assist them to translate the Bible from English to our language, Ngonde.... I accepted and then I knew that God wanted me to come here to make sure I participated in that particular exercise.

Similarly, Thengo Maloya has dedicated his life to religion.

I decided to leave politics. I didn't stand [for MP]... Since then I decided that God will decide my future. I've put myself in the hands of God. I have decided to be a devout follower of Christ. A devout Christian, so that I forget the past and the mistakes I have made in the past.... I was at a mission school. I could have been a minister by now of religion. But politics swayed me aside. And the actions at that time, even among the Christian white people - so by allowing myself to say a white man is acting like a government official, he is not a Christian, but I made a mistake. Black people, white people we all have one saviour and that is Jesus Christ. The white man has sinned. The black man has sinned. We are all equal at the feet of Christ on the cross. And when we meet at the cross there is no colour. It's a question of a sinner asking for salvation, forgiveness and salvation. Indeed, white, black, red or any other colour, we come to the cross for our salvation.

Machipisa Munthali became a pastor of his church after his release from prison. James Mwagomba also became very religious. Mordecai Gondwe has been a long standing clerk of the CCAP church and church elder. Augustine Msiska is deeply involved in his church and preaches sermons.

8.4 No Compensation and Rehabilitation

The National Compensation Tribunal was created as part of the discussions around Malawi's transition to multiparty democracy. Like other institutions created in this period it was corrupted by those who graduated from the Banda school to the new government in the democratic dispensation. Most exiles were denied compensation and the Malawi government never requested available United Nations assistance for the resettlement of returning refugees. Funds were clearly limited, but some very dubious large claims early in the process diminished the credibility of the process, especially when the majority of people who submitted claims were either refused or received a token K20,000.

Carson Kayuni was an activist throughout his years in exile. The treatment he received and the way his attempt to claim compensation was frustrated left him angry and bitter.

When we came in with these people [Kapote and the Lesoma leadership], we were a threat. They were feeling inferiority complex. They knew these people had met international leaders and that they had accumulated enough knowledge how to handle the situation. So much so that today, when we talk of democracy, they are the same repeated [recycled] people who when the change came they jumped and got on to here.

….. And of course here we are. They [the Yatuta Brigade] died. They did the job. Which is why today, those who never even sacrificed, are in the forefront to church. Those who suffered, still suffer.... I had over 1000 heads of

cattle. I made an application through Bazooka Mhango, the lawyer.... Instead when I asked him to help me, he said you pay something in advance. I said, If I had something to pay you, why would I be claiming to the government? From that time I stopped depending on anyone....

Now George Kanyanya was a minister.... I tried to go through him... I tried through a social welfare officer in Karonga. He was very useless. I went up to Chairman of the National Compensation Tribunal. My file number is 6680, only to be told funds are exhausted..... In number, they used to say we were 24,000 [claimants].... I have tried to talk with the government of Muluzi, nothing, nothing. There came the government of Bingu.... Some came to interview me and I gave them my statement. They went even to see the job I am doing. I am growing potatoes at this age in order to survive.....

We are forgotten guys. Some of my very important documents I gave to these people who came to interview me and they were never returned.

For these new regimes, nobody talks of Chisiza or Chipembere. I have been asking for compensation, and [I suspect that] someone else may have taken my compensation. Even under Joyce Banda, we are not getting anywhere.

Carson Kayuni in his root cellar

I have lived to be very [un]happy. I returned in 1994, 20 June. The people in the village refused to welcome me. They accused me of killing someone. We came in 1966. We were 16 and we wanted to start from Fort Hill. We were well dressed.

That was the story repeated by many people. The exiles, in particular felt that they had been deliberately omitted.

On a more positive note, the international community, particularly Germany and the European Union, had supported Machipisa in his return to civilian life. The longevity and the severity of his detention evoked a great deal of international support. He was able to settle back in his home at Mlowe, build a couple of houses and establish several small businesses that allowed him a comfortable life in his later years.

Although the NGO, Committee for Human Rights and Rehabilitation, included resettlement and compensation as part of their mandate as a human rights organisation, they were never able to make rehabilitation a priority in their programming and activities.

8.5 Dispossession

Detainees and exiles were almost without exception dispossessed of their positions and their possessions. Civil servants were dismissed from their jobs, university staff from their posts, businesspeople stripped of their enterprises never to regain them. Chief Mwase, his induna, GK Mpango and the other chiefs and indunas from the 1973 Manoah Chirwa incident lost all their cattle and wealth, their chieftaincies and in many cases their homes. Mordecai Gondwe had a thriving shop and a prosperous business, which was almost totally dissipated by the time he returned to his home from his periods of detention. Mpango talks of his loss and the fact that at 90 plus years of age he was deprived of a nest egg to retire on and is still obliged to work in his fields to produce crops to sustain his family.

Any land owned by an exile was subject to confiscation without compensation. Molly Dzabara explains:

We had left houses. Augustine had bought a house on the way to Chileka which was occupied by Dumbo Lemani now. We don't know how he got it. And my husband bought a house somewhere behind this hill which a Greek man built named Trataris who was then running a bakery. He had a beautiful house. We bought that one... we paid in installments through the National Building Society - a mortgage, so we only paid for three months [when] we ran away. So we could not claim it when we came back, because it was a little money. My other brother bought a house near Chigumula in Newlands. It was a beautiful house which Harry had bought. It was built by an architect. So he bought and paid and Augustine bought and paid for his house before we ran away and [they] finished paying for their houses, both my brothers. And they never got their houses back...

Tujilane Chizumila, daughter of Professor Michongwe, tells of her father's piece of land at Seven Miles, where her relatives are buried. To this day, the new owner has not allowed them to visit the family graves and honour their ancestors' memories. This despite their claim for restitution being supported by original title deeds and related documents.

The MCP took away his [her father's] land and froze his accounts. The land was given to an MCP diehard. Grandfather is buried there after dying in detention... Grandfather, grandmother, aunties and dad's brother all were detained.... They left detention with terrible bronchitis.

My grandfather and aunties are buried there and the man refuses to allow us to visit the graveyard. It is so painful. I used to drive to Zomba via Zalewa to avoid driving by the land that was taken from us. We tried to get the land back through the National Compensation office and the Ombudsman office.

G.K. Mpango in 2012

G.K. Mpango is now over 90 years old. The memoires of his loss are still very much alive.

For the seven years that we were in detention at Mikuyu, I lost everything I owned. Before I left I had sixteen cows. But I only found 2 remaining when I returned. All this because of the cruelty of Dr Hastings Kamuzu Banda.... When Mwase was detained, his headquarters were demolished. The throne was destroyed and the chieftainship abolished and.... The Mwase chieftainship was reduced to an ordinary village headman, but all the powers of the big chief were given to Kaomba.... other parts to Lukwa.... Since our return from detention, I have continued to face great difficulties. I have no assistance, I need to have young men assist me in the gardens. I am still going into the gardens myself, to clear the land and till it, so it is very problematic.

8.6 Alienation

Resettlement in Malawi, after the exile experience, can be complicated as adults and children alike deal with a number stressful issues. A major problem of exile is the stress of losing contact with family at home. Refugee families often experience anxiety over family members who remained in Malawi. Refugee children must leave behind all they have ever known, including friends, communities, schools, homes, and family members. They are faced with the challenge of adapting to a new environment while coping with this loss. In exile, differences can arise between parental and host country values and create rifts between the refugee child and his/her family.

Traditional family dynamics in refugee communities are disturbed by cultural adaptation which destabilize important cultural norms, which can create a rift between parent and child. Parents expect their children to remain loyal to ethnic values despite being expected to master the host culture in school and social activities while in exile. Families that settled in Tanzania and Zambia absorbed the culture of free speech and support of progressive policies of popular development and support for the national liberation struggles of Southern Africa. In response to these demands, children may over-identify with their host culture to avoid being marginalised by their peers.

The phenomenon occurs in reverse when returning to Malawi after a prolonged absence. The long separation from family can manifest itself in many unfortunate ways. It is not unusual for young people to have a decreased familiarity with Malawi, its language and cultural heritage. Nor do they share the sense of ethnic identity and group identification that evolved in Malawi during Dr Banda's thirty-year rule. Upon their return to Malawi they can face stigma and even discrimination on the part of family who remained under Kamuzu and absorbed the prejudices his regime fostered about the exiles. After a childhood and adolescence of adapting to their host country's language, culture and political values, children returning from exile can find themselves alienated by a Malawian culture that maintains most of the essentially conservative and elitist elements of life under Kamuzu. Others, who grow up in the affluent countries of the West, often experience difficulties adjusting to life in Malawi, one of the world's poorest country with all its problems.

The clash between values acquired in exile and the popular culture of Malawi often leads to alienation. After becoming fluent in Swahili or other languages and only hearing the family mother tongue spoken by older family and members of the community, they must learn and function in Chichewa often with an accent in what is supposed to be their first language. Despite calling Malawi their home, they nonetheless face a sense of alienation or "being the other."

It was very tragic for many of the refugees who dreamed of coming home and settling with their families to then find that their children raised abroad had little or no interest in returning to deal with the Malawian reality. They rejected their parents' ancestral home and fled to countries and environments where they felt more comfortable or "at home." For many families, the children were scattered across many continents. Mary Mwambetania has a child in Scotland, four remained in Dar es Salaam where they grew up and another in Capetown, while she herself commutes between her husband's home in Karonga and her children in Dar es Salaam. Some, like Zifa Kazeze, returned to Malawi while his children moved to the United States. That means they find themselves with little or no family support in Malawi to help with family issues and provide the normal support one would expect from adult children as they grow older.

Even when children followed their families home there were problems of alienation with other family members. Tujilane provides an overview of the loss of Malawian identity that contributed to this alienation.

I went to Tanzania when I was about 12. I left Tanzania when my firstborn son was almost 12. So it has been a lifetime. I think that is why a lot of people here think I am a Tanzanian. They don't believe I am a Malawian.... Again it goes back to the culture. We lost the Malawian culture. We lost the accent. We lost almost everything.

Tujilane explained that in many ways friends in exile became more like family than the families who remained in Malawi and rejected their relatives upon their return.

.... Another impact. We spoke Chinyanja at home at all times and we could talk well. It was wonderful to come home with my two children.

[However] *My own relatives,* [would say] *you and your little Swahili brats you don't know the Malawi culture. I went behind his chair and he shouted at me. Is this what you learned in Tanzania... going behind people's backs?*

My children were brought up as Tanzanians... they couldn't take the elderly women kneeling before them... The boys would hide in the bush to avoid the elderly having to kneel, they were embarrassed by it.

The dress code - the African attire was my style imposed by my father who forbid mini-dresses.... I have to explain my roots to people to be accepted.

The strain on families that had been separated over a long period of time has manifested in different ways. Tujilane speaks about it when she explains the close relations with the other former refugees and her old friends in Tanzania.

We lost relations - They distance themselves from you because you are now a Swahili.... The ones born while we were away are our cousins but they don't know us. We did not grow up together. We are closer to the other refugees than our blood family.... My children ask why the family doesn't come to visit. So we depend on friends and we have remained very close with the Tanzanian friends.

Nettie Dazabara was shocked at the way old and out-dated customs had remained so deeply enshrined under the conservative reign of Dr Banda.

Women are disadvantaged in this country. I'll tell you an example. I came from Zambia. I am a pharmacist. I have come with that mentality... where I am treated not because I am a woman, but because I am a human being first and foremost and a professional.

So I came for a holiday.... A cousin or someone had died. I was told to serve food to this group of mourners who were in this special room. There were ladies. There were gentlemen and I was passing the water [for handwashing]. I passed the water to this lady, very elderly, who was the nearest. She said, "No, koma bambo awo" [No – that gentleman over there] *I crossed the room and it was, "No! No! No!" So here I am* [frustrated] *so I just put it in the middle of the room and I walked out....*

Even families of ex-detainees who remained in the country faced enormous family stress. Victoria attributed her marriage breakdown and the soured relations with in-laws as a result of the climate of suspicion that Dr Banda engendered.

Khwauli Msiska relates how the cultural differences manifested themselves in the professional world.

You are not 100% accepted, and also I see as a challenge... I will give as an example because of that gap, people will be discussing certain issues and mentionning certain names and they assume you know them. And you feel it is rude to say, "I don't know such a person," because you missed out and these are great people, that you are supposed to know. If you had been here and you had gone to the same university here, you had worked here, you would have known these people. And because you feel it is rude to say this person they are discussing, I don't know him.

And sometimes also your mannerisms and your way of thinking and the way you talk. Sometimes people think you are rude. I know my wife for example would caution me, "Here when you talk to people, don't be so forthright. They will think you are a crook of some kind." Especially here you are supposed to be a bit meek and humble, but this is not how I have grown. In Tanzania and Kenya, you look people in the face and you talk forthright and you tell them what you think. Tell your mind. And people [here] misconstrue that. They think that you are a crook, that you are proud. So you have certain mannerisms that are not really that acceptable.

Maybe you are going into Cabinet, there is a certain way of... you may have a brilliant idea, but you don't just say it. It is how you present it and maybe you have to wait. Certain people have to speak first. So I have had to learn. It is not easy.

8.7 Contributions of the Returnees

The returnees and survivors of the terror displayed amazing resilience despite the pain and suffering they have had to deal with. They overcame their difficulties in a variety of ways. Ollen Mwalubunju provides an excellent reflection on what some returnees have done to keep Malawian democracy evolving in a transparent and constructive direction.

Perhaps I should share with you that when we returned and being denied jobs, we formed a group called the Centre for Human Rights and Rehabilitation, basically to contribute to the consolidation of democracy in Malawi and also promote people's rights and also to push for accountability.... there were a number of institutions that were created under the new constitution which was put in place in 1994 and adopted in 1995, the Human Rights Commission, the Ombudsman, Law Commission. So there were a lot of processes that needed consolidation. The other aspect was that most people were not fully aware of their rights, roles and responsibilities, because this was all new, having been denied space for over 30 years, therefore we thought we could contribute to move forward that process through the Centre for Human Rights and Rehabilitation. I was its founding director from 1995 up to 2005.

I would say that it is one of the organisations that has contributed a lot towards the consolidation of democracy and also trying to hold the state... accountable. And to educate people about democracy, good governance and so forth. Also it has taken a much greater leadership role from 1995 up to date. It is one of the organisations which is a household name in areas of rights. It is highly respected both by the local people as well as people in government.

For example in 2000, President Muluzi wanted to amend the Constitution for a third term and it was the Centre for Human Rights which contributed a lot alongside church faith-based organisations to mobilise people to reject the third term because it was unconstitutional. The constitution has two terms of five years limit, so he wanted to go further. Through the Centre and other groups we tried to mobilise parliamentarians and successfully.

So we have been part and parcel of civil society activism and human rights activism. Changes are there in the sense that the Malawians are increasingly able to speak out when things are not going well. The media has been in the forefront in terms of exposing issues of bad governance, corruption and so forth....

During the period of the second term of Bingu wa Mutharika there was a lot of bad governance, disrespect of the rule of law and civil society stood up, organised some demonstrations. A lot of pressure was given to government. Of course [the government] was arrogant, but still civil society manged to conscientise the people, put some pressure, conscientise the donor community, as a means of weakening the regime. The country depends 30% of its budget from donor support which was based on good governance. It was suspended.... You can see some indicators that it's actually building up. Also there are debates, radio debates, people can talk without fear, those ones who are courageous. So one could say that [in] some aspects we are there if one compares with other countries.

In the process of living with their pain and coping with their re-integration into Malawi, former detainees and refugees displayed a mix of reactions, but all showed amazing resilience. Some are living comfortable retirements, while others face tragic poverty and struggle to survive. Some younger professionals have carved out new careers and made remarkable progress. While others are suffering in poverty and despair because of their psychological and physical scars. The common thread among them all is their sense of bitterness, which is reflected in how they see Malawi's current political and economic situation, what we refer to as the "democracy bubble."

Chapter 9 – The Promised Land and the Democracy Bubble

9.1 The Banda Legacy

9.2 Denial of the Legacy

9.3 Truth and Justice

9.4 The Democracy Bubble

9.5 The Impact of the Banda Legacy on Youth

When considering the question "Should we remember?" it is very important to firstly ask, has any victim forgotten? Could they ever forget? Secondly we should ask, who wants to forget? Who benefits when all the atrocities stay silent in the past?

(Roberto Cabrera – Guatemalan human rights activist)[1]

We asked all our respondents what they thought of the Malawi of today and what legacies remain from the Banda era. Almost without exception, they were very critical of the political evolution over the last few years and ascribed the nation's ills to the 30 year reign of Dr Banda. Most were very critical of the rehabilitation of Dr Banda's image as a hero and saviour. Their comments speak for themselves.

9.1 The Banda Legacy

Frank Jiya protests how the promoters of Banda's hero qualities position themselves on

....the topmost on the platform say[ing], "I admire Dr Banda." Admire Dr Banda? But admire to what point? Because yes he started well, but he became oppressive and dictatorial. His system maimed people, killed people and forced them into exile. So what do you admire?... So okay, those who sit down and declare someone a hero. Where? How do you describe a hero? A hero today. Tomorrow a traitor. He becomes a hero again; the next a traitor. We are still in the old days like it was under Dr Banda. Most of the projects are from the top down. No people who sit down here plan and ask the executive to give them land. But the executive will decide.

.... For example, is it normal for an Ndirande man, a chief, to stand up and say, "Your Excellency. We just want to complain a little. We are asking

---

[1] Quoted in Richard Carver. (2000) *"WHO WANTS TO FORGET?" Truth and Access to Information About Past Human Rights Violations*, published by Article 19 – The Global Campaign for Free Expression, London

for one or two boreholes?"... They just sing a song. They are not themselves, they are still parotting the songs.... We still go to sing and dance for leaders at the airport or at a rally. No production. No nothing. That is not what we were fighting for.... We have to deBandanise ourselves before we can move forward.

Ceciwa Khonje has been a strong supporter of our project since she first heard of it. She immediately wrote us two pieces. She elaborates in more detail how the influence of Dr Banda still permeates the ruling classes of Malawi today. This is an abridged extract of a longer letter, which she entitled:

Malawi & The Aftermath Of Her Dictatorship

After he returned to Malawi from exile in 1994, my brother, the late Dr Harry Bwanausi, once said, "It will take 100 years for Malawi to get back to normal after the dictatorship of Kamuzu Banda." Observing developments in Malawi even from Pretoria, I can see what he was talking about. In the 30 years of his dictatorship, a generation of Malawians was born and the only form of government they knew was the dictatorship. The people we left in the country as adults got so brain-washed they started believing everything the dictator said. Even those that did not necessarily like the dictatorial tendencies, they swallowed everything from the dictatorship and never contradicted in order to save their necks.

In the 30 years such a situation lasted, they subconsciously began to **believe** what they were taking in. That is why to this day, roads, the Capital City airport, hospitals, are all named after the man who hanged Chesilombela in public! That is why even President Joyce Banda, as democratic and as human rights protecting as she sounds, she renames her State House "Kamuzu" Palace. She even publicly states she was impressed with Kamuzu's achievements. What achievements? Sending a letter bomb to Dr Atati Kumpakati in Maputo and severing his fingers and finally following him all the way to Harare and shooting him dead there? How can the President not know about the torture that went on [nyakula] in Kamuzu's prisons like Dzereka and Mikuyu?

The reason why the democratic dispensation has not brought about correction of the distorted history of Malawi is because what the leaders know about government and how it's run is what they saw Kamuzu do. We should never forget that Muluzi who took over from Kamuzu had been Secretary General of the Malawi Congress Party, serving the dictatorship during a period that covered the kidnapping of Orton Chirwa and family and the shocking primitive trial of Chirwa that followed in Malawi. How much democracy can we expect from a key participant of such a crime?

Mutharika, who took over from Muluzi, is someone my whole extended family knows from the days he was a primary school boarder at the Henry Henderson Institute in Blantyre. When I was in the UN he was also in Addis

Ababa serving the UN. To cut a long story short, many mistake Mutharika as having been a refugee in Zambia. Before leaving Malawi, he went to say goodbye to Kamuzu, telling him he was looking for greener pastures in Zambia. No prospective refugee can take leave of his oppressor.

As the English say, "The proof of the pudding is in the eating." When Bingu became president, one of the first things he did was to build a mausoleum for Kamuzu – honouring the man who fed his live political opponents to crocodiles! Would any genuine exile, anybody horrified by such acts, honour such a sadistic killer? **Birds of a feather flock together!**

The reason why Malawi's development was stymied and remains even more untenable today is because from the time of Kamuzu's dictatorship, the focus of all activity in the country was on politics and nothing else. The core of that focus was the elimination of opposition and the aggrandisement of the leader. Hence the establishment of the one party state with a life president; the substitution of educated cabinet ministers for uneducated boot-lickers to worship the leader and facilitate smooth dictatorship. Change will happen only when the leader of the country completely severs all links to Kamuzu. When they realize he was a human rights abuser and one of the worst dictators the world ever had.

Ollen Mwalubunju was part of the group of returned exiles who decided to stay in civil society and monitor the political health and evolution of Malawi after the democratic dispensation. At the time of writing this book he was the Executive Director of the National Initiative for Civic Education (NICE) Trust. He reflects on the problems left by the Banda regime.

Closing the mindset of people to think inside the box, because the system was not allowing people to think free and Banda was bombarding them with Malawi is the best. During his time, people were not able to access information. Even listening to an international radio station was a crime. So it was a closed society and also in the educational system even today is not preparing the students to have critical analytical thinking. So we have ended up producing people who have accumulated knowledge, but that knowledge is not... being effectively utilised. It is what I call primitive accumulation of knowledge. If you have knowledge, you should be able to use that knowledge to help you to move, and things seem not to move in government as well as in the university, because it is just the same, even among scholars themselves. There are very few scholars who have come out on national issues and making arguments critically that we can build on these ideas.

Margaret Khonje echoes Professor George Shepperson in his quoting of Shakespeare "The good that men do dies with them, the evil lives on…." She says

I went through adulthood with Dr Banda. The one thing that I learned out of that regime was that a leadership must be focussed. It is good for

leadership to have strong strategies. It is good for leadership to build based on what a person can do, based on expertise and not based on where people come from. We saw that out of Kamuzu… If people are not free, people will not remember the strong things that people did. People will always think of the negative, the weak areas. For example, let's say Bingu built roads and things, but he will be remembered for killing innocent young people. So it is the same with Kamuzu. When you talk about Kamuzu, you think about crocodiles, the negative things and yet the person did a lot of good things. No matter how good your planning is, if people don't have freedom, if they are not free citizens….

When we interviewed Khwauli Msiska, he was Member of Parliament for Karonga North and a deputy minister. As such, he has privileged insight into the workings of the current government when he critiques the Banda legacy.

I think that the greatest damage that Kamuzu did to this country was… the type of people that he produced. The Kamuzu era was mainly responsible for having destroyed…or it did not nurture entrepreneurship. That spirit of assertiveness. They did not create go-getters, people who can take their destiny in their own hands… He created yes men, and we lack that self-reliance, type of people. Now is when I appreciate why Nyerere kept talking about ujamaa, that you have to rely on yourselves. Be independent. Be self-reliant. We are yet to achieve that and it is not something we can magically achieve. I think it will take yet another protracted struggle.

From her background growing up in Dar es Salaam, Tujilane Chizumila had an interesting perspective on the differences between the cultures of the two societies.

I grew up a Tanzanian for 30 years. That's half of my life. I always compare notes. We went through economic hardships. When our economy went to the dogs. I look at the level of kindness, simplicity and cleanliness in Dar es Salaam.

I want to move and be free [in Malawi] but I can't do anything for myself… It's our background here as Malawians. In those days, women had to wear three piece suits and men had to wear three piece suits to go to work or whatever. I cannot even talk to the messenger in the office or people will talk about you breaking protocol. We are having problems moving away from that elite culture… Nyerere encouraged equality in society. The elite culture of Kamuzu is still alive.

9.2 Denial of the legacy

There is still a strong tendency, even amongst people who suffered at the hands of the Banda regime, to deny that Dr Banda was responsible for the atrocities or that he even had knowledge of what was going on. Like many people, Mathews Kalambo refuses to accept that a man as well educated as Dr Banda could perpetrate the atrocities that occurred during his regime.

I thought Dr Banda was a well educated person and I wondered how his government can do things like this, detaining educated people. Until I came out. I found out that it was not him at all. It was the people who surrounded him, the people he worked with, not Kamuzu. These people who work with him spoiled him.

By contrast, Justin Malewezi dealt with Dr Banda face to face regularly in his last years as President and was very clear in his assessment of Banda's capacities and control of the matters of state even as he was in his nineties.

…. He was still in charge…. He was old but still sharp….

As one of the last of the Secretaries to the President and Cabinet, Justin saw Dr Banda often and was supposed to be present at various functions. There were certainly power manipulators behind the throne, but Justin saw Dr Banda run the affairs of state himself. Banda knew what was going on in all sectors of the country.

… You must take notes, be attentive and follow up. You must do that. After every meeting I would go to Sanjika. If he had promised anything or someone else had promised anything, I would have it in written form at his desk. If it didn't come you were in trouble. He would remember.

9.3 Truth and justice

Malawi has not squarely faced the truth about the past nor dealt with the injustices inflicted on the country's people during the 30 years of Dr Banda's dictatorship. To paraphrase an old adage, if we have not learned the lessons of the past then we are doomed to repeat the many negative practices that Kamuzu implanted.

When asked about truth and justice, Ollen Mwalubunju is clear on this point:

For some of us that is very fundamental. You are seeing around people who have murdered, who have killed your relatives, your friends who have gone scot-free. How do you reconcile? How do you forgive if there is no accountability mechanism. The truth should be known then forgiveness and reconciliation come through. So it is just like a time-bomb. The people who were perpetrators are continuing benefiting, the perpetrators of human rights [abuse]… [while] victims are continuing suffering.

Most of the detainees, the returnees have not been resettled, [not] been compensated. A handful of politicians who were part of perpetrating abuses but who fell [out] with the regime went into the new political parties at a senior level. A few of them got millions as part of compensation, but a common Malawian who suffered is continuing his suffering. They have not been compensated. So where is justice? Yes, the 1994 Constitution... we had the National Compensation Tribunal which had about a ten year life span. After 2004 it was dissolved while not fulfilling what it was supposed to do, and the government did not even extend its lifespan. One would say perhaps that the group of people who suffered was a small group that it cannot impact on the political process. But you don't do that. Justice. Justice.

For example, the government spent so much money building the mausoleum for Dr Banda whose system made Malawians suffer. He is honoured by a K77 million mausoleum, while the victims, 80 to 90% of them, have not received a penny. Is there any justice? Are we serious as a people? The answer is no and this will be the source... of trouble in the future. Because the more people are being enlightened, the more the anger is growing up. Of course people are saying that Malawians are submissive... but anything can happen.

These are very fundamental aspects.... It is not about entitlement, it is about justice.

Frank Jiya offers an answer to what happened to the National Compensation Tribunal.

Money was given to the tribunal and unfortunately, people with advance information, because some of them, those who were in government at that time were the people who benefitted. Immediately the money was given to the tribunal, it was taken right away by those people in the know and the rest of the people got nothing before the Tribunal's mandate expired. The majority especially those from exile did not benefit. I will not go into details, but we should demand that we should publish the names of the people who benefited.

9.4 Democracy Bubble

President Joyce Banda praised Dr Banda twenty years after his dictatorship had been overthrown. George Kasakula hit the nail on the head in his *Nation* article of July 2014 entitled: *Give Malawians a break on Kamuzu Banda* and reprinted in full in the introduction to this book. *Going through statements from various quarters, including one President Joyce Banda made in Kasungu, canonising Kamuzu Banda as a holy patron saint of development and women liberation, you would think that this is not the same man who for over 30 years ruled Malawi with an iron fist.* This is what we call the Democracy Bubble.

The promised democracy is a shallow facade. There are elections every five years, a free and combative press, political detentions are a thing of the past, but real or fundamental change has not occurred. The habits of Dr

Banda live on in the leadership of today. Praise singers are bussed in to clap their hands, ululate and sing when elections occur and throw their votes to the candidate who offers them a few kwacha for their votes. Five presumed free elections have simply replaced dictatorship with endemic corruption, because these past practices shape current behaviour. The people are still shut out of the political process, which remains decidedly top down, authoritarian and tribute based. Frank Jiya's assessment is that we have

[N]ot yet Uhuru... and Malawi has not yet embraced multipartyism completely. We are in a multiparty dispensation, but the way we govern, the way we behave, the way we do our things is still one party. We need to come up with a project to deBandanise ourselves.

It is a luta continua [the struggle continues]. We have to struggle, keep on fighting until we get to a real democracy. Other countries which could not feed themselves and now feed themselves. Do you mean Malawi cannot do the same? Just two kilometres out of Lilongwe and that is where poverty is. There is still poverty and illiteracy just outside of the city. In 1961, I taught my mothers to read and think and here 50 years later we are more illiterate than before....

Thengo Maloya was involved with the patriotic fervour of the nationalist struggle and looking back from his vantage point sees that it is sadly lacking today.

Malawi of today. Well I would say that the young people haven't seen the struggle for independence and freedom. If you tell them about thangata they wouldn't know. If you tell them about the humiliation under the white man they wouldn't know it. They go to school with the white man and the Indians as well... I don't blame them for not knowing. They didn't know what went on.... but Malawians, I feel they are beginning to lose their democracy by forgetting that this country was fought for. People must be aware that some people fought for this country not on a selfish level. They fought for this country because they loved this country. They wanted the people of Malawi to be very free. Free as any other people in any other nation. When people lack this spirit, patriotism I will call it in short... you find that they will receive bribes. They will do anything. They will quarrel with us. They blame Banda for staying on as President for lifetime when they themselves don't want to step down as chairman. Patriotism is lacking.

Khwauli Msiska was the Deputy Minister of Economic Planning and Development and MP for Karonga North at the time of this writing.

We are not yet there. We are not yet there. Looking at what we fought for out there. Let there be freedom. Let there be democracy. That we should come back here and participate in the voting, participate in the politicking, multiparty dispensation. That to some extent has been achieved, but I think we are yet to have inclusive participation in our democracy.... I feel the struggle has been hijacked to some extent. I don't see that inclusive participation. The challenge is to build a democratic culture. We need that.

Professor George Michongwe sees another result of the Kamuzu era that has polluted the political landscape. The fear instilled by the regime has left people deeply suspicious of others.

I think I must start by saying that I was not fully convinced that this country would be as peaceful as I had left it. But now I am convinced. When I was coming I was still doubtful. Although what I discovered was, and I think it was quite natural, people were not very keen on those of us that were out, that we should be given good jobs in government....

Without going into details, I must start by saying no, it was not the kind of Malawi I expected to find. Indeed as I said before, I found it peaceful, but I still found... suspicion. In fact, I annoyed several people telling them face to face that this country was full of suspicion. Everybody suspects everybody else. They are not happy to see somebody being promoted and not them. That's what I found. And I have been telling some of the people involved that that is our weakness. Some are very unhappy. They can't listen to me now.

Two. I discovered... that our Malawians now they don't know the history of Malawi. They don't know their history. They don't know how we got independence. Who did what for independence. They don't know.

…. they think [Kamuzu did everything], but Kamuzu, when he came, we were almost independent. We brought him because we were almost independent. Not in order to make us independent. No. No....

One thing I found which was positive was that people are no longer killing each other. At least that was not there. No longer going into people's houses and beating each other. That has gone.

But they are still suspicious, A) against those of us that had been out. Some of the senior civil servants and politicians thought we were coming to grab their jobs from them. And that, I think is still true up till now. Some of them are still not very happy about our being here.

Secondly, something which makes me very unhappy is that we don't know each other....

The professor explained that he was never sought out for his knowledge, expertise or advice despite long experience in the civil service even before independence.

Without being prompted on the issue, the late Willie Chokani described how the progressive ministers cut their salaries 50 years ago in order to show how serious they were in dealing with the funding problems that had led to the proposed *tikkey* fee on hospital visits before the 1964 Cabinet Coup. He also denounced the shameful get-rich-quick mentality of today's venal and greedy political leaders and civil servants.

*The disappointing thing is this **corruption**. Whereas, right at the word 'Go' we fought for the country, for the people... these people fought for themselves as individuals.... Yes I think an element of democracy has come. People can say, "No!" People can march. You couldn't do that in Dr Banda's time. You would be all gone... Now people don't care, whether they oppose the government or not.*

The sad thing is this group, the middle group, they don't know. You tell them about democracy and they say what democracy? They are after a job. It's sad! Sacrifice? You read for example of MPs wanting a higher salary. In our time it was not like that. It was the reverse. We would rather say, "I'll do it for nothing." We used to maintain the road from Blantyre mission here up to Ndirande some two miles away for nothing. In fact, a cousin of mine was in charge of the group. They got nothing. Today you can't ask someone to do that without their allowances. This is something that is painful to us.... It's not there anymore. It's a shame...

You need a very strong leadership who can teach social responsibility.... It's a shame ... quite a number of chaps in positions of leadership, they look at success in terms of how much have they accumulated.... Who have they put into offices....

Nettie Dzabara was equally eloquent about the problems facing Malawi in her concluding remarks when asked if the Malawi of today is what she had anticipated.

***NO**.... Wow! Where do I start? Malawi has become a very frustrating country. This is because all the politicians that come they have a vision about a better Malawi for the people, but all of them seem to do one thing. They surround themselves with opportunists, corrupt people and we end up feeling that we have been cheated again.*

Mluzi came in. What happened? Bingu came in. On paper, he had very nice theories but execution....

Now the case of Joyce Banda is extra special, because Joyce Banda is a very hardworking person, extremely hard working woman with the best of intentions. But Malawians, we are still at that stage where we do not want to be led by a woman. That's the truth. Women are disadvantaged in this country.

When asked if this sexism is part of the Kamuzu legacy, Nettie replied:

I think probably we can say yes, because we have not emancipated [ourselves] at the rate we are supposed to have emancipated our thinking. For example, it took me ages to get the salesladies in my shop to stop kneeling when they talked to me. They actually go and kneel, and it is so entrenched in them. I just say oh my God.... This is not Malawian culture. It will take ages to get that thinking out.

And with the President being a woman they will do things just because she is a woman. She said this when we met in Addis. We had a caucus and she said to us that because I am a woman, there are a lot of things that I cannot get away with which are done by men and the country accepts. But because I am a woman they will challenge anything that I do. And to make matters worse, Malawian women will not support another woman. She mentionned this that she did a survey that only 35% of the professional women actually support me... So this is not the Malawi that I was hoping to build.

Ollen Mwalubunju provided insight into why the situation has deteriorated in the democracy bubble.

One could say that the struggle was highjacked.... Our expectation was not the outcome of the process. It was not what we would have liked to start building a new Malawi....

Of course, one would like to have much more, a better Malawi, but looking at the destruction that Dr Banda had made and also looking at the change of guards through Muluzi, Bingu himself and through the current president [Joyce Banda at the time], we have leaders who are transactional rather than transformatory in nature. Because of the lack of transformatory leadership, we are not achieving much progress. We are just moving around the circle. Business as usual and so those are some of the challenges.

Chifipa Gondwe, with his years of experience at the UN's Economic Commission on Africa, is able to provide more than a simple drive-by view. He points out the problem lies with:

... government policies towards the rural people. Poverty is massive. Government policies towards commodities is not very helpful to the rural people. Mangoes are just rotting but it is all wasted.... I can't understand why the government doesn't have a vision. They don't talk to people. They don't ask what we can do here.... Conditions under Dr Banda were moving well according to UNDP Human Development Reports but now Mozambique, Zambia and Tanzania have... overtaken Malawi.

Malawi has the lowest rate of rural electrification in the world at 3% and the next country up has 11 or 12%. Most Malawians still spend nights in darkness. The implication is that most of our little children as soon as it is dark they can't read they have no television.... The second aspect in terms of industrial development, Malawi is way behind the region and behind in many other things. According to the BBC, Malawi has the highest rates of footprints, people without shoes in the world.... Our road system is very bad....

Chifipa concluded his reflection by noting the root of these problems was deep-seated.

Malawi is corrupt. Things started a long time ago. Swindling government resources started a long time ago. It is not new.... I am sad. Sometimes I ask why I should be a Malawian....

Tom Chabwino Nyirenda also articulates these sentiments.

We do not have a government that yet appreciates what they put us through it. All the leaders we have today, the people who had the mentality of Dr Banda are still there. I don't think I can trust any government that comes from such people. They don't torture anymore, now they are killing. It will take another 40 years for Malawi to change....

You old people are being denied. You fought for this but you have been forsaken. Those people who were mistreating us are still enjoying. And those people don't even believe that there is democracy in this country. Financially it's all economical. It's the same [nothing has changed] for you people. You are forsaken, you people.

He points at Kapote and he is referring to the opposition leadership that toiled in exile and struggled to bring about democracy and remove the dictatorship.

9.5 The Impact of the Banda Legacy on Youth

Macheza Dzabala is a recent university graduate. He was born in exile, the son of Nettie Dzabala, and in 1995, at 6 years old, he came to Malawi. He sat and listened intently as we interviewed his grandmother, Molly. He asked us if he could contribute to this project. It is an excellent intervention from the point of view of a young person, the youth of today. When asked how the dictatorship of Dr Banda impacted his family, he replied:

Macheza Dzabala

It has taught many valuable lessons along the way. We have learned the fine art of humility.... We have seen history being misinterpreted for a very long time. It is a history that is very vital. It is important for a lot of people to know. For example, people praise Dr Banda as a national hero and in a way we understand how that comes about. But then they forget and they leave out the parts about what this man actually did and how he destroyed people's lives....

Malawians are generally a peaceful people which is very good, but I think that the youth have lost that vision, the drive. The youth have reached a place of mediocrity and they are satisfied in it. They think this is the way things are and this is the way they will always be. Funnily enough we live in a democratic nation and in a place where we are free to speak... but we do not speak, even when we see things going wrong.

But if you look at the past, for example, my family's history and what they went through, that should be drive enough that when we see something wrong we are able to stand up [against] it...

The youth in this country have the problem... of being satisfied with mediocrity... with things that are being served as injustices... We are satisfied and we have gotten to the realm of okayness.

When asked if the struggles his family went through and what he sees in Malawi today reflects the efforts that people like them went through, he replied:

I do [see the changes], but I think Malawi should be more, this country itself should be more. Too many people have suffered and too many people have lost their lives for this country. Too many people have been chased away. Too many people do not know their home because they have fled. Yes, in the sense of democracy, but then the country should give back to the people who actually fought for it. Who actually contributed to what it is today.

But the country itself and especially our leaders, the ones who came in after Kamuzu Banda, could have done more to help drive this country forward. To get this country to where it was is a struggle. And I think that to not commemorate, to not acknowledge the people as well, who made this country what it is is a severe injustice.

For example, I could safely say that no one knows the history of the MCP,... as my grandmother who had to explain the history of the MCP all over again. No one really knows who fought for this country. No one really knows who lost their lives for this country. We pick up one of two names and we are fine with that and we think we know it all but we do not delve deep into the essence of this country, its core.

This country has not developed into what my grandfather wanted, what my grandmother wanted, what my uncles, what everybody who fought for this country wanted... We still have certain things as Malawians that we failed to achieve.

We still go through phases like, for example the last president, the late Ngwazi, Professor Bingu wa Mutharika. He was also a semi-dictator.

So this country hasn't really reached that stage that we can safely say that it is what the people who fought for it wanted. I do not think so and I think the key lies with the young ones, the coming generation.

It's going to take a lot of eye opening. There is an English saying that in order to know where you are going, you must know here you come from. That is true. The youth are just going to roam around aimlessly. They are going to be satisfied. They are just going to get by for them and them alone. They do not understand to get where we are today, people had to fight, not only for themselves but for others. Until the young ones realise that we do *not live for ourselves, but for the people around us too, this country will never advance in the way it is supposed to.*

It is fair to note that Malawi is not alone in dealing with these kinds of transitional issues. The news out of South Africa perpetually revolves around the scandalous abuse of power and the outrageous wealth accumulation of the post-apartheid leadership. The former Soviet Union and Eastern Bloc countries also demonstrate how painful and slow change can be when systems change. Our respondents were all very critical of this current phase. Their situation is even more dismal than at independence. It is our belief that Malawi can do better.

Chapter 10 Conclusion

In a very insightful interview with The Nation newspaper, senior journalist, James Chavula asked Doug and Kapote the question, "Why do the smart, educated people you interviewed not write their history themselves? Why did you feel you have to do it?" We were briefly taken aback, since our mission had seemed so obvious to us.

The respondents readily agreed to participate in this project and are remarkable for their courage and honesty. That they feel forsaken and forgotten is evidence of how the residue of the Banda period continues to enforce the regime's rule of silence. The dearth of serious writing on the repression and suffering also confirms this legacy. Others before us have tried to publicise these issues but slowly and inexorably the cloak of silence about the crimes committed against the Malawi people envelopes the conversation and smothers public discussion and memory. The current trend to rehabilitate the dreadful legacy of Dr Banda and his acolytes is extremely offensive to the many people of Malawi who suffered detention, exile and a daily state of terror.

As this conclusion was being redrafted for the third time at the behest of our editor, a Malawian expatriate and a longtime supporter called to insist that we refund his donation from 2013. He no longer wished to be associated with the project and wanted to use his money for other purposes. We were very hurt and disappointed, but pursued the conversation long enough to establish his motives. First, he was unhappy that it was taking too long for the book to appear. More telling was how very upset he was about the current state of affairs in Malawi. As far as he was concerned, the current rulers are so bad that life was much better under the dictatorship and as a result he did not want to hear the stories of Banda's abuse.

Our Long Journey

We agree and regret that this project has taken such a long time to produce. We humbly offer as an excuse that we are two retired seniors on limited, fixed incomes living continents and oceans apart. It must also seem very long for the people we interviewed, some as long ago as 2012. We are especially saddened that several have fallen by the way as time and age have overwhelmed them.

Our original goal when we set out in 2010 was to write the history of Lesoma before that phase in Malawi's history became any more distant in people's memories. As we pursued our work, our sense of urgency over Lesoma evolved into a sense of indignation at the current leadership classes rehabilitating the image of the dictator as a saviour. We are indignant because too many of our friends and comrades paid with their lives or their well-being under the brutal repression Dr Banda unleashed upon the people of Malawi.

Why is this rehabilitation happening? Because many of the people who held positions of power and influence and who prospered under Banda's regime still wield power today. They also bring with them the political and social culture of that era. This has been made possible, in large part, because the history of what truly happened during the Banda years has been buried, a calamity that we have tried to redress in this book.

We have called the 30 years of Dr Banda's dictatorship the Lost Years. The years in detention were Lost Years. The years in exile were Lost Years for the many refugees forced to leave their homeland, when they should have been inside Malawi working to overcome the stifling poverty inflicted on the people. Professors, doctors, nurses, lawyers, ophthalmologists, agronomists, statisticians – rather than contributing to overcoming underdevelopment in Malawi, they were in Tanzania, Zambia and other countries, which happily harnessed their talents. Beyond the individual cases of the detainees and exiles, the whole country suffered the consequences of the Lost Years. The individual stories, while tragic, pale beside the daily grinding poverty to which the Banda regime condemned the entire population.

By requesting a refund of his money, our friend highlighted the sad irony of the link between the malaise of today and the cancer of the past. The most obvious sign of the continuity of the disease was the restoration of Dr Banda's name to all the roads, bridges, airports, hospitals and public institutions under the rule of Bingu waMutharika. More insidiously, Dr Banda taught the lessons that are emulated by today's rulers. Their current behavior is nothing less than an extension and logical outcome of his example.

Our respondents joined our project willingly and selflessly. They stand as living testimony to how the abuse of the past continues to fester today. They came from all walks of life, but shared the common story of mistreatment. Thomas Nyirenda, crippled and with poor eye-sight, is especially upset that the people who suffered have been left with nothing, while the Tembos and Kadzimiras are still rich and continuing to prosper from their role in Banda's misrule. Carson Kayuni is in his eighties and despite an enormous sacrifice and 30 years of exile still must work in the fields growing potatoes to feed himself and his family. Chief Mwase's *induna*[1], G.K. Mpango, is in his nineties and complains bitterly that he still has to work in the fields because his years of detention in Mikuyu left him a poor man. To rub salt in the wounds of Mpango's suffering, he lives within sight of Dr Banda's extravagant palace on the lower slope of Kasungu Mountain. Ngulu wa Nawambe stands largely unoccupied today and serves to showcase Banda's abuse of power and the inequitable accumulation of wealth his policies promoted.

---

1 Chief's counsellor

Our respondents are growing older, and many are in failing health – often directly due to their harsh treatment during the Banda years. Consequently, it is urgent to record and publicise their stories. We regret that the book format limits how much of each person's story we could use. We selected portions of their interviews that were representative of the issues we explored and only included one or two examples in cases where many people made the same point.

Their stories also reveal that they were not alone or isolated despite their trials and tribulations. Many other unsung heroes and heroines, high and low, helped them escape or supported them through exile and detention. Kennedy Msonda's grandfather confronted the security apparatus head-on to ensure that his clansman, Machipisa Munthali, had not been killed in prison. Relatives and friends hid Jando Nkhwazi and ferried him by bicycle at night through the bush to safety across the Songwe River in Tanzania. Women, in particular, carried an extra burden and were deeply involved in the struggle for change even as they suffered in the silence imposed by the state apparatus. They endured, were strong and defied the abuse. Without them, many of our respondents would not have survived to tell their stories. In retrospect, Victoria Sibanda speaks with pride of having survived all her trials, "Psychologically, I was very strong. I didn't break down after all these hassles. I felt very strong."

The stories our collaborators shared with us reveal the essential contributions of many important heroes and heroines of the independence and nationalist struggle who are still ignored and largely unacknowledged. Rose Chibambo and Willie Chokani were deeply involved and brought the youthful energy and commitment needed to liberate their country from the injustices of colonial rule over Malawi in the 1950s. Machipisa Munthali, John Jando Nkwasi, and Frank Jiya described how they and their comrades resisted the move to dictatorship. Young militants like John Phiri and Ollen Mwalubunju talked about their role as part of the organised opposition in the 1980s that older activists like Atati Mpakati, Professor Michongwe, Kapote and John Jando Nkwhazi had set in motion.

They put to rest the myth that Malawians sat in passive silence and acquiesced in their oppression. They were developing and promoting an alternative vision to the course Dr Banda had set the country on. Their willingness to quickly return and immerse themselves in the transitional process also attests to their commitment to bring peace and transformation to a tormented nation. That radical tradition has been almost completely extinguished, not by repressive measures, but by a smothering blanket of denial and the continuation of many of the undemocratic habits of the Banda regime in the practices of government of today.

Banda as Dictator

From his return to the country in 1958 until his removal from power, Dr Banda established himself as the unquestionned ruler of the country. The respondents clearly demonstrated the brutal ruthlessness he used to assume this absolute power. From our respondents it was clear that his actions as prime minister and then president in the early sixties were meant to establish him as the sole person in charge, while the savage repression unleashed on the country after the 1964 Cabinet Crisis was meant to enforce his totalitarian rule and eliminate the radical tradition. Kings Phiri narrowly escaped imprisonment in 1976, but described the fear of daily life under "state terrorism." Chifipa Gondwe, Kirby Mwambetania, Makhumbira Munthali, Augustine Msiska, Mathews Kalambo, James Mwagomba tell their stories of being picked up and held in terrible conditions without any charges or due process. Their misery was entirely due to the capricious and malicious whims of people who wielded absolute power without any controls or checks.

Regrettably, many people, including some who suffered at the hands of the regime, have succumbed to the pretension that Dr Banda was a good man, and any misdeeds were committed by the people who exploited their positions of proximity to the throne. Deep into his nineties, after 30 years as absolute ruler, Dr Banda still maintained control over the pinnacle of government and micromanaged all aspects of political life. Justin Malewezi illustrates how even his very senior position did not protect him and he feared every encounter with Dr Banda.

Regionalism

The tribal and regional differences evident today are another sad legacy of the distrust engendered by the regime. Rose, Willie, Ceciwa and others attest to how the period of the nationalist struggle brought people together despite the diversity of their linguistic, ethnic or regional origins. However, the current rulers continue to promote their group at the expense of others.

The spectre of tribalism has been re-introduced and elevated to the public platform, arousing the old fears of minority groups. The 1964 installation of dictatorship marked the introduction of the Centre against the South and the North. It is significant that the overthrow of the Banda dictatorship in 1994 coincided with the Rwanda genocide. That tragedy demonstrates how ethnic divisions between people can be exacerbated into full-scale massacres. This lies behind the fears of many people in Malawi's minority groups. They are anxious that the noise on the podium will move beyond words to violence.

Wealth and Corruption

The most egregious consequence of the Banda legacy plaguing the body politic of Malawi today is the ostentatious and inequitable wealth accumulation of the small circle of people close to power. The 2013 Cashgate scandal has provided public evidence of this unbridled looting of the country's wealth. A position of power provides entitlement to loot. From the most mundane police roadblocks to the highest seats of power, any position of power entitles the occupant to line his or her pockets at the expense of fellow citizens.

Our respondents showed how this practice had its roots early in the Banda reign and decried the current widespread corruption as shameful. They also attest to how this mentality has come to dominate public life and quite literally smothered the sense of duty and service that motivated the Young Turks as nationalist leaders. The late Willie Chokani described how the young cabinet ministers selflessly cut their salaries in order to show Dr Banda that they were serious about saving money and forestalling Banda's intention to charge Malawi's poor citizens user fees for medical help. Once they had been eliminated, Banda went on to become the richest person in the country and used government to enforce his personal right to accumulation.

By contrast, during his reign, the majority of Malawi's citizens remained mired in poverty. This part of Banda's legacy has continued as Malawi's current rulers shamelessly ignore the plight of their fellow citizens who today still lack access to education, health, clean water and many other basic services. Chifipa Gondwe spoke of Malawi holding the appalling title of the country with the highest rate of barefootedness and the lowest rate of rural electrification.

Truth and Justice

President Julius Nyerere of Tanzania said: *If you hide your disease, death will expose you.* It is our point that the political, economic and social paralysis we see today in Malawi that frustrates the country's march to democracy comes directly from the disease of the past. Mary Mwale and Ollen Mwalubunju very eloquently decried the lack of honesty and truth-telling about the injustices of the past. Ollen was clear about the need for some form of truth and reconciliation, otherwise the problems of the past will continue to fester and haunt the present.

The lack of public truth-telling and reconciliation also has an impact on the transparency and accountability of government. Richard Carver noted, a mere six years after the democratic dispensation of 1994, that the failure to undertake an honest accounting for past abuses explains a number of the current problems:

[T]here is also a very strong pragmatic argument for fact-finding exercises.... the democratic government of Malawi since 1994 has not been a model of openness, efficiency or good governance. Why? Largely because it continues with the methods and the low standards of probity and accountability that characterized the years of single-party rule. One result of this is that donors' money is spent inefficiently and often corruptly. Surely a thorough investigation that documented the nature of abuses under the old

*regime could lead to reforms that would facilitate better governance under the new.*²*

Many people, both inside and outside of the country, point to how the transition to democracy was peaceful. The testimony of the victims of the past clearly demonstrates that it was not peace that Banda installed but a brutal system of fear and repression. Hiding this history does not bring peace. Silence does not create or represent peace, and there can be no peace without justice. As the stories revealed in this book so painfully demonstrate, the wounds of dictatorship run deep and still fester. There is an urgent need to tell the truth by way of some form of truth and reconciliation process in order to achieve restorative justice, reconciliation, and forgiveness. But for forgiveness to be forthcoming from the victims, those who committed the crimes have to acknowledge that they did indeed do something wrong.

Rather than acknowledging their role, the wrongdoers are seeking to forget or bury the past, or worse, rewrite it by rehabilitating the dictator's legacy. For this to be challenged, the voices in this book must be heard. Opening this door is a challenging and painful process, but other countries have been bold enough to grapple with their tortured past, and as this book has demonstrated, Malawians certainly have the courage and wherewithal to do the same.

When dramatic regime change occurs in any country, a number of different reactions can occur. In the Czech Republic, the new post-communist government passed a law forbidding members of the secret police and the old communist party from being members of the civil service and its related bodies such as the police. South Africa's Truth and Reconciliation Commission was established to allow people who had been wronged to recount the injustices they had faced and call to account the person or organisation who had wronged them. Wrongdoers could acknowledge their crimes and avoid prosecution. In Sierra Leone, a blanket amnesty was issued to all parties to the brutal civil war with the exception of some of the major actors who were brought to trial before a special international tribunal set up to deal with them. This meant victims of atrocities often returned to their homes and found themselves living side by side and having to make uneasy peace with neighbours who had caused them great personal harm. The Gachacha courts in Rwanda were meant to dispense justice expediently at a local level, to heal the wounds of victims and to hold accountable the perpetrators of atrocities.

The Romanian, Malawian and Northern Ireland examples point to what happens when the same people who were highly placed members of a previous regime remain in power after the transition. In her radio documentary, *State Secrets*, Oana Lungescu interviewed people about why Romania was facing

---
2 Richard Carver 2000 *"WHO WANTS TO FORGET?" Truth and Access to Information about Past Human Rights Violations*, Article 19, London.

so many problems many years after the fall of the Ceausescu regime. One of her interview subjects provided a compelling answer:

The problem is the communists are very strong. They still control the economy and more important the property. They had the money. They had the vested interests, they had the relations. In effect they remain. A lot of the same people are still around. There is a lot of political infighting and people are more involved with the current struggles than with the past.

After decades of oppressive rule under the Ceausescu regime, the interviewee felt that there was "still a little bit of Ceausescu in all of us" and that it would take some time to change the bad old habits of the past that had been so firmly ingrained throughout the society. As many of our respondents so eloquently revealed, there is still a little bit of Dr Banda in many Malawians as well. Frank Jiya emphasised that we must deBandanise ourselves if we want to see any real change. A collective exercise in exorcising his negative legacy would be a crucial first step in breaking his lasting power.

At independence, in 1964, we had a golden opportunity to make a truly significant change in the lives of all Malawians. The brilliant young nationalists had laid the foundation with their progressive struggle against colonialism. Dunduzu Chisiza helped articulate it with his economic symposium but that was aborted by his premature death and Dr Banda's embrace of the World Bank paradigm of permanent underdevelopment. Thirty years of dictatorship later and the failure of all World Bank policies has left Malawi a basket case of maldevelopment and unforgivable poverty.

We had another golden opportunity in 1994 to turn the failures around and begin anew, but that chance was also squandered. The lessons of the past were not assimilated into the democratic dispensation and the rulers of the country carried on with business as usual in the Banda mould. The old corrupt practices have burst the democracy bubble and left Malawi a tragic failed state.

All our respondents showed us great respect and many expressed keen interest and encouragement. Their testimonials tell a different history of Malawi, one that holds the key to a very different future. Our fervent hope is that current and future generations will use that key to open the door to the kind of change and vision so eloquently expressed and fought for by our informants and untold others.

The Next Step

Oral history democratises history by giving it back to the people who lived it. We have carefully archived the interviews with our collaborators and are making arrangements to house the digitally recorded interviews to allow scholars, students and others interested people to hear the respondents' full testimonies. The goal would be to continue the work of collecting this history from as many victims of the regime as possible and archiving it for future purposes. We would appreciate if others were able to extend this history to inform the world about people as worthy as the ones we spoke to in order to help draw a much more complete history of the terror of the time.

Appendix

Living Our Faith
Pastoral Letter of the Catholic Bishops of Malawi
Lent 1992

Dear Brothers and Sisters in Christ,

As we commence this time of the Lord's favour, we, your bishops, greet you in the name of Our Lord and Saviour Jesus Christ.

Introduction

As a community journeying in faith and hope we recognize and accept the Lord's invitation proclaimed again in this time of Lent. On Ash Wednesday we receive ashes with the prayer: "Repent and believe the Good News." This prayer introduces the period of Lent when we shall enter once more into the saving mysteries of the Lord's death and resurrection.

Christ began his public ministry by proclaiming: "Repent and believe the Gospel" (Mk 1: 15). In this proclamation he states the programme of his ministry: to call all humankind in and through His life, death and resurrection to conversion and witness. People in every age and culture are called to this conversion and to respond in commitment and faith.

In this conviction we, your leaders in the faith, come to share with you what this faith invites us to as a church in the Malawi of today. We place this exhortation under the guidance of the Holy Spirit am the patronage of Mary, Queen of Malawi and of Africa.

The Dignity and Unity of Humankind

Man and woman, created in the image and likeness of God (Gen 1:26), carry in themselves the breath of divine life. Each created person is in communion with God. He or she is 'sacred', enjoying the personal protection of God. Human life is inviolable since it is from God and all human beings are one, springing as they do from a single father, Adam, and a single mother, Eve, "the mother of all those who live" (Gen 3:20).

The unity and dignity of the human race have been definitively sealed in Christ the Son of God who died for all, to unite everyone in one Body. Rejoicing in this truth we proclaim the dignity of every person, the right of each one to freedom and respect. This oneness of the human race also implies equality and the same basic rights for all. These must be solemnly respected and inculcated in every culture, every constitution and every social system.

The Church and Society

Because the Church exists in this world it must communicate its understanding of the meaning of human life and of society. As Pope Paul VI says: "the Church is certainly not willing to restrict her action only to the religious field and disassociate herself from man's temporal problems" (The Evangelization of Peoples, no. 34).

In this context we joyfully acclaim the progress which has taken place in our country, thanks in great part to the climate of peace and stability which we enjoy. We would, however, fail in our role as religious leaders if we kept silent on areas of concern.

The Aspiration to Greater Equality and Unity

In our society we are aware of a growing gap between the rich and the poor with regard to expectations, living standards and development. Many people still live in circumstances which are hardly compatible with their dignity as sons and daughters of God. Their life is a struggle for survival. At the same time a minority enjoys the fruits of development and can afford to live in luxury and wealth. We appeal for a more just and equal distribution of the nation's wealth.

Though many basic goods and materials are available, they are beyond the means of many of our people. One of the reasons for this is the deplorable wage structure which exists. For many, the wages they receive are grossly inadequate, e.g. employees in some estates, some domestic workers, brick-makers, etc., and this leads to anger, frustration and hopelessness. Another example of glaring injustice is the price paid to producers, especially subsistence farmers, for some of their crops. We wish to state that every person has a right to a just reward for work done, a wage which will ensure a dignified living for his or her family.

Not only has the worker a right to be paid justly by his employer, but he also has a duty honestly and responsibly to do the work for which he is employed. We would like to remind all Christian workers that their first duty on receiving their earnings is to look to the adequate support of their family. All too often workers spend their salaries for selfish purposes.

Bribery and nepotism are growing in political, economic, and social life. This causes violence and harm to the spirit of our people. Honesty, righteousness, respect, equal opportunity for all: these must be the qualities which guide our nation as it grows and develops into the future.

One of the cornerstones of the nation is "unity". This reflects the will of our Creator that we live in mutual respect and oneness. Tribalism, apartheid (whether economic or social), regionalism and divisions are contrary to the call and truth of humankind. We call all the faithful to celebrate our common birth and destiny in mutual respect, acceptance, justice and love.

The Right to an Adequate Education

A society which values its future affords the highest priority to providing education for all its young people. As it is commonly put: "Young people are the future of the nation". A sound education will aim at the following:

i. creating an environment favourable to the physical, emotional, intellectual, relational and spiritual development of pupils.
ii. developing in each student a respect for others and a recognition of civic responsibilities.
iii. promoting the creative potential of students. The unique and diverse talents of every individual are recognized and encouraged.
iv. instilling an appreciation of the students' cultural heritage, i.e. the linguistic, musical and artistic legacy inherited from the past.
v. providing the students with appropriate training and skills which will equip them to make a living in the actual circumstances of our country.
vi. seeking excellence, while aiming to provide education for everyone.

Problems of Our Educational System

At the outset, we wish to record how greatly we esteem and applaud the efforts which have been made by the government to provide education at all levels. The work of the Churches in this field has also contributed greatly to the advancement of our people.

Nevertheless we feel it necessary to draw attention to some of the problems which beset our educational institutions at present:

a. Illiteracy

Illiteracy is one of the principal causes of poverty and lack of development. It cannot be said that we have succeeded in promoting the creative potential of our citizens while there remains a large scale problem of illiteracy in our society. It must be recognized that this is a problem which cannot be solved by state initiatives alone. Since a great responsibility lies with parents, we urge them to recognize their duty by sending their children to school.

b. Falling Standards, Overcrowding and Shortage of Teachers and Materials

It is more and more widely recognized that standards of education are not only not rising, but are actually falling. Clearly there can be little hope of creating an environment favourable to the emotional, intellectual and spiritual development of pupils when schools are grossly overcrowded and suffer from a serious lack of teachers. While the present acute shortage has been made much worse by the policy of requiring all teachers to remain in their own regions, final solutions to these problems will also demand generous increases in the resources made available to education. This will have very practical implications for the way in which our national priorities are established and the budget distributed.

c. Unequal Access to Education

The criteria used in selection of pupils for secondary schools and third-level institutions should be known to all and be seen to operate fairly. Nor should they work to the disadvantage of particular individuals or groups. Access to education should not depend on whom the candidate knows nor on how much money he possesses.

d. Discipline

We believe that indiscipline is a major problem in secondary schools. It will not be solved by threats of punishments. There is a need to examine the underlying reasons for this state of affairs. Among them are:

i. failure of parents to exercise their responsibility towards their children as they grow older.

ii. lack of co-operation between parents and school authorities.

iii. frustration due to poor or uncertain job opportunities.

iv. manipulation of the selection process to include undeserving students.

v. lack of support from higher authorities when action has been taken, or needs to be taken, by the school.

Church-State Partnership in Education

Improvements will come about in the educational system only if there is mutual trust and genuine partnership between the different interested groups in society, i.e. parents, teachers, the Church and the State. In particular, we recognize the importance of Church-State participation in this area. On the one hand, the Church has a responsibility to support in every way possible the educational goals of the government. On the other, the government has a duty to respect the rights and legitimate aspirations of the Churches. Only through such a mutual recognition of rights and responsibilities will a fruitful partnership between Church and State be realized in practice.

Adequate health services for all

Equality among citizens and the demands of justice call for policies which aim to provide adequate health care for all without distinction. The following principles have always guided us in this vital area of concern:

i. Life is sacred. It is a gift from God to be valued from the moment of conception until death.
ii. Human beings can never be reduced to the status of objects. We recognize that our bodies ate temples of the Holy Spirit.
iii. Every person is of equal dignity. The value of life is not to be measured by one's age, possessions or position in society.

Difficulties Experienced in Our Health Services

We wish to pay tribute to the achievements of the government of Malawi in extending health services with the aim of providing the best possible care for all. Particularly worthy of mention has been the establishment of an excellent system of primary health care. The notable contribution of the churches through their extensive network of hospitals and health centres is deserving of special praise.

At the same time we are aware of the severe difficulties which the health services are experiencing at present:

a. Overcrowding and Lack of Personnel

Without doubt the most serious problem Is the acute shortage of health centers to cater for the population. One cannot claim to uphold the principle of the sanctity of life if provision has not been made for even minimal health care for every person. This is a priority which a society cannot ignore if it wishes to be a caring and compassionate community. It must be recognized that if this problem is to be tackled, it will demand the allocation of more resources from the State.

b. The Vocation of Caring for the Sick

Caring for the sick is a calling from God of a special dignity and importance. It can never be seen as just another job or another way of earning one's living. While we greatly value the generous dedication to service of many of those who work in the medical field, we cannot ignore that the quality of medical care is often seriously inadequate, e.g. patients being unattended to for long periods of time; the lack of commitment on the part of some personnel; the failure to recognize each patient as one's brother or sister in need, etc. We therefore invite all health workers to serve every patient without exception with responsibility and true dedication.

c. Inequality in Medical Treatment

Absolute equality of access to health care for all citizens is difficult to achieve. However, this is an ideal which must always be striven for. The guiding principle determining whether a patient will receive priority treatment ought not to be his apparent usefulness or his position in society. Rather, every person, whether rich or poor, educated or not, blood relative or not, has equal right to receive health care. The practice of stealing and re-selling medicines seriously threatens this right.

The Tragedy of AIDS

It is heartening to note the extensive health education programmes currently in operation in the state. One cannot fail to stress the importance of preventive measures particularly in respect of contagious diseases. The current epidemic of AIDS is a case in point. All recognize that in the present circumstances where no cure for AIDS is available, prevention in that form of health education is the only way of combating this problem.

We want to encourage the efforts undertaken in that direction and hope they can still be intensified: true facts about the disease should be made public more readily; information made available to all; personnel and resources freed for the treatment and counseling of the victims and their families.

However, preventive methods must respect God's law and enhance the dignity of the human person. It is most regrettable that little attention is paid to the fact that faithfulness to the Gospel's teaching on conjugal fidelity is the single most effective method of preventing the spread of this tragic illness. We strongly object to the dissemination of the view that the use of condoms is the remedy against this epidemic.

Besides the immorality involved in the indiscriminate distribution and use of condoms, we must be aware how much they contribute to spreading a false sense of security and encouraging a promiscuity which can only aggravate the existing problem. We appeal to Christian parents to protect and counsel their children against such practices and to guide them to a true Christian understanding of sexuality.

Participation of All in Public Life

In their writings to the Christians, both the apostles Peter and Paul note how the Holy Spirit grants the members of the Christian community gifts of all sorts for the benefit of the community. "On each one of us God's favour has been bestowed in whatever way Christ has allotted it... To some his gift was that they should be apostles; to some prophets; to some evangelists; to some pastors and teachers..." Whatever the gift, the purpose is one: "to knit God's holy people together for the work of service to build up the Body of Christ" (Eph 4:7-16; cf I Pet 4:10-11).

African society has traditionally recognized that what is true of the Church is also true of any society: its strength resides in recognizing the gifts of all and in allowing these gifts to flourish and be used for the building up of the community. "Mutu umodzi susenza denga". No one person can claim to have a monopoly of truth and wisdom. No individual - or group of individuals -

can pretend to have all the resources needed to guarantee the progress of a nation. "Mtsinje wopanda miyala susunga madzi." The contribution of the most humble members is often necessary for the good running of a group. "Wopusa anaomba ng'oma wochenjera navina."

Freedom of Expression and Association

Moreover human persons are honoured - and this honour is due to them - whenever they are allowed to search freely for the truth, to voice their opinions and be heard, to engage in creative service of the community in all liberty within the associations of their own choice. Nobody should ever have to suffer reprisals for honestly expressing and living up to their convictions: intellectual, religious or political.

We can only regret that this is not always the case in our country. We can be grateful that freedom of worship is respected; the same freedom does not exist when it comes to translating faith into daily life. Academic freedom is seriously restricted; exposing injustices can be considered a betrayal; revealing some evils of our society is seen as slandering the country; monopoly of mass media and censorship prevent the expression of dissenting views; some people have paid dearly for their political opinions; access to public places like markets, hospitals, bus depots, etc., is frequently denied to those who cannot produce a party card; forced donations have become a way of life.

This is most regrettable. It creates an atmosphere of resentment among the citizens. It breeds a climate of mistrust and fear. This fear of harassment and mutual suspicion generates a society in. which the talents of many lie unused and in which there is little room for initiative.

Fostering participation

We urgently call each one of you to respond to this state of affairs and work towards a change of climate. Participation in the life of the country is not only a right; it is also a duty that each Christian should be proud to assume and exercise responsibly. People, in positions of authority, in government and administration, have a particular duty to work for the restoration of a climate of trust and openness. However participation will remain a fiction without the existence of adequate channels of expression and action: an independent press, open forums of discussion, free association of citizens for social and political purposes, and the like...

"The Truth will Set You Free"

A first step in the restoration of the climate of confidence may be taken by recognizing the true state of the nation. "The truth will set you free" (Jn 8:32). These words of Christ do not have an exclusively religious meaning. They also express a deep human reality.

For too long we have refused to see that, besides the praiseworthy achievements of the last decades, our country still suffers from many evils: economic and social progress does not trickle down to the mass of the people; much still remains to be achieved to make adequate education and health services available to all; the AIDS problem presents an incredible challenge; recurrent unfavourable climatic conditions often account for poor crops and subsequent misery for the people....

People will not be scandalized to hear these things; they know them. They will only be grateful that their true needs are recognized and that efforts are made to answer them. Feeding them with slogans and half- truths - or untruths! - only increases their cynicism and their mistrust of government representatives. It gives rise to a culture of rumour mongering. Real progress can only be attained when the true problems and the real needs are identified and all resources are channelled towards solving them.

Let us add here that people in positions of responsibility have an obligation to know the actual conditions in which their people live and to work tirelessly for their betterment. They should be willing to allow their performance to be judged by the people they serve. Accountability is a quality of any good government. People are entitled to know how their representatives fulfil their duties. No disrespect is shown when citizens ask questions in matters which concern them.

A System of Justice which Works Fairly

We would like to draw your attention to another area of life in our society. We cannot ignore or turn a blind eye to our people's experience of unfairness and injustice, for example those who, losing their land without fair compensation, are deprived of their livelihood, or those of our brothers and sisters who are imprisoned without knowing when their cases will be heard.

In a just society, a citizen must have easy access to an independent and impartial court of justice whenever his rights are threatened or violated. In particular, before a penalty is imposed, it is in the interest of justice and human dignity that the accused be informed in good time of the charge against him and be granted opportunity for a fair trial, and where necessary, the possibility of legal counsel. We call upon all and particularly those responsible for the administration of justice to ensure not only that procedures are respected but also that impartial judgment is rendered to the accused person. This will only be possible if the administration of justice is independent of external influence, political or other. Our bond of brotherhood and sisterhood in the one body of Christ and our solidarity as a people should, in love, compel us to hunger for the justice and righteousness of the Lord in our society.

In this context, we recall the words of Jesus at the beginning of his ministry:

"The Spirit of the Lord is on me, for he has anointed me to bring the good news to the afflicted. He has sent me to proclaim liberty to captives, sight to the blind, to let the oppressed go free, and to proclaim a year of favour from the Lord" (Luke 4:18-19).

This appeal for fair treatment should also be heard within the Church. We want to recall the importance of adhering to procedures which have been instituted to promote justice and protect the rights of the faithful. Our Church communities do need well established and competent forums for hearing various cases, complaints and grievances of their members. Those of us who have to pronounce judgment on persons and situations are to view the exercise of their authority as a service of the truth for the common good as well as for the well-being of the individual. In particular, we exhort the people of God to respect the right of defence of those accused of having committed offences.

Conclusion

"Love tenderly, act justly, walk humbly with your God" (Micah 6:8)

The issues raised in this letter will obviously require an ongoing and more in depth reflection. It is the Church's mission to preach the Gospel which effects the redemption of the human race and its liberation from every oppressive situation, be it hunger, ignorance, blindness, despair, paralyzing fear, etc. Like Jesus, the advocate of the poor and the oppressed, the believing community is invited, at times obliged in justice, to show in action a preferential love for the economically disadvantaged, the voiceless who live in situations of hopelessness.

The human rights and duties identified in this pastoral letter for our reflection are only some of the issues that God invites us to consider seriously. In our response to God, we humbly recognize that though a gifted and blessed people, we are not a perfect community. If some of our personal weaknesses, biases and ambitions are not purified by the word of God and just laws, they can very easily destroy peace and harmony in our societies and communities. We hope that our message will deepen in all of us the experience of conversion and the desire for truth and the light of Christ. This will prepare us for the worthy celebration of Easter, the feast of the risen Lord in whom we see ourselves as a risen people with dignity restored.

The Catholic Bishops of Malawi

Archbishop J. Chiona	Bishop A. Chamgwera
Bishop F. Mkhori	Bishop G. M Chisendera
Bishop M.A. Chimole	Monsignor J. Roche
Bishop A. Assolari	

List of references

Colin Baker, 2008, *Chipembere: The Missing Years*, Kachere Books no.25, Zomba.

Richard Carver, 1990, *Where Silence Rules: The Suppression of Dissent in Malawi*, An Africa Watch Report of Human Rights Watch, New York.

Richard Carver, 2000, *"Who Wants To Forget?" Truth and Access to Information about Past Human Rights Violations*, Article 19 - The Global Campaign for Free Expression, London.

Catholic Institute for International Relations, July 1993, *Malawi a Moment of Truth,* Nottingham.

Reuben Makayiko Chirambo, 2010, *"A Monument to a Tyrant," or Reconstructed Nationalist Memories of the Father and Founder of the Malawi Nation, Dr. H. K. Banda*, article in Africa Today, Volume 56, Number 4, Summer 2010, pp. 2-21.

Reuben Makayiko Chirambo, 2011*, Vipers who minute our twitches: Psychopath's that served Banda's Malawian dictatorship in Jack Mapanje's Prison Poetry,* quoted in *Spheres Public and Private: Western Genres in African Literature*, ed. Gordon Collier, *Matatu* 39, Editions Rodopi, Amsterdam & New York.

Vera Chirwa, 2007, *Vera Chirwa: Fearless Fighter – an autobiography*, Zed Books, London with Amnesty International and Danish Institute for Human Rights.

Dunduzu K. Chisiza, 1962, *Africa - What Lies Ahead*, The African-American Institute, New York.

Oana Lungescu, December 2009, *State Secrets Part Two*, The Documentary Podcasts http://www.bbc.co.uk/programmes/p005cbw4, London.

John Lloyd Lwanda, 1993, *Kamuzu Banda of Malawi: A Study in Promise, Power and Paralysis*, Glasgow, Dudu Nsomba Publications.

Peter Mackay, 2008, *We have tomorrow: Stirrings in Africa 1958 – 1967*, Michael Russell Publishing Ltd., Norwich.

Jack Mapanje, 2011, *And Crocodiles are Hungry at Nights: a Memoir*, Ayebia Clarke Publishing, Oxfordshire.

John McCracken, 2012, *A History of Malawi*, James Curry, Suffolk.

Guy C.Z. Mhone, (ed.) 1992, *Malawi at the Crossroads: The Post-colonial Political Economy*, Harare, SAPES Books.

Justice Michael Harris Mtegha, December 1994, *The Republic of Malawi Commission of Inquiry Mwanza Road Accident Report*, Limbe.

A.K. Mwakasungura, 1986, *The Political Economy of Malawi: A critical analysis*, Chr. Michelsen Institute – DERAP, Bergen, Norway.

Robert I Rotberg, ed. 2001, *Hero of the Nation – Chipembere of Malawi: An Autobiography*, CLAIM Kachere Book No.12, Zomba.

Andrew Ross and T. Jack Thompson, 2009, *Colonialism to cabinet crisis: a political history of Malawi*, Kachere Books #44, Zomba.

George Shepperson, 1998, *Memories of Dr. Banda*, The Society of Malawi Journal, Vol. 51, No. 1 (1998), pp. 74-84, Blantyre.

Philip Short, 1974, *Banda*, Routledge and Kegan Paul, London and New York.

A.T. Williams, 1978, *Malawi: The Politics of Despair*, Cornell University Press, Ithaca and London.

www.ingramcontent.com/pod-product-compliance
Lightning Source LLC
Chambersburg PA
CBHW050531300426
44113CB00012B/2049